FINANCIAL
SHOCK

FINANCIAL
SHOCK

A 360° Look at the Subprime Mortgage Implosion, and How to Avoid the Next Financial Crisis

MARK ZANDI

Vice President, Publisher: Tim Moore
Associate Publisher and Director of Marketing: Amy Neidlinger
Executive Editor: Jim Boyd
Editorial Assistant: Heather Luciano
Development Editor: Russ Hall
Digital Marketing Manager: Julie Phifer
Publicity Manager: Laura Czaja
Assistant Marketing Manager: Megan Colvin
Marketing Assistant: Brandon Smith
Cover Designer: Chuti Prasertsith
Operations Manager: Gina Kanouse
Managing Editor: Kristy Hart
Project Editor: Chelsey Marti
Copy Editor: Krista Hansing Editorial Services
Proofreader: Water Crest Publishing, Inc.
Indexer: Lisa Stumpf
Compositor: Jake McFarland
Manufacturing Buyer: Dan Uhrig

FT Press offers excellent discounts on this book when ordered in quantity for bulk purchases
or special sales. For more information, please contact U.S. Corporate and Government Sales,
1-800-382-3419, corpsales@pearsontechgroup.com. For sales outside the U.S., please contact
International Sales at international@pearson.com.

ISBN-10: 0-13-714290-0
ISBN-13: 978-0-13-714290-3

Pearson Education LTD.
Pearson Education Australia PTY, Limited.
Pearson Education Singapore, Pte. Ltd.
Pearson Education North Asia, Ltd.
Pearson Education Canada, Ltd.
Pearson Educatión de Mexico, S.A. de C.V.
Pearson Education—Japan
Pearson Education Malaysia, Pte. Ltd.

Library of Congress Cataloging-in-Publication Data

Zandi, Mark M.
    Financial shock : a 360° look at the subprime mortgage implosion, and how to avoid the next
financial crisis / Mark Zandi.
        p. cm.
    ISBN 0-13-714290-0 (hardback : alk. paper) 1. Mortgage loans—United States. 2. Hous-
ing—United States—Finance. I. Title.
    HG2040.5.U5Z36 2009
    332.7'220973—dc22
                                                                              2008024348

For Ava, Bill, Anna, and Lily

Contents

Acknowledgments

This book would not have been possible without the support and help of a number of people.

Paul Getman, my friend, business partner, and sounding board for a quarter century, has been instrumental in guiding me through the tricky parts of putting this work together. He taught me the basics of banking back in the 1980s when it wasn't taught in graduate school. His insights have been key to guiding my thinking on the topics addressed in this book.

Andy Cassel also deserves a substantial amount of credit for his tireless efforts turning my prosaic prose into something hopefully worth reading.

I had invaluable help from Zoltan Pozsar who culled through endless reports and documents and hunted down the most arcane of information. His enthusiasm and interest in the topic made my job much more interesting.

I would also like to thank Jim Boyd, my editor, who gave me very kind encouragement throughout the entire process. His cool demeanor was important to keeping my cool.

To my father, and my brothers and sister, Richard, Karl, Peter, and Meriam. My father has been the proverbial, loving pain in the side, cajoling me to write a book; I surely wouldn't have done it otherwise. I haven't lived with my brothers and sisters for almost thirty years, but I think of them every day, and their influence is enduring.

Finally, I must acknowledge my dear wife and children. Their love and patience is key to anything I'm able to accomplish.

About the Author

Mark Zandi is Chief Economist and co-founder of Moody's Economy.com, Inc., where he directs the firm's research and consulting activities. Moody's Economy.com is an independent subsidiary of the Moody's Corporation and provides economic research and consulting services to global businesses, governments and other institutions. His research interests include macroeconomic and financial economics, and his recent areas of research include an assessment of the economic impacts of various tax and government spending policies, the incorporation of economic information into credit risk analysis, and an assessment of the appropriate policy response to real estate and stock market bubbles. He received his PhD from the University of Pennsylvania, where he did his PhD research with Gerard Adams and Nobel Laureate Lawrence Klein, and his BS degree from the Wharton School at the University of Pennsylvania.

Introduction

"If it's growing like a weed, it's probably a weed." So I was once told by the CEO of a major financial institution. He was talking about the credit card business in the mid-1990s, a time when lenders were mailing out new cards with abandon and cardholders were piling up huge debts. He was worried, and correctly so. Debt-swollen households were soon filing for bankruptcy at a record rate, contributing to the financial crisis that ultimately culminated in the collapse of mega-hedge fund Long-Term Capital Management. The CEO's bank didn't survive.

A decade later the world was engulfed by an even more severe financial crisis. This time the weed was the subprime mortgage: a loan to someone with a less-than-perfect credit history.

Financial crises are disconcerting events. At first they seem impenetrable, even as their damage undeniably grows and becomes increasingly widespread. Behind the confusion often lie esoteric and complicated financial institutions and instruments: program-trading during the 1987 stock market crash; junk corporate bonds in the savings & loan debacle in the early 1990s; the Thai baht and Russian bonds in the late 1990s; and the technology-stock bust at the turn of the millennium.

Yet the genesis of the subprime financial shock has been even more baffling than past crises. Lending money to American homebuyers had been one of the least risky and most profitable businesses a bank could engage in for nearly a century. How could so many mortgages have gone bad? And even if they did, how could even a couple of trillion dollars in bad loans come so close to derailing a global financial system that is valued in the hundreds of trillions?

Adding to the puzzlement is the complexity of the financial institutions and securities involved in the subprime financial shock. What are subprime, Alt-A, and jumbo IO mortgages, asset-backed securities, CDOs, CPDOs, CDSs, and SIVs? How did this mélange of acronyms lead to plunging house prices, soaring foreclosures, wobbling stock markets, inflation, and recession? Who or what is to blame?

The reality is that there is plenty of blame to go around. A financial calamity of this magnitude could not have taken root without a great many hands tilling the soil and planting the seeds. Among the elements that fed the crisis were a rapidly evolving financial system, an eroding sense of responsibility in the lending process among both lenders and borrowers, the explosive growth of new, emerging economies amassing cash for their low-cost goods, lax oversight by policymakers skeptical of market regulation, incorrect ratings, and of course, what economists call the "animal spirits" of investors and entrepreneurs.

America's financial system has long been the envy of the world. It is incredibly efficient at investing the nation's savings—so efficient, in fact, that although our savings are meager by world standards, they bring returns greater than those nations that save many times more. So it wasn't surprising when Wall Street engineers devised a new and ingenious way for global money managers to finance ordinary Americans buying homes: Bundle the mortgages and sell them as securities. Henceforth, when the average family in Anytown, U.S.A. wrote a monthly mortgage check, the cash would become part of a money machine as sophisticated as anything ever designed in any of the world's financial capitals.

But the machine didn't work as so carefully planned. First it spun out of control—turning U.S. housing markets white-hot—then it broke, its financial nuts and bolts seizing up while springs and wires flew out, spreading damage in all directions.

What went wrong? First and foremost, the risks inherent in mortgage lending became so widely dispersed that no one was forced to worry about the quality of any single loan. As shaky mortgages were combined, diluting any problems into a larger pool, the incentive for responsibility was undermined. At every point in the financial system, there was a belief that someone—*someone else*—would catch mistakes and preserve the integrity of the process. The mortgage lender counted on the Wall Street investment banker who counted on the regulator or the ratings analyst, who had assumed global investors were doing their own due diligence. As the process went badly awry, everybody assumed someone else was in control. No one was.

Global investors weren't cognizant of the true risks of the securities they had bought from Wall Street. Investors were awash in cash because global central bankers had opened the money spigots wide in the wake of the dotcom bust, 9/11, and the invasion of Iraq. The stunning economic ascent of China, which had forced prices lower for so many manufactured goods, also had central bankers focused on fighting deflation, which meant keeping interest rates low for a long time. A ballooning U.S. trade deficit, driven by a strong dollar and America's appetite for cheap imports, was also sending a flood of dollars overseas.

The recipients of all those dollars needed some place to put them. At first, U.S. Treasury bonds seemed an easy choice; they were safe and liquid, even if they didn't pay much in interest. But after accumulating hundreds of billions of dollars in low-yielding Treasuries, investors began to worry less about safety and more about returns. Wall Street's new designer mortgage securities appeared on the surface to be an attractive alternative. Investors were told they were safe—at most a step or two riskier than a U.S. Treasury bond but offered significantly higher returns—which itself should have served as a warning signal to investors. But with more and more U.S. dollars to invest, the quest for higher returns became more concerted and investors warmed to increasingly sophisticated and complex mortgage and corporate securities, indifferent to the risks that they were taking.

The financial world was stunned when U.S. homeowners began defaulting on their mortgages in record numbers. Some likened it to the mid-1980s, when a boom in loans to Latin American nations (financed largely with Middle Eastern oil wealth) went bust. That financial crisis had taken more than a decade to sort through. Few thought that subprime mortgages from across the U.S. could have so much in common with those third-world loans of yesteryear.

Still more disconcerting was the notion that the subprime mortgage losses meant investors had badly misjudged the level of risk in all their investments. The mortgage crisis crystallized what had long been troubling many in the financial markets; assets of all types were overvalued, from Chinese stocks to Las Vegas condominiums. The subprime meltdown began a top-to-bottom reevaluation of the risks inherent in financial markets, and thus a repricing of all investments, from stocks to insurance. That process would affect every aspect of economic life, from the cost of starting a business to the value of retirees' pensions, for years to come.

Policymakers and regulators had an unappreciated sense of the flaws in the financial system, and those few who felt something was amiss lacked the authority to do anything about it. A deregulatory zeal had overtaken the federal government, including the Federal Reserve, the nation's key regulator. The legal and regulatory fetters that had been placed on financial institutions since the Great Depression had been broken. There was a new faith that market forces would impose discipline; lenders didn't need regulators telling them what loans to make or not make. Newly designed global capital standards and the credit rating agencies would substitute for the discipline of the regulators.

Even after mortgage loans started going bad en masse, the confusing mix of federal and state agencies that made up the nation's regulatory structure had difficulty responding. After regulators finally began to speak up about subprime and the other types of mortgage loans that had spun out of control, such lending was already on its way to extinction. What regulators had to say was all but irrelevant.

Yet even the combination of a flawed financial system, cash-flush global investors and lax regulators could not, by itself, have created the subprime financial shock. The essential final ingredient was hubris: a belief that the ordinary rules of economics and finance no longer applied. Everyone involved—homebuyers, mortgage lenders, builders, regulators, ratings agencies, investment bankers, central bankers— believed they had a better formula, a more accurate model, or would just be luckier than their predecessors. Even the bursting tech stock bubble just a few years earlier seemed to hold no particular lessons for the soaring housing market; this time, the thinking went, things were truly different. Though house prices shot up far faster than household incomes or rents—just as dotcom-era stock prices had left corporate earnings far behind—markets were convinced that houses, for a variety of reasons, weren't like stocks, and so could skyrocket in price without later falling back to earth, as the Dow and NASDAQ had.

Skyrocketing house prices fed many dreams and papered over many ills. Households long locked out of the American dream finally saw a way in. While most were forthright and prudent, too many weren't. Borrowers and lenders implicitly or explicitly conspired to fudge or lie on loan applications, dismissing any moral qualms with the thought that appreciating property values would make it all right in the end. Rising house prices would allow homeowners to refinance again and again, freeing cash while keeping mortgage payments low. That meant more fees for lenders as well. Investment bankers, empowered by surging home values, invented increasingly sophisticated and complex securities that kept the money flowing into ever hotter and faster growing housing markets.

In the end there was far less difference between houses and stocks than the markets thought. In many communities, houses were being traded like stocks, bought and sold purely on speculation that they would continue to go up. Builders also got the arithmetic wrong as they calculated the number of potential buyers for their new homes. Most of the mistakes made in the tech-stock bubble were repeated in the housing bubble—and became painfully obvious in the subsequent bust and crash. The housing market fell into a self-reinforcing vicious cycle as house price declines begat defaults and foreclosures, which begat more house price declines.

It's probably no coincidence that financial crises occur about every ten years. It takes about that long for the collective memory of the previous crisis to fade and confidence to become all pervasive once-again. It's human nature. Future financial shocks are assured.

There were a few naysayers along the way. I take some pride in being one of those, but I was early in expressing my doubts and had lost some credibility by the time the housing market unraveled and the financial shock hit. I certainly also misjudged the scale of what eventually happened. I expected house prices to decline and for Wall Street and investors to take some losses, but I never expected the subprime financial shock to reach the ultimate frenzy that it did. Some on Wall Street and in banks were also visibly uncomfortable as the fury intensified. But it was hard to stand against the tide; too much money was being made, and if you wanted to keep doing business, there was little choice but to hold your nose. As another Wall Street CEO famously said just before the bust, "As long as the music was playing, you had to get up and dance." A few government officials did some public hand-wringing, but their complaints lacked much force. Perhaps they were hamstrung by their own self-doubts, or perhaps their timing was off. Perhaps history demanded the dramatic and inevitable arrival of the subprime financial shock to finally make the point that it wasn't different this time.

Any full assessment of the subprime fiasco must also consider the role of the credit rating agencies. Critics argue that the methods and practices of these firms contributed to the crisis, by making exotic mortgage securities seem much safer than they ultimately proved to be. Others see a fatal flaw in the agencies' business model, under which the agencies are paid to rate these securities by the issuers of these securities. The global business of rating credit securities is dominated by three firms: Moody's, Standard & Poor's, and Fitch. In 2005, the company I co-founded was purchased by Moody's, and I have been an employee of that firm since then. To avoid any appearance of a conflict of interest, I have no choice but to leave discussion of this facet of the subprime shock to others. The views expressed in this book are mine alone and do not represent those held or endorsed by Moody's. It is also important for you, the reader, to know that my royalties from the book will be donated to a Philadelphia based non-profit, The Reinvestment Fund (TRF). TRF invests in inner-city projects in the Northeast United States.

Understanding the roots of the subprime financial shock is necessary to better prepare for the next financial crisis. Policymakers must use its lessons to reevaluate the regulatory framework that oversees the financial system. The Federal Reserve should consider whether its hands-off policy toward asset-price bubbles is appropriate. Bankers must build better systems for assessing and managing risk. Investors must prepare for the wild swings in asset prices that are sure to come, and households must relearn the basic financial principles of thrift and portfolio diversification.

The next financial crisis, however, won't likely involve mortgage loans, credit cards, junk bonds, or even those odd-sounding financial securities. The next crisis will be related to our own federal government's daunting fiscal challenges. The U.S. is headed inexorably toward record budget deficits, either measured in total dollars or in proportion to the economy. Global investors are already growing disaffected with U.S. debt, and even the Treasury will have a difficult time finding buyers for all the bonds it will be trying to sell if nothing changes soon. Hopefully, the lessons learned from the subprime financial shock will be the catalyst for facing the tough choices regarding taxes and government spending that we collectively will have to make in the not-too-distant future.

This book isn't filled with juicy financial secrets; it may not even spin a terribly dramatic yarn. It is rather an attempt to make sense of what has been a complex and confusing period, even for a professional economist with 25 years at his craft. I hope you find it organized well enough to come away with a better understanding of what has happened. While nearly every event feels like the most important ever when you are close to it, I'm confident that the subprime financial shock will be judged one of the most significant financial events in our nation's economic history.

1

Subprime Précis

Until recent events, few outside the real estate industry had even heard of a subprime mortgage. But this formerly obscure financial vehicle has grabbed its share of attention because of its ravaging effect on the U.S. economy and global financial markets.

Simply defined, a subprime mortgage is just a loan made to someone with a weak or troubled credit history. Historically, it has been a peripheral financial phenomenon, a marginal market involving few lenders and few borrowers. However, subprime home buyers unable to make good on their mortgage payments set off a financial avalanche in 2007 that pushed the United States into a recession and hit major economies around the globe. Financial markets and the economy will ultimately recover, but the subprime financial shock will go down as an inflection point in economic history.

Genesis

The fuse for the subprime financial shock was set early in this decade, following the tech-stock bust, 9/11, and the invasions of Afghanistan and Iraq. With stock markets plunging and the nation in shock after the attack on the World Trade Center, the Federal Reserve Board (the Fed) slashed interest rates. By summer 2003, the federal funds rate—the one rate the Fed controls directly—was at a record low. Fearing that their own economies would slump under the weight of the faltering U.S. economy, other major central banks around the world soon followed the Fed's lead.

In normal times, central bankers worry that lowering interest rates too much might spark inflation. If they worried less this time, a major factor was China. Joining the World Trade Organization in November 2001 not only ratified China's arrival in the global market, but it lowered trade barriers and accelerated a massive shift of global manufacturing to the formerly closed communist mainland. As low-cost Chinese-made goods flooded markets, prices fell nearly everywhere, and inflation seemed a remote concern. Policymakers even worried publicly about deflation, encouraging central banks to push rates to unprecedented lows.

China's explosive growth, driven by manufacturing and exports, boosted global demand for oil and other commodities. Prices surged higher. This pushed up the U.S. trade deficit, as hundreds of billions of dollars flowed overseas to China, the Middle East, Russia, and other commodity-producing nations. Many of these dollars returned to the United States as investments, as Asian and Middle Eastern producers parked their cash in the world's safest, biggest economy. At first they mainly bought U.S. Treasury bonds, which produced a low but safe return. Later, in the quest for higher returns, they expanded to riskier financial instruments, including bonds backed by subprime mortgages.

Frenzied Innovation

The two factors of extraordinarily low interest rates and surging global investor demand combined with the growth of Internet technology to produce a period of intense financial innovation. Designing new ways to invest had long been a Wall Street specialty: Since the 1970s, bankers and traders had regularly unveiled new futures, options, and derivatives on government and corporate debt—even bonds backed by residential mortgage payments. But now the financial innovation machine went into high gear. Wall Street produced a blizzard of increasingly complex new securities.

These included bonds based on pools of mortgages, auto loans, credit card debt, and commercial bank loans, sliced and sorted according to their presumed levels of risk. Sometimes these securities were resliced and rebundled yet again or packaged into risk-swapping agreements whose terms remained arcane to all but their authors.

Yet the underlying structure had a basic theme. Financial engineers start with a simple credit agreement, such as a home mortgage or a credit card. Not so long ago, such arrangements were indeed simple, involving an individual borrower and a single lender. The bank loaned you money to buy a house or a car, and you paid back the bank over time. This changed when Wall Street bankers realized that many individual mortgages or other loans could be tied together and "securitized"—transformed from a simple debt agreement into a security that could be traded, just as with other bonds and stocks, among investors worldwide.

Now a monthly mortgage payment no longer made a simple trip from a homeowner's checking account to the bank. Instead, it was pooled with hundreds of other individual mortgage payments, forming a cash stream that flowed to the investors who owned the new mortgage-backed bonds. The originator of the loan—a bank, a mortgage broker, or whoever—might still collect the cash and handle the paperwork, but it was otherwise out of the picture.

With mortgages or consumer loans now bundled as tradable securities, Wall Street's second idea was to slice them up so they carried different levels of risk. Instead of pooling all the returns from a given bundle of mortgages, for example, securities were tailored so that investors could receive payments based on how much risk they were willing to take. Those seeking a safe investment were paid first, but at a lower rate of return. Those willing to gamble most were paid last but earned a substantially higher return. At least, that was how it worked in theory.

By mid-decade, such financial innovation was in full frenzy. Any asset with a cash flow seemed to qualify for such slice-and-dice treatment. Residential mortgage loans, merger-and-acquisition financing, and even tolls generated by public bridges and highways were securitized in this way. As designing, packaging, and reselling such newfangled investments became a major source of profit for Wall Street, bankers and salesmen successfully marketed them to investors from Perth to Peoria.

The benefits of securitization were substantial. In the old days, credit could be limited by local lenders' size or willingness to take risks. A homeowner or business might have trouble getting a loan simply because the local bank's balance sheet was fully subscribed. But with securitization, lenders could originate loans, resell them to investors, and use the proceeds to make more loans. As long as there were willing investors anywhere in the world, the credit tap could never run dry.

On the other side, securitization gave global investors a much broader array of potential assets and let them precisely calibrate the amount of risk in their portfolios. Government regulators and policymakers also liked securitization because it appeared to spread risk broadly, which made a financial crisis less likely. Or so they thought.

Awash in funds from growing world trade, global investors gobbled up the new securities. Reassured by Wall Street, many believed they could successfully manage their risks while collecting healthy returns. Yet as investors flocked to this market, their returns grew smaller relative to the risks they took. Just as at any bazaar or auction, the more buyers crowd in, the less likely they are to find a bargain. The more investors there were seeking high yields, the more those yields fell. Eventually, a high-risk security—say, a bond issued by the government of Venezuela, or a subprime mortgage loan—brought barely more than a U.S. Treasury bond or a mortgage insured by Fannie Mae.

Starved for greater returns, investors began using an old financial trick for turning small profits into large ones: leverage—that is, investing with borrowed money. With interest rates low all around the world, they could borrow cheaply and thus magnify returns many times over. Investors could also sell insurance to each other, collecting premiums in exchange for a promise to cover the losses on any securities that went bad. Because that seemed a remote possibility, such insurance seemed like an easy way to make extra money.

As time went on, the market for these new securities became increasingly esoteric. Derivatives such as collateralized debt obligations, or CDOs, were particularly attractive. A CDO is a bondlike security whose cash flow is derived from other bonds, which, in turn, might be backed by mortgages or other loans. Evaluating the risk of such instruments was difficult, if not impossible; yet investors took comfort in the high ratings given by analysts at the ratings agencies, who presumably were in the know. To further allay any worries, investors could even buy insurance on the securities.

Housing Boom

Global investors were particularly enamored of securities backed by U.S. residential mortgage loans. American homeowners were historically reliable, paying on their mortgages even in tough economic times. Certainly, some cities or regions had seen falling house prices and rising mortgage defaults, but these were rare. Indeed, since the Great Depression, house prices nationwide had not declined in a single year. And U.S. housing produced trillions of dollars in mortgage loans, a huge source of assets to securitize.

With funds pouring into mortgage-related securities, mortgage lenders avidly courted home buyers. Borrowing costs plunged and mortgage credit was increasingly ample. Housing was as affordable as it had been since just after World War II, particularly in areas such as

California and the Northeast, where home ownership had long been a stretch for most renters. First-time home buyers also benefited as the Internet transformed the mortgage industry, cutting transaction costs and boosting competition. New loan products were invented for households that had historically had little access to standard forms of credit, such as mortgages. Borrowers with less than perfect credit history—or no credit history—could now get a loan. Of course, a subprime borrower needed a sizable down payment and a sturdy income—but even that changed quickly.

Home buying took on an added sheen after 9/11, as Americans grew wary of travel, with the hassles of air passenger screening and code-orange alerts. Tourist destinations struggled. Americans were staying home more, and they wanted those homes to be bigger and nicer. Many traded up.

As home sales took off, prices began to rise more quickly, particularly in highly regulated areas of the country. Builders couldn't put up houses quickly enough in California, Florida, and other coastal areas, which had tough zoning restrictions, environmental requirements, and a long and costly permitting process.

The house price gains were modest at first, but they appeared very attractive compared with a still-lagging stock market and the rock-bottom interest rates banks were offering on savings accounts. Home buyers saw a chance to make outsized returns on homes by taking on big mortgages. Besides, interest payments on mortgage loans were tax deductible, and since the mid-1990s, even capital gains on most home sales aren't taxed.

It didn't take long for speculation to infect housing markets. Flippers—housing speculators looking to buy and sell quickly at a large profit—grew active. Churning was especially rampant in condominium, second-home, and vacation-home markets, where a flipper could always rent a unit if it didn't sell quickly. Some of these investors were disingenuous or even fraudulent when applying for loans, telling lenders they planned to live in the units so they could obtain better mortgage terms. Flippers were often facilitated by home builders who turned a blind eye in the rush to meet ever-rising home sales projections.

Speculation extended beyond flippers, however. Nearly all homeowners were caught up in the idea that housing was a great investment, possibly the best they could make. The logic was simple: House prices had risen strongly in the recent past, so they would continue to rise strongly in the future.

Remodeling and renovations surged. By mid-decade, housing markets across much of the country were in a frenzied boom. House sales, construction, and prices were all shattering records. Prices more than doubled in such far-flung places as Providence, Rhode Island; Naples, Florida; Minneapolis, Minnesota; Tucson, Arizona; Salt Lake City, Utah; and Sacramento, California.

The housing boom did bring an important benefit: It jump-started the broader economy out of its early-decade malaise. Not only were millions of jobs created—to build, sell, and finance homes—but homeowners were also measurably wealthier. Indeed, the seeming financial windfall for lower- and middle- American homeowners was arguably unprecedented. The home was by far the largest asset on most households' balance sheet.

Moreover, all this newfound wealth could be readily and cheaply converted into cash. Homeowners became adept at borrowing against the increased equity in their homes, refinancing into larger mortgages, and taking on big home equity lines. This gave the housing boom even more economic importance as the extra cash financed a spending splurge.

Extra spending was precisely what the central bankers at the Federal Reserve had in mind when they were slashing interest rates. After all, the point of adjusting monetary policy is to raise or lower the economy's speed by regulating the flow of credit through the financial system and economy. Nevertheless, by mid-2004, the booming housing market and strong economy convinced policymakers it was time to throttle back by raising rates.

Housing Bust

Signs that the boom was ending appeared in spring 2005, in places such as Boston and San Diego. After several years of surging house prices and nearly a year of rising interest rates, many home buyers simply could no longer afford the outsized mortgages needed to buy. Homes that had been so affordable just a few years earlier were again out of reach.

The frenzy began to cool. Not only did bidding wars among home buyers vanish, but many sellers couldn't get their list prices as the number of properties for sale began to mount. Moreover, many sellers found it extraordinarily painful to cut prices. Flippers feared the loss of their capital, and other homeowners with big mortgages couldn't take less than they needed to pay off their existing mortgage loans. Realtors were loath to advise clients to lower prices, lest they destroy belief in the boom that had powered enormous realty fees and bonuses.

Underwriting Collapses

As they anxiously watched loan-origination volumes top out, mortgage lenders searched for ways to keep the boom going. Adjustable-rate mortgage loans (ARMs) were a particularly attractive way to expand the number of potential home buyers. ARMs allowed for low monthly payments, at least for awhile.

Although borrowers have had access to such loans since the early 1980s, new versions of the ARM came with extraordinarily low initial rates, known as teasers. In most cases, the teaser rate was fixed for two years, after which it quickly adjusted higher, usually every six months, until it matched higher prevailing interest rates. Homeowners who took on these exploding ARM loans are the ones who are now losing their homes the most quickly.

Lenders also began to require smaller down payments. To allow home buyers to avoid paying mortgage insurance (generally required for large loans with low down payments), lenders counseled borrowers to take out second mortgages. For many such borrowers, the amount of the first and second mortgage together equaled the market value of the home, meaning there was no cushion in case that value declined. Moreover, although payments on the second mortgage may have been initially lower than the cost of the insurance, most loans also had adjustable rates, which moved higher as interest rates rose.

Such creative lending worked to support home sales for awhile, but it also further raised house prices. Rising prices together with higher interest rates (thanks to continued Fed tightening) undermined house affordability even more. Growing still more creative—or more desperate—lenders offered loans without requiring borrowers to prove they had sufficient income or savings to meet the payments. Such "stated income" loans had been available in the past, but only to a very few self-employed professionals. Now they went mainstream, picking up a new nickname among mortgage-industry insiders: liars' loans.

By 2006, most subprime borrowers were taking out adjustable-rate loans carrying teaser rates that would reset in two years, potentially setting up the borrowers for a major payment shock. Most of those borrowers had put down little or no money of their own on their homes, meaning they had little to lose. Many had overstated their incomes on the loan documents, often with their lenders' tacit approval. By any traditional standard, such lending would have been viewed as a prescription for financial disaster. But lenders argued that as long as house prices rose, homeowners could build enough home equity to refinance before disaster struck.

For their part, home appraisers were working to ensure that this came true. Typically, their appraisals were based on cursory drive-by inspections and comparisons with nearby homes that had recently been sold or refinanced—in some cases, homes they themselves had appraised. Lenders, meanwhile, were happy to see their subprime borrowers refinance; most subprime loans carried hefty penalties for paying off the mortgage early, and that meant more fee income for lenders.

Regulators and Rating Agencies

Federal and state regulators may have been nervous about runaway mortgage lending, but they failed to do much about it. They certainly had reason to worry; their own surveys showed that most mortgage borrowers understood little about the financial obligations they were taking on. Many ARM borrowers did not know their mortgage payments were likely to increase, much less when they would adjust higher or by how much.

Meanwhile, hamstrung government regulators couldn't keep up with lenders who were constantly devising ways to elude oversight. Some of the most egregious lending was done not by traditional mortgage lenders, such as commercial banks and savings and loans, but by real estate investment trusts (REITs). The Securities and Exchange Commission (SEC), the agency that regulates stock and bond sales, also regulates REITs. Yet the SEC was focused on insider trading at the time, not predatory mortgage lending. An even more important factor was a philosophical distaste for regulation that seemed to pervade the Federal Reserve, the nation's most important banking regulator. Without Fed leadership, the agencies that monitor smaller corners of the banking system, such as the Office of the Comptroller of the Currency, the Federal Deposit Insurance Corporation, and Office of Thrift Supervision, were deterred from taking action. State regulators also had a say, but they were no match for a globally wired financial industry.

Regulators' reluctance to intervene in the mortgage market may have also been based on their trust in the acumen of the rating agencies. These companies provide opinions about the creditworthiness of securities and are paid by the issuers of these securities. Global banking regulators had only recently given the agencies' opinions a quasi-official status, by making their opinions count toward determining whether banks had an appropriate amount of capital to safeguard depositors. The rating agencies were also the only institutions outside of the mortgage or banking business with enough data and information to make an informed judgment about the securities' safety. If the agencies gave them an A-rating (meaning that they saw very little chance of default), regulators weren't going to argue.

Yet the rating agencies badly misjudged the risks. Poor-quality data and information led to serious miscalculations. The agencies were not required to check what the originators or servicers of the mortgage loans told them, and this information was increasingly misleading. The agencies also had the difficult task of developing models to evaluate the risk of newfangled loan schemes that had never been through a housing slump or economic recession. Without that experience, the models were not up to the task they were asked to perform. The ratings were supposed to account for the range of things that could go wrong, from rising unemployment to falling house prices, but what went wrong was much worse than they had anticipated.

Delusional Home Builders

Despite the developing stress lines, home builders retained their congenital optimism about the housing market. Most could afford it; they still had plenty of cash and bank lines built up during the boom. So they kept on building, putting up a record number of homes through summer 2006. The home-building industry had been transformed during the previous decade, as large, publicly traded firms took market share away from smaller, privately held builders. The big builders now did most of the construction in the largest markets. Observers thought this would mean more disciplined building; the large builders would have better market information, and shareholders would demand that builders pull back at the first sign of weakness. That, too, turned out to be a delusion.

The big publicly held builders and their stockholders showed no such discipline. They ignored the weakening market, putting more shovels into the ground and projecting future sales growth to keep their stock prices up. When challenged by investment analysts or reporters, construction executives proffered theories about why the housing market would remain strong. Some said lots of immigrants were coming to the U.S. and would keep buying no matter what; unfortunately, after 9/11, there were fewer immigrants. There were also variations on the old saw about land—that they're not making more of it. True, in some places developable land was in increasingly short supply; many beachside resorts are short on spare lots. But, of course, developers don't need much vacant land to put up a condo tower, which were sprouting skyward along much of the nation's coasts.

Undaunted, some builders even established their own mortgage lending affiliates to ensure that credit kept flowing even if traditional lenders became skittish. These affiliates were particularly aggressive, even offering down payments to buyers as gifts. (They recouped the cost in a higher house price.) And if that still failed to entice purchasers, the builders could offer a marble counter top, a bigger deck, or a built-out basement to close a deal. Yet despite all their efforts, as spring 2006 turned to summer, fewer deals closed and cancellations ballooned.

Lenders Cave

Eventually, the mortgage lenders caved. With housing affordability collapsing, there was no longer a way to squeeze marginal home buyers into mortgages—at least, not without some disingenuous slight of hand. Not only was it tough to make a new loan, but a growing number of recent borrowers, mostly flippers, weren't even making their first few mortgage payments. Even though the lenders didn't own the loans (they had already been sold for securitization), the terms of those deals left lenders on the hook for any losses that occurred soon after the sale. This was a modest attempt to dissuade fraud. Now these early-payment defaults became a call to arms for nervous regulators, who finally took action and issued new rules to limit some of the more aggressive types of lending.

As their losses began to mount, some mortgage lenders sold out and found buyers for their businesses in still-confident investment banks. The Wall Street firms calculated that the loan originators' losses would be short term and that they themselves would be well compensated in the long run through the extra securitization business their ownership would bring in. But by the end of 2006, even the investment banks began to lose heart, and loss-plagued loan companies found nobody wanted to buy them. The only recourse for many lenders was bankruptcy and, ultimately, liquidation.

Subprime Shock

Global investors were very slow to notice the mounting troubles in the U.S. housing and mortgage markets. After some volatility early in 2007, when the Chinese stock market briefly stumbled, global stock and bond prices rocketed to new highs. But fissures were developing in some esoteric corners of the financial markets, such as the credit default swap market (a market for insurance contracts on bonds— mostly corporate bonds, but also mortgage-backed bonds), but this meant little to all but the handful of investors who traded in them.

But by late spring, the cracks could no longer be ignored. A string of venerable investment banks, including the now-defunct Bear

Stearns, announced that some of their hedge funds, which had invested aggressively in mortgage-related securities, were hemorrhaging cash and facing failure. Investors weren't prepared for the news. Most global stock, bond, and real estate markets were trading near record highs, reflecting investors' complacent view of the risks involved. As the extent of the financial system's exposure to subprime mortgages came into relief in the following weeks, these same investors began running for the door. By summer 2007, the subprime financial shock was reverberating across the globe.

Some parts of the market for mortgage-backed securities effectively shut down. Bonds backed by the Federal Housing Administration, which is part of the federal government, and Fannie Mae and Freddie Mac, two publicly traded companies created by Congress, continued to be issued. But banks abruptly stopped issuing other mortgage-backed bonds, especially those backed by subprime loans. At the peak of the boom, such bonds had accounted for half of all mortgage originations.

Money Stops Flowing

The mortgage securities market wasn't the only casualty of the subprime shock. Very quickly, global money markets began to suffer as well, thanks to a complex chain of financial links that few outside these markets had noticed or understood previously. Over the course of several years, major U.S. and European money center banks had established so-called structured investment vehicles, or SIVs. These are entities set up to invest in a wide range of assets, including subprime mortgage securities, with money they raise by selling short-term commercial paper. Commercial paper (historically used by businesses to purchase inventory that will soon be sold, or other short-term financing needs) is a mainstay of the money markets because it is regarded as both safe and liquid. Millions of savers who use money markets as an alternative to passbook bank accounts or certificates of deposit are investing in commercial paper, whether they know it or not.

In a time of low interest rates and easy credit, SIVs could easily and cheaply issue short-term commercial paper and use the proceeds to buy longer-term mortgage-backed securities. Now, however, money market funds and other investors began to lose faith in the commercial paper SIVs issued. The SIVs were effectively out of business.

It is a truism to say that financial markets work on trust. Each party to a deal must trust that the other side will honor its commitments. Lenders must trust that their loans will be paid back; investors must trust that they will see a return on their investment. But no market depends more on trust than a money market, in which the transactions are large and are held for short periods of time. Without trust, money markets quickly break down. By late summer 2007, trust in the SIVs had evaporated. Investors shunned their commercial paper, forcing the SIVs to sell their assets at increasingly distressed prices, thus accelerating the downdraft in financial markets generally.

Short-term lending within the global banking system was also disrupted, as a string of banks began to report losses on their mortgage-related holdings. The distress appeared particularly acute in Europe, as several prominent German and British institutions stumbled. But these high-profile affairs were assumed to be just the tip of the iceberg. With U.S. mortgage security holdings so widely dispersed, and with little information about who was suffering losses and to what extent, banks shrank from doing business with each other. Fewer thought it prudent to borrow or lend, and those that would demanded substantially higher interest rates to compensate for the greater risk they now believed existed.

Banking Buckles

Pressure now mounted on the banks. Not only were they struggling to raise funds in money markets and to straighten out their troubled SIVs, but their mortgage holdings also suddenly turned toxic. They couldn't even count their losses because trading had collapsed in the mortgage securities market; thus, pricing their mortgage assets was all but impossible. Banks began feverishly writing down the value of these assets, although it was unclear how large those write-downs should be.

The banks were further hurt as investor angst over mortgage credit quality spilled over into corporate credit, particularly for lower-rated loans and bonds. These "junk" loans and bonds had financed a wave of leveraged corporate buyouts and had been very lucrative for the banks, but they were supposed to be temporary; banks expected to quickly resell them to investors. Now investors stopped buying, so the loans were stuck on the banks' balance sheets. That puts the banks at significant risk if the businesses involved in these leveraged buyouts begin to falter, a growing likelihood in a weakening economy. At the very least, these loans tie up scarce capital—the dollars regulators require banks to set aside in case of credit problems. This impairs the bank's capability to extend credit to other borrowers. A bank's capability to lend depends on how much capital it has; less capital means less lending.

Other parts of the credit market were now feeling the stress, as investors grew wary of all risk. Prices for lower-quality bonds backed by auto and credit card loans fell sharply, as did prices for the commercial mortgage securities used to finance the purchase and construction of office towers, shopping malls, and hotels. Bond issuance declined substantially, with junk corporate bond issuance stalling and even well-performing emerging economies pulling back on the debt they were willing and able to sell.

Bond Insurers at the Brink

Financial guarantors faced especially sharp problems. These institutions sell insurance on bonds, guaranteeing to make investors whole if the bonds ever default. Providing insurance on municipal bonds has long been their principal business; because state and local governments almost never default, it has been very profitable, if a bit dull.

The government agencies that issue municipal bonds, from the Port Authority of New York to the state of California, are willing to insure their bonds only if such insurance costs less than the added interest they would pay with no insurance. The formula normally works because the guarantors have their own top-grade seal of approval, which the pension funds and endowments that invest in risk-free assets such as insured municipal bonds demand.

Now, however, it appeared that the guarantors had undermined their own financial viability by expanding beyond their core municipal insurance sphere of business. In search of bigger profits, the guarantors wrote hundreds of billions of dollars in insurance contracts in the credit default swap market, a market in which investors buy and sell insurance on a wide array of bonds and CDOs. They promised to compensate buyers if their mortgage-related bonds ever defaulted. As the calamity in the housing and mortgage markets unfolded, these payouts began to look as if they would cut deeply into the insurers' capital base.

The rating agencies that rate the bond insurers' debt warned the guarantors to shore up their capital or see their ratings downgraded. Downgrades would almost certainly put the insurers out of business, rendering their insurance worthless. Investors with a mandate to purchase only risk-free assets would have no choice but to sell their insured municipal holdings, at whatever price they could get.

The formerly staid muni market launched into turmoil as the odds of this scenario rose. Rock-solid municipalities found themselves in the unlikely position of having to pay interest rates reserved for only high-risk borrowers. Waves from the subprime financial shock had now engulfed state and local governments.

Liquidity-Squeezed Broker-Dealers

The financial shock hit its apex in spring 2008 when rumors swirled over potential liquidity problems among Wall Street's so-called broker dealers. These are investment firms that buy and sell securities both for customers, and for themselves. They often are highly leveraged, borrowing to make big bets on securities ranging from U.S. Treasury bonds to exotic and risky securities backed by mortgages. When they bet right their profits can be huge—but when they bet wrong, they can end up like Bear Stearns.

Bear Stearns bet big on the residential mortgage market. It not only issued mortgage securities, it had acquired mortgage lending firms that originated the loans that went into those securities. Bear "made a market" in mortgage securities, meaning it would either buy or sell, whichever a customer wanted. It prospered during the housing bubble, but as the housing and mortgage markets collapsed, each of Bear's various business segments soured in turn, and confidence in the firm's viability weakened. Unlike commercial banks that collect funds from depositors, a broker dealer relies on other financial institutions to lend it the money it invests. If those other institutions lose faith and begin withdrawing their money, the broker dealer's only options are bankruptcy, or—as in Bear Stearns' case—selling out.

Over a tumultuous weekend in mid-March, the Federal Reserve engineered the sale of Bear Stearns to J.P. Morgan Chase. The Fed acted out of fear of what a bankruptcy could have meant for the financial system, given Bear's extensive relationships with banks, hedge funds, and other institutions around the world. Policymakers were legitimately worried that the financial system would freeze. To make the deal work, the Fed had agreed to absorb any losses on tens of billions of dollars in risky Bear Stearns securities that J.P. Morgan acquired in its takeover of the failed firm. The Fed also established new sources of cash for these hard-pressed institutions to forestall a similar fate befalling another one.

Recession

The Fed's actions signaled that policymakers, including Congress and Bush Administration were working hard to stem the financial crisis. It was too late for the rattled economy. With the entire financial system hemorrhaging losses, and with every corner of the credit markets in disarray, loans to consumers, businesses, and even state and local governments became scarcer and more costly. Banks aggressively ratcheted up their lending standards; borrowers who normally were considered good credits and could readily get a loan, now could not. Not only was a subprime loan out of the question, but even prime borrowers were struggling to get credit.

Without credit, home sales buckled, and subprime borrowers who had hoped to refinance before their mortgage payments exploded higher could not do so. Foreclosure seemed the only option. Inventories of unsold homes surged and house prices collapsed.

Commercial property markets froze as tighter bank underwriting and problems in the commercial mortgage securities market undermined deals. Just a year earlier, transaction volumes and real estate prices had been at record highs. Now property deals could not be consummated, weighing on commercial real estate prices and impairing developers' ability to finance new projects.

Even small and midsize companies in far-flung businesses completely unrelated to housing or mortgage finance found themselves in tough negotiations, with lenders demanding more stringent and costly terms. Financing investment and hiring was suddenly more difficult.

Previously stalwart stock investors, who had held on admirably through the turmoil in the credit markets, finally capitulated. They began to discount a recession. Financial shares of commercial and investment banks, mortgage insurers, and financial guarantors were crushed. The financial system's problems were daunting when the economy was still growing; with the economy in recession, they were overwhelming. The massive losses investors and insurers had already recognized on their mortgage holdings now seemed inadequate.

Credit is the mother's milk of a well-functioning economy, and with credit no longer flowing freely, the economy stalled. The nation's GDP barely grew at the end of 2007, and unemployment began to rise. A weakening job market mixed with the financial turmoil was too much for households to bear; consumer confidence plunged to lows last seen in the early 1980s when both unemployment and inflation were well into the double-digits. Vehicle sales plunged, and scared consumers reined in their buying. All this made businesses even more nervous, prompting less hiring and more unemployment. The self-reinforcing negative cycle that characterizes recession was now in full swing. The presidential candidates who just a few months earlier were distinguishing themselves by their positions on the Iraq war began debating the merits of fiscal stimulus and a housing bailout.

2

Sizing Up Subprime

Imagining how something as obscure as a subprime mortgage loan could have brought the global financial system to its knees and pushed the U.S. economy into recession might be hard. It's particularly strange because such loans, designed for people with a dark mark on their credit records, were, at most, marginal financial products for most of their quarter-century history.

Yet in the last year, the word *subprime* has come to stand for something much bigger: an unprecedented, broad-based erosion of credit standards. During the subprime lending frenzy, practically anyone could get a mortgage. Loans were streamlined, stripped of most controls, and offered freely under conditions that would have given most traditional bankers nightmares. Lenders even handed checks to people without requiring proof that they had a job or the income necessary to pay back the loan. The subprime phenomenon grew far beyond home mortgages, to include auto loans, credit cards, and even student loans.

Despite the clear risks, lenders also no longer required borrowers to obtain mortgage insurance. Such insurance used to be required of anyone attempting to buy a home without a substantial down payment. Instead, lenders now advised borrowers to skirt the insurance requirement by taking out two loans: a first mortgage small enough not to need insurance, and a second to cover the rest of the purchase price. The borrowers' incentives were clear: Payments on the second mortgage were less than the insurance—at least for awhile.

A requirement that borrowers also save for the expenses of home ownership also fell by the wayside. Lenders no longer required an escrow account for property taxes, which were rapidly escalating with housing values. The same applied to homeowners' insurance, which was growing more expensive, particularly in storm-prone coastal areas.

Mortgages grew more complex, evolving from plain-vanilla fixed-rate loans into myriad adjustable-rate and variable-payment form loans. Adjustable-rate mortgages (ARMs) that included only interest in the monthly payments—even loans in which such payments didn't cover the interest, with the difference added back to the principal—became increasingly common. Only someone adept at financial planning and spreadsheets could reasonably map out what these loans meant for a homeowner's future mortgage bill.

Examining the terms under which homebuyers were able to get loans in the housing boom is essential to understanding why so many are now losing their homes. The smorgasbord of terms offered to borrowers during the boom is confusing but necessary to sort through.

Government vs. Private

The menu of mortgages available to home buyers begins with those the government offers. Government plays a surprisingly large role in the nation's housing market; more than 40% of all mortgage loans outstanding have some form of federal backing.[1]

Washington supports mortgage lending most directly through the Federal Housing Administration and the Veterans Administration.[2] These agencies don't make loans themselves; they insure lenders against default. In exchange, the agencies impose some modest standards covering down payments, income, and other conditions. Despite the easy terms, FHA and VA lending faded to a trickle during the housing boom, as private subprime lenders offered borrowers much more attractive terms. More recently, the agencies have made a come-back as subprime lending has evaporated and as policymakers have ex-panded the FHA's lending authority.

Government's role in the housing market is also evident in its im-plicit backing of Fannie Mae and Freddie Mac. The Federal National Mortgage Association (Fannie Mae, for short) was established during the Great Depression to improve the flow of mortgage credit and in-crease home ownership. The Federal Home Loan Mortgage Corp. (Freddie Mac) was set up in 1970 to do essentially the same thing, to provide competition to Fannie Mae. Both were so successful that they were spun into publicly traded companies in 1989. The government no longer formally backs them and has no legal obligation to help if they stumble, yet it is clear from recent events that the federal govern-ment would not let either company go down. So strong is the belief in Washington's support, in fact, that Fannie and Freddie are able to raise funds more cheaply than other private financial institutions.

Fannie and Freddie are heavily regulated, and their charters re-quire that they promote home ownership among lower-income and disadvantaged groups. As such, until recent policy changes, they were barred from backing "jumbo" loans (those over $417,000) in most parts of the country. Loans below that size and those that also meet (conform to) other Fannie and Freddie requirements are known as "conforming" loans.

Prime vs. Subprime

Government's role in the mortgage market is still large, but it has steadily diminished over the past quarter-century. Private sources of mortgage credit overtook government sources at the start of this decade and now account for some 60% of mortgage debt outstanding.

The private mortgage market can be sliced in numerous ways; the most obvious is based on borrowers' credit scores. The market distinguishes between prime and subprime borrowers using such scores, which reflect how an individual has managed his debts in the past. Scores are derived using statistical techniques based on information in borrowers' credit files. Borrowers with a record of late debt payments receive a lower score. Borrowers with a lot of credit cards and other financial obligations receive lower scores, as do borrowers who actively use most of the credit lines available to them.

Many types of credit scores exist—almost as many as there are lenders—but the most common is the FICO score, named after the firm Fair Isaacs, which was the first to successfully commercialize its use. The FICO score ranges from a low of 350 to a perfect 850. The lower the score, the higher the likelihood the borrower will not manage new credit well. Until recent years, credit scores were primarily used to make decisions about credit cards. In the past decade, however, scoring has become common across all consumer lending, including mortgage loans.

As the term suggests, a prime borrower is someone lenders are eager to do business with because the person has a good history of debt repayment. Prime borrowers may have missed a payment or two in the past, but never by more than a month. A bill two months past due causes borrowers' credit scores to drop, jeopardizing their prime status. By contrast, a subprime borrower has a significantly blemished credit history, or none at all. During the housing boom, many first-time home buyers had never received credit.

A wide range of in-betweens exists—not quite prime, not quite subprime. Some of these borrowers receive labels such as "alternative-A," or eligible for an A or prime loan, but with something not quite right. These alt-A borrowers generally have solid credit scores, but another credit issue might precludes them from being considered prime. For example, an investor or borrower whose income has not been documented and verified may be classified as alt-A.

No credit score officially distinguishes a prime borrower from a subprime borrower, but most lenders and regulators consider someone with a score of less than 620 subprime. (The average national credit score across all borrowers is about 700.) Credit scores for subprime borrowers moved higher during the housing boom, but largely because lenders were aggressively pushing subprime loans—loans that carried higher rates and fees—to people who might well have been eligible for cheaper conventional mortgages. The average FICO score among subprime borrowers who took out loans to purchase homes in 2006 had risen to about 650 (see Table 2.1).

TABLE 2.1   What Is a Subprime Mortgage? Characteristics of Securitized Mortgage Purchase Loans, 2006

	Subprime	Alt-A	Jumbo
Basic Characteristics			
Avg. FICO Score	646	717	748
Avg. Combined Loan-to-Value Ratio	95.0%	89.0%	79.0%
Avg. Debt to Income Ratio	42.0%	38.0%	36.0%
Avg. Loan Size	$205,410	$302,404	$584,545
Product Type			
Interest-Only Fixed Rate	1.0%	13.2%	15.1%
Other Fixed Rate	8.5%	7.5%	40.5%
Interest Only ARM	22.0%	39.6%	38.4%
Negative Amortization ARM	0.0%	23.2%	0.2%
Other ARM	68.5%	6.5%	5.9%
Type			
Fixed Rate	9.4%	30.7%	55.6%
1-Year Arm	0.7%	21.1%	0.3%
2-Year Arm	75.9%	2.1%	0.0%
3-Year Arm	10.5%	4.1%	0.9%
5-Year Arm	2.8%	31.5%	21.5%
7-Year Arm	0.1%	5.7%	10.7%
10-Year Arm	0.5%	4.8%	11.0%

**TABLE 2.1   What Is a Subprime Mortgage? Characteristics of
Securitized Mortgage Purchase Loans, 2006**

	Subprime	Alt-A	Jumbo
Occupancy Status			
Owner Occupied	91.7%	78.0%	87.9%
Investor	5.9%	14.8%	1.5%
2nd Home	2.4%	7.2%	10.6%
Documentation			
Full Doc	48.5%	18.1%	46.6%
Low Doc	51.1%	78.2%	49.3%
No Doc	0.3%	3.6%	4.1%
N/A	0.0%	0.1%	0.0%
Piggyback Second Mortgage Loans			
With Piggybacks	55.4%	57.0%	29.4%
Without Piggybacks	44.7%	43.1%	70.6%
Property Type			
Single-Family	67.7%	53.4%	66.4%
Condo/Coop	8.7%	13.5%	13.5%
2-4 Units	7.8%	7.0%	1.5%
Other	15.8%	26.1%	18.6%
40-Year Mortgage			
40-Year FRM	0.2%	0.2%	0.0%
40-Year ARM	2.9%	6.1%	0.1%
Not a 40-Year Mortgage	96.6%	93.7%	99.9%

Subprime lending took off everywhere across the country, but ground zero was in California and Florida. More than one-third of the loans made in 2006 in the Central Valley of California and throughout south Florida were subprime (see Figure 2.1).[3] The border areas of Texas and around Detroit were also hotbeds of such lending. Subprime was less prevalent in areas where credit scores were higher, such as New England and much of the farm belt. The lowest average credit scores in the country are along the Texas-Mexican border; Wisconsin households have the highest credit scores in the nation.[4]

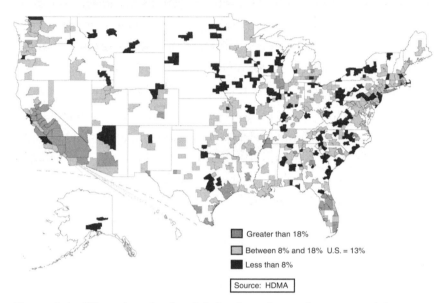

Figure 2.1 Where is subprime? Subprime share of mortgage debt outstanding, 2006.

Fixed vs. Adjustable

Subprime borrowers' financial woes were worsened by the fact that most took out adjustable-rate mortgages (ARMs). ARMs have existed for a quarter-century, but lenders historically have offered them only to home buyers with good credit, bigger down payments, and stable incomes. This changed quickly during the housing boom; 90% of subprime loans made in 2006 carried adjustable rates.

The fixed-rate mortgage loan, in which monthly mortgage payments never change, no matter what happens to interest rates or financial markets, is a uniquely American financial instrument. It is the predominant type of mortgage, accounting for three-fourths of mortgage debt outstanding. Thirty-year, fixed-rate loans were born in the wake of the Great Depression and fostered by the federal government, via the FHA and Fannie Mae, as a way to promote home ownership.

Fixed-rate mortgages have succeeded in putting and keeping households in their homes. Households with fixed mortgages can accurately budget their housing costs, making payment problems unusual. When long-term interest rates decline (fixed mortgage rates are commonly pegged to the rates on ten-year U.S. Treasury bonds), borrowers can easily and cheaply refinance at the lower rate.

Fixed-rate loans have obvious advantages for borrowers, but they can be unaffordable when inflation and interest rates are high. ARMs were developed in the early 1980s, a period of double-digit inflation and interest rates, to help with these affordability problems. Lenders can offer borrowers lower rates to start, pegging the interest rate to short-term market rates, which are generally lower than long-term rates. Borrowers don't know for sure what their future mortgage payments will be, but they accept the greater uncertainty in exchange for an initially more affordable mortgage.

Policymakers have also encouraged the use of ARMs over the years. During the 1980s, regulators viewed ARMs as a way for lending institutions to reduce some of the interest-rate risk they continually struggle with. The savings and loan crisis of the early 1990s grew out of the mismatch between the fluctuating interest rates savings depositors demanded and the fixed interest payments S&Ls received on the mortgages they held. Regulators believed ARMs would help solve lenders' problems matching their borrowing costs with their interest income on their loans.

Federal Reserve Chairman Alan Greenspan was still singing the praises of ARM loans as recently as this decade. Greenspan argued that most people remain in their homes less than ten years, so why should they pay the added interest expense associated with a fixed-rate loan based on a ten-year bond? ARM loans that adjusted after three, five, or even seven years would be cheaper and fit better with American families' lifestyles.

Yet ARM loans also shift substantial risk to borrowers when rates fluctuate. Falling short-term rates are not a problem for borrowers, but rising rates can quickly create a major financial headache. Indeed, homeowners with ARM loans are much more likely to have credit problems than those with fixed-rate loans. Even in the best of times, the delinquency rate on ARM loans is 50% greater than on fixed-rate loans.[5]

The fact that most subprime and alt-A loans made in recent years are ARMs is disconcerting. ARMs account for a fourth of total mortgage debt outstanding, but they make up three-quarters of subprime loans and almost two-thirds of alt-A loans. Most subprime ARM loans are designed to "reset" after two years. That is, their interest rates remain fixed for the first 24 months; after that, the monthly payment is tied to a benchmark index. Payments generally adjust every six months. The bulk of subprime loans made in 2006 began to reset in early 2008.

The size of a reset depends on prevailing interest rates. Homeowners who took out ARMs in 2005 saw their payments soar in 2007 because short-term rates were very high early that year. Most subprime loans have an adjustment cap of 2 percentage points, meaning that the rate can't reset by more than that. In early 2007, many ARM loans hit the cap. Monthly payment on these loans jumped by an average of $350, taking the average homeowner's monthly payment from $1,200 to $1,550.

In a quest to improve affordability, lenders heavily marketed ARM loans with features that shifted even more interest-rate risk to borrowers. One such feature was the "teaser" rate, an extraordinarily low initial rate designed to enable borrowers to qualify for a loan. At times, teasers were offered at rates of only 1% or 2%. Borrowers qualified for loans based on the monthly payments implied by the low teasers, even though the payments would rise substantially when the ARM began to reset. That was a problem for another day.

"Interest-only" and "option" ARMs also became popular ways to arrange low initial monthly payments. Interest-only ARMs allow borrowers to forgo principal payments. Option ARMs give borrowers a choice; they may make standard interest and principal payments, pay only the interest, or pay only a minimum amount that doesn't even cover the interest due. Interest not paid is added back into the loan principal. This is known as negative amortization, a reverse of the way most mortgage loans behave. Most loans self-amortize over their life, typically 30 years. Not surprisingly, most borrowers who take out option ARMs use the negative-amortization payment option.

Interest-only and option ARMs are very effective ways to significantly lower monthly payments early on, but they impose much higher borrowing costs in the future. The larger the amount of negative amortization and the longer the period over which it occurs, the larger the increase in the payment needed later to fully amortize the loan.

In the teeth of the housing boom, teaser rates on subprime loans were common. Interest-only loans grew in use. Option ARM loans had not yet become common for subprime borrowers, although lenders were beginning to consider them. Yet the housing and mortgage markets unraveled before they had a chance.

Risk Layering

With so many borrowers with sketchy credit getting increasingly complex ARMs, a growing number faced difficulty staying current on their loans. Yet for millions to actually begin losing their homes, something else had to be at work. Credit risk managers call that something else "risk layering." This was the combination of subprime borrowers and their unmanageable ARMs with little or no down payment, unverified and thus unreliable incomes, and already burdensome debt loads.

Down payments were the first traditional lending standard to crumble. For many potential borrowers, the principal impediment to purchasing a home was saving that initial stake. Typically at least 20% of the purchase price, the down payment represented the owners' equity, their stake in the home. The down payment was large enough to convince lenders that a new owner was truly committed and would not risk losing the investment. This standard steadily eroded. Down payments shrank to 10 percent and then 5 percent; in the midst of the housing boom, many subprime borrowers were down putting little, if anything.

To compensate for a low down payment, borrowers in the past had been required to purchase mortgage insurance. Without much of a financial stake in the home, a borrower was more likely to default; insurance was necessary to cover the lender and pay any associated costs in a foreclosure. This insurance was costly, however, so creative lenders came up with an alternative: Take out two loans. Buyers could obtain a first mortgage equal to 80% of the home's purchase price, and a second mortgage that covered the remaining 20%. These so-called "piggyback" second loans, which usually took the form of home equity lines of credit, were cheap, particularly when the Federal Reserve Board was easing monetary policy. Rates on most home equity lines were linked to short-term lending rates, as opposed to longer-term (and usually higher) rates that governed standard home mortgages.

Putting a "piggyback" loan on top of a standard mortgage was a very sweet deal for a home buyer. To have a house of your own, you needed little or no money; all you had to do was sign some papers. Essentially all the money paid to the seller of a house was borrowed. For lenders, however, this was an exceptionally risky proposition. Before the housing bubble, the average American homeowner's mortgage debt equaled 40% of the home's purchase price. Excluding families that already had paid off their mortgages, the average U.S. mortgage still equaled only 65% of a home's market price. But by 2006, the average subprime borrower had mortgage debt equal to 95% of the home's purchase price. That was a recipe for disaster: If home prices fell, many of those homeowners would owe more on their loans than their homes were worth. That's exactly what happened.

Most homeowners will work to make good on their mortgage even in tough circumstances. If they also have to struggle with a substantial increase in their mortgage payment or a disruption to their income, however, they will find it all but impossible to keep the house. If, in addition, their own equity stake in the house is gone—because the amount they owe on their mortgages exceed the market value of the home, putting it "under water," in the parlance of the trade—they might easily lose hope and simply decide to walk away.

Not only did lenders stop asking for down payments, but they also stopped asking for proof of income. Asking for a W-2 form or a tax return had always been a standard part of making a loan. In some cases, a self-employed borrower didn't have the necessary documentation, but they were uncommon, and lenders had enough other information to feel comfortable that the borrower could support the loan. This changed during the boom. Lenders stopped asking for proof of income altogether. By 2006, well over half of subprime loans were so-called "stated income" loans; the borrower simply stated the income, and the lender accepted that number. Some borrowers lied outright, and many more stretched the truth to stretch into a mortgage.

In most cases, the mortgage they stretched into put a heavy burden on their stated income, even at the teaser ARM rate. The average recipient of a subprime mortgage in 2006 was committing more than 40% of his or her income to mortgage payments. Of course, most borrowers had liabilities beyond their mortgages. Staying current on credit cards, auto loans, student loans, and other debts required more than half these borrowers' incomes.

Alt-A and jumbo borrowers weren't quite as layered up, but they weren't far behind. In 2006, for example, nearly 15% of alt-A borrowers were investors; they bought a house not to live in, but to sell quickly at a profit. These buyers were much more likely to walk away from a bad mortgage deal.

To Securitize or Not to Securitize

To fully understand a subprime mortgage, you need to know how it is financed. Fundamentally, loans either are financed directly by financial institutions such as commercial banks and thrift institutions, or are repackaged as bonds (that is, securitized) and sold to investors, who keep or trade them in global financial markets. The overwhelming majority of subprime loans have been securitized.

A quarter-century ago, most mortgage loans were funded the old-fashioned way: Commercial banks or savings and loans loaned the money they had received from depositors. Only a tenth of mortgage loans were securitized, and the securities market was dominated entirely by the government-related agencies Fannie Mae, Freddie Mac, and Ginnie Mae, the agency that insures mortgage securities backed by FHA and VA loans (see Figure 2.2).

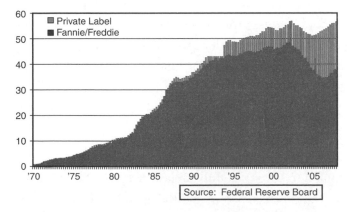

Figure 2.2   Securitization flourishes: share of mortgage debt that is securitized

This all changed during the 1980s and 1990s. Securitization flourished, partly because the S&L industry had all but collapsed. That collapse, in turn, can be traced to how S&Ls had mismanaged the fixed-rate mortgage loans they originated. Meanwhile, Fannie and Freddie were flourishing. Both had become publicly traded companies in the late 1980s; the move unfettered them from the government but did not take away the advantage they enjoyed as "government-sponsored enterprises." Both were able to raise money cheaply from investors who assumed they were safer than other banks. As a result, both grew rapidly in size and scope. By the mid-1990s, more than half of all mortgage loans had been securitized.

The securities market also underwent a substantial transformation beginning in the 1990s, when private financial institutions (mainly investment banks) became substantial players. Fannie and Freddie were barred from making subprime, alt-A, and jumbo loan business, so these other institutions moved in, expanding these markets as well. At the peak of activity, just before the subprime shock, these private-label securities financed one-fifth of all mortgage loans.

The benefits of securitization appeared substantial. For institutions that originated loans (commercial banks, but also nonbank mortgage lenders and others), securitization reduced their risk and freed up cash for additional lending. For global investors, it provided an opportunity to invest in a much broader array of assets and to precisely calibrate the amount of risk in their portfolios. Wall Street loved the hefty fees involved in packaging and selling the securities. Policymakers also liked securitization because it appeared to spread risk broadly among global investors.

By mid-2008, as the effects of the subprime shock spread, mortgage lending seemed to have gone full circle. Private-label securitization had collapsed, and banks, S&Ls, and the agencies were trying to fill the void. The volume of mortgage securities issued by Fannie, Freddie, and Ginnie Mae was slowly reviving. And while banks and thrifts weren't making subprime and alt-A loans, they were beginning to make prime jumbo loans.[6] How this trend developed became critical in determining when and how quickly the U.S. housing market revived.

Sizing Subprime

The home sales and mortgage lending craze lasted from spring 2004 to fall 2007. Throughout this period, the market was flooded with the riskiest varieties of subprime, alt-A, and jumbo ARM loans, the types of loans lenders' would have been too nervous to make even a few years before.

The frenzied lending hit an apex in 2006. Of the $3 trillion in loans extended to all mortgage borrowers that year, $615 billion were subprime, $475 billion were alt-A, and $395 billion were jumbo ARMs. An incredible $250 billion in the riskiest stated-income, no-down-payment subprime ARM loans were originated.

In truth, barely anyone expected these loans to be around very long. The expectation was not that they would default, but that they would be refinanced before trouble hit. The thinking was that house prices would continue to rise strongly, creating new wealth in the form of housing equity for even borrowers who had put down no money. This equity would be enough to convince future lenders to replace the existing loan with a new one, with possibly even better terms for the borrower.

House prices peaked just as lending was at its most crazed, in spring 2006, and then began to fall. By mid-2008, they were back to levels that had prevailed in early 2004. That left most subprime borrowers who had received loans with little or no down payment during the boom in a dangerous situation, owing more than their properties were worth. Refinancing was no longer an option because a new loan could not be enough to pay off the old one.

Ten million American homeowners, a fifth of all mortgage holders, are now in this untenable financial situation. The face value of
their mortgages is a whopping $2.75 trillion, equal to nearly a quarter
of all mortgage debt outstanding. Half of this, equal to $1.25 trillion,
consists subprime debt, another $1 trillion is alt-A, and jumbo ARMs
account for the remaining $500 billion (see Figure 2.3).

Given the millions of homeowners and trillions of dollars involved,
it was perhaps inevitable that the global financial system would react.
But what happened next was bigger than anyone had foreseen.

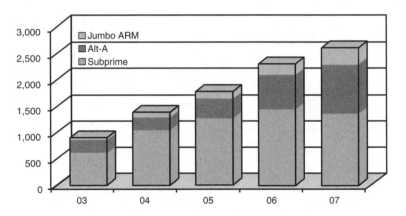

Figure 2.3   Lots of subprime: mortgage debt outstanding, $ bil, year-end

3

Everyone Should Own a Home

The roots of the subprime financial shock begin in the American psyche and run through the typical household's balance sheet. Most of us define financial success by the size and quality of our home. The pecuniary and psychological benefits we attach to home ownership are unique; no other country values hearth and home more highly. Most of us spend far more on housing than we do on anything else, and American wealth is critically linked to the home—a house is the typical family's largest asset, and the mortgage is the largest liability.

Most economic policies since the Great Depression have been designed to help people acquire homes. Nothing receives more tax breaks than a house, from the ability to deduct mortgage interest and property taxes, to the low tax rate on the profits from a home sale. A host of government agencies and related institutions, such as the Federal Housing Administration (FHA), Fannie Mae, and Freddie Mac, exist to ensure that almost anyone who wants a home can own one.

The national obsession with home ownership reached a crescendo in this decade's housing boom. Home sales, housing construction, and house prices surged nearly everywhere. Most of us understood that home prices wouldn't go straight up forever, but many accepted the notion that they would never fall. At the height of the frenzy, we were all investing aggressively in our homes. We expected this to pay off big—certainly bigger than any other investment opportunities. We were all speculating.

Renters in places such as Los Angeles and Boston, who thought they'd never be able to own a home, were finally able to get in the door. Soaring house prices were no longer an impediment; a first-time home buyer could obtain a mortgage with little money down and a (just barely) low enough monthly payment. The loan might have been complicated and hard to understand, but lenders seemed sure it was affordable.

The market also brought trade-up buyers, people who had purchased their first home a few years earlier and now wanted something bigger. Others wanted to upgrade their current house, adding a bigger deck, a swimming pool, or a built-out basement. And why not? With real estate prices rising quickly and cheap credit readily available, didn't it make financial sense to aggressively invest in your home? And with 9/11 just a recent memory, spending more time at home—in a bigger, better home—seemed the prudent thing to do.

Older people, especially higher-income baby boomers, were thinking ahead to their retirements. If they didn't move quickly, that second home on the golf course or near the beach might soar out of reach. And with stocks gyrating in the wake of the tech bust, and CDs and money markets paying rock-bottom rates, where better to put your savings than in real estate?

On the far end of the market were so-called "flippers," who bought and sold houses quickly for profit. They were pure speculators who cared nothing about home values beyond a few months into the future. No investment had offered better returns since the collapse of the Internet bubble, and all that easy credit meant you were putting someone else's money at risk.

By summer 2005, the housing boom was at its apex. Nearly everyone believed there was no place like home. The housing market had come unhinged from the underlying forces that determine sales, construction, and house prices. The subprime financial shock, or something similar to it, was inevitable.

Hearth and Home

Outside of employment, nothing determines the economic well-being of most American households more than a house. Most of us spend as much on our home as our incomes and wealth allow. Substantial financial incentives—the most obvious being the tax code—enable this, although our preoccupation with houses is more deep-seated. Owning a home is a basic theme of nearly everyone's American dream.

Perhaps the best measure of the nation's economic success is the home ownership rate—the percentage of households who own their homes. From a historical perspective, we've done well. From just before World War II to 2005, the home ownership rate rose a stunning 25 percentage points.[1] It rose even faster for groups with historically lower rates of home ownership, such as younger, African-American, and Hispanic households.

After World War II, returning GIs took advantage of the period's low borrowing costs and new, no-down payment mortgages backed by the Veterans' Administration (VA).[2] Home ownership surged, rising from 44% of households in 1940 to 55% by 1950 (see Figure 3.1). The rate rose more slowly after that but still increased another 10 percentage points during the next quarter-century. A key factor was the expansion of the interstate highway system in the 1960s and 1970s, which helped turn millions of urban renters into suburban homeowners.

Housing struggled during the 1980s and early 1990s. Double-digit borrowing costs and unemployment weighed heavily on home ownership early in the period. Then the savings and loan crisis and resulting credit crunch in California and the Northeast caused housing prices to fall sharply in these areas. The home ownership rate in 1995 was not much higher than in 1965.

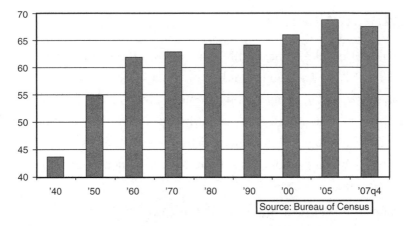

Figure 3.1   Steadily rising homeownership: The % of households that own their own home

In the late 1990s, however, falling mortgage rates, low housing prices, and rapidly increasing access to mortgage credit brought housing back to life. As the market grew increasingly frenzied after 2000, the home ownership rate rocketed higher. From 1995 to 2005, the home ownership rate jumped 5 percentage points to an all-time high of 69%.

No Place Like Home

A home is the largest budget item for most American households. From the mortgage payment and property taxes, to heating oil and furniture, the average family devotes a third of its spending to the house.[3] Nothing else comes close, even cars. Most households own at least two vehicles, and purchase, operations, maintenance, and all other transportation-related costs account for only a seventh of the average household budget. Food, including restaurant dining, accounts for a tenth.

Spending on homes makes Americans unique. By comparison, households in New Zealand devote about a fourth of their budgets to housing. For French households, it's a fifth, and only a seventh for the Japanese and Koreans.

Housing is equally important to rich and poor Americans. Spending on houses increases lockstep with incomes; the highest-earning homeowners devote as large a slice of their budgets to housing as do middle- and lower-income households. We spend as much on our homes as our incomes, wealth, and mortgage lenders will allow.

A home is most households' largest asset. Collectively, homeowners owned $20 trillion in residential real estate at the peak of the housing boom in 2006.[4] This was more than double the amount a decade earlier. Most of us finance our homes with mortgage loans, although a surprising fourth of homeowners owe nothing on their homes. Collectively, homeowners are on the hook for more than $10 trillion in mortgage debt. Homeowners' equity—the value of all homes minus the mortgage debt owed on them—totals about $10 trillion.

The average homeowner's equity was $75,000 at the peak.[5] Housing wealth is distributed relatively evenly; it's not that a few wealthy homeowners own most of the equity. More than three-fourths of homeowners had equity worth more than $30,000. Housing wealth does vary substantially across the country. On the Monterey Peninsula in California, the average homeowner had more than $400,000 in equity, although homeowners in Indianapolis had only $25,000.

Although we seem to spend more time thinking about stocks, most of us shouldn't. No more than half of all households own any stock, and the value of all U.S. stock holdings, held directly or through pension funds, amounts to less than $17 trillion. The average household owns stock worth about $40,000, and stock ownership is distributed very unevenly; only about half of all investors' portfolios exceed $30,000. Except during the height of the Internet bubble at the turn of this century, housing has always been the most important asset owned by households (see Figure 3.2).

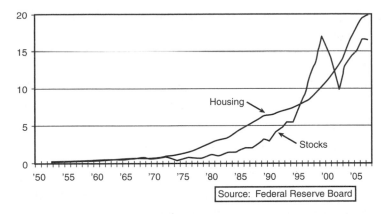

Figure 3.2 Households most prized asset: Household's holdings, Trillions $

Incentives to Own

Buying a home is a goal for most Americans, and government policies provide big incentives to do so. Ever since the Great Depression cost millions of people their homes, promoting home ownership has been a central objective of public policy. Home ownership is believed to be good for communities because homeowners are expected to care more about their neighborhoods. Policymakers have also long believed that it was good macroeconomic policy as housing plays such a fundamental role in the economy's growth prospects.

The government most clearly promotes housing through the tax code. The U.S. Treasury gives up $150 billion each year in revenue, thanks to the tax breaks housing enjoys. The biggest tax break is the mortgage interest deduction. Part of the income tax code since its inception in 1913, the mortgage deduction wasn't initially designed to promote home ownership. Only 1% of the population earned enough money to pay income tax a century ago, and very few homeowners even had a mortgage. The interest deduction was instead aimed at businesses paying taxes on their profits. For tax purposes, profits were defined as revenues minus expenses, and interest payments were defined as an expense. The same formula was extended to individuals; taxable income was defined to exclude interest. Later amendments took the privilege away from nonmortgage debt, so taxpayers cannot deduct credit card or auto loan interest. But mortgage interest is still deductible. And today nearly 40 million taxpayers take advantage of this unintended consequence of the original tax code.

Other key tax breaks include deductions for state and local property tax payments and the treatment of capital gains on home sales.[6] Capital gains taxes on sales of a primary residence were significantly reduced a decade ago; profits of less than $250,000 ($500,000 for a married couple) are not taxed. Even before this addition, homeowners could take a once-in-a-lifetime exclusion on all the profit earned from selling a home. Sellers also received a big break early in the decade when President George W. Bush lowered the tax rate on capital gains.

Taken together, tax benefits on housing lower the effective mortgage rate to borrowers by nearly a full percentage point. If you buy a home today, putting down 10% and taking out a prime, fixed-rate mortgage of $225,000, the tax code saves you $150 per month, lowering your monthly payment from $1,425 to $1,275.[7] Importantly, the full benefits of these tax breaks go to only those who itemize deductions on a tax return; therefore, higher-income households tend to be the biggest winners.

The government also boosts housing by providing a reliable source of cheap mortgage credit. This isn't particularly important in good times, but in tough times it's vital. During the Great Depression, commercial banks and savings institutions, the traditional sources of mortgage loans, found themselves losing depositors; without deposits, they couldn't make loans. The Federal Home Loan Bank (FHLB) system was established to fill this breach. As a government-backed entity, it could raise funds cheaply from investors and loan money at low interest rates to member banks, which then made loans to households and businesses. The FHA and Fannie Mae were also set up during this period to provide funds to the distressed housing market.[8]

We recently learned the importance of these institutions. When the private mortgage lending industry fell into disarray and funding sources dried up, lenders turned in near desperation to the FHLB system. FHLB lending then ballooned. FHA lending, which mortgage lenders had all but forgotten about during the housing boom, grew rapidly and was considered essential for solving the housing crisis.

Policymakers also turned to Fannie Mae and Freddie Mac. Now private companies with their own financial problems, these institutions still enjoyed implicit government backing and had public charters, and they came under intense pressure to provide more credit. They were granted greater authority to insure bigger mortgage loans and to purchase more mortgage securities.

Even the Federal Reserve Board (the Fed) was drafted to support the flow of mortgage credit. The U.S. central bank started its own new scheme to aid cash-strapped financial institutions, taking mortgage security holdings as collateral for loans. The Fed hoped to stabilize the value of those assets, shore up the mortgage securities market, and keep the credit crunch from getting worse.

First-Timers

Of course, obtaining credit was not a problem during the housing boom, and no one seemed to benefit more from free-flowing mortgage loans than the first-time home buyer. First-timers enjoyed a once-in-a-lifetime opportunity: All the traditional hurdles to home ownership—including credit scores, down payments, and high monthly mortgage bills—crumbled in the home-lending frenzy.

In many places across the country, first-timers had found it nearly impossible to afford the American dream. This was true even early in the decade, when mortgage rates were as low as they had been in a generation and before housing prices had taken off. Before subprime lending became widespread, a first-timer with good credit who was earning the median household income and able to put down 10% still didn't have enough income to purchase the median-priced starter home. Things had been even tougher in the early 1980s, when mortgage rates were at their highest and affordability at its lowest; a median household income was only about half of the amount needed to afford a median-priced home. ("Median" means that half of all houses would be priced higher and half would be priced lower.)

This all changed with the subprime lending explosion. As if by magic, the average first-timer now had just enough income to afford to purchase a median-priced starter home. How could that be? Incomes weren't higher; the median household had barely seen any real gains in earnings. And housing prices weren't lower; indeed, prices had soared in many areas of the country. The difference was that no-down payment, subprime, teaser-rate adjustable rate mortgage (ARM) loans were ubiquitous. And despite higher mortgage rates and much higher housing prices, the initial rate on a subprime loan was low enough to enable first-time buyers to squeeze into a typical home.

This affordability math was even more compelling for potential first-timers in the nation's priciest housing markets. In Los Angeles and Miami early in this decade, when mortgage rates were low but subprime loans were still uncommon, a first-timer with a median income had only about 60% of what was needed to buy the median-priced starter home. By early 2006, when the most aggressive subprime loans were readily available, the same Los Angeles and Miami home buyers had 85% of the income needed to buy a median-priced home, even though that house had nearly doubled in price from a few years earlier. And with a bit of financial sleight of hand, such as a no-documentation loan, a first-timer could close the deal and move into that home.

All this was too much for many first-timers to pass up. Many saw it as a rare opportunity. With mortgage rates on the rise and housing prices appreciating rapidly, if they didn't walk through the proverbial door now, wouldn't they be locked out for good?

It's clear now that many first-timers who walked through the door with a teaser-rate, subprime ARM did not understand that their mortgage payments would rise sharply a couple years later. The Fed conducted borrower surveys and found a substantial amount of misunderstanding regarding all ARM loans.[9] Some borrowers did not know their mortgage payments would ever rise, and others were confused about how much and when. Lower-income people, less educated people, and members of minority groups were much less likely to understand the terms of their ARM loans (see Table 3.1).

TABLE 3.1   Percent of Homeowners Who Don't Understand Various Features of Their ARM Loan

	Per-Period Cap	Lifetime Cap	Index
All ARM Borrowers	35	41	28
Age of Mortgage Borrower			
25-44	33	37	33
45-64	33	41	19
Income of Mortgage Borrower			
Less than $50k	40	53	40
$50k-$150k	35	34	23
More than $150k	13	21	8
Education			
College education	27	34	14
Less than college	42	47	43
Race or Ethnicity			
White, non-Hispanic	26	37	24
Non-white or Hispanic	59	52	38

TABLE 3.1   Percent of Homeowners Who Don't Understand Various Features of Their ARM Loan

	Per-Period Cap	Lifetime Cap	Index
Subprime			
Yes	37	42	25
No	23	36	45
Mortgage Debt Service Ratio			
15% of less	32	40	26
15-28%	35	35	27
Greater than 28%	41	51	36

Source: Federal Reserve Board—Based on Survey of Consumer Finances conducted by the Federal Reserve—Subprime is defined as having a mortgage rate more than 3 percentage points above the annual rate on comparable 30-year Treasury.

However, many other first-timers understood the financial implications of their mortgage, particularly in the high-priced markets. Yes, lenders likely told them they could refinance into a new loan before their mortgage payment rose. And, yes, they might not have known that refinancing would be exorbitant, given the prepayment penalties on their loans, but they also knew they were taking a gamble. It seemed like a good one at the time.

Trade-Up Buyers

With a flood of first-time home buyers coming into the market, it seemed to be an opportune time for others to trade up. First-timers are generally in their 30s, and trade-up buyers are dominated by 40-somethings. In 2005, the population count was more than 45 million American 40-somethings—people born at the peak of the post–World War II baby boom (see Figure 3.3). More 45-year-olds lived in the United States that year than any other single age group. Many had children in school and housing needs that had grown beyond the size of their starter homes.

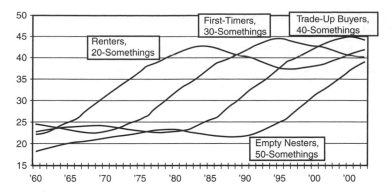

Figure 3.3   How many homebuyers? (Millions)

Interestingly, the number of American 30-year-olds—the prime demographic base of first-time home buyers—was much smaller during the housing boom. Most of the baby boomers had celebrated their thirtieth birthdays in the mid-1990s, and the number of 30-year-old Americans has been steadily shrinking since. Yet despite this substantial demographic drag, first-time home buyers fueled the housing boom—proof that the subprime loan was the catalyst for the explosion.

Terrorism also provided a substantial lift to home buying. As with nearly everything else, fallout from the World Trade Center attack on September 11, 2001, significantly shaped the housing market. This is clearest among trade-up buyers, who had the financial means to travel but largely stopped doing so out of fear that more attacks would come. Air travel was particularly nerve-wracking, and going overseas seemed downright foolhardy. Instead of traveling, households stayed home. As this nesting took hold, household spending on bigger and better homes surged.

Home builders became particularly reliant on trade-up buyers. They were building homes for first-timers, but the real money was in putting up larger homes for the more affluent trade-up market. The average size of a new home ballooned to nearly 2,500 square feet, 25% bigger than a decade before and twice the size of homes built in the

1950s.[10] Nesting 40-somethings were trading up to big, brand-new homes.

But by 2008, the trade-up buyer was fading fast as a source of housing demand. Terrorism fears had abated, and although travel still included numerous hassles—a falling U.S. dollar, rising gasoline prices, airport delays, and security screening—the nesting impulse had cooled. Demographics were changing as well. More boomers were reaching their 50s and beginning to consider life without children at home. These empty nesters would soon be trading down.

Investors

Most home buyers are normally motivated simply by the need for shelter. This changed during the housing boom. For many, the house was not just to live in; it was also a great investment. At the peak of the boom, Americans invested aggressively in their homes, effectively shifting money out of other financial investments such as stocks and bonds.

It's easy to see why investment in housing took off early in the decade. Housing brought much bigger returns than stocks, bonds, or cash. The stock market was especially unattractive after the dotcom bust in 2000. Stock prices peaked soon after Y2K; three years later, the major stock indices had been sliced nearly in half. Some $7 trillion in household wealth evaporated in the collapse, and the market has yet to fully recover. Needless to say, most households were not interested in making a major commitment to stocks during this period.

Holding cash also made little sense. The Fed had slashed short-term interest rates following the stock market crash, 9/11, and the invasion of Iraq. Soon after U.S. troops occupied Baghdad, the federal funds rate was at 1%, a rate not seen since just after World War II. Most money market accounts and CDs didn't pay enough to even match the period's low rate of inflation.

Long-term bonds offered better returns, but not significantly better; yields were historically very low. A 10-year Treasury bond in summer 2003 offered less than 3.5%, historically a rock-bottom rate. High-grade corporate and mortgage-backed bonds carried slightly higher yields, but most households had few easy ways to directly invest in them.

A house looked like a no-lose proposition by comparison. National housing prices were rising each year, posting high single-digit gains, and many parts of the country saw prices rising far faster. Even without rising housing prices, investors early in the decade found they could earn double-digit returns simply by buying a home and renting it out. This compares with 7% on an investment in an office building, 5% on a long-term Treasury bond, and 3% on an investment in the S&P 500 (see Figure 3.4).

Cash Yield

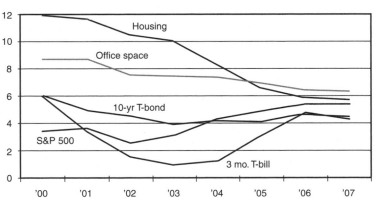

Figure 3.4   Housing loses its investment luster: cash yield

Investment returns on housing were even more attractive because the typical home was highly leveraged—most of the investment consisted of borrowed money. Leverage multiplies investment gains: For example, if you buy a house with 10% down and the value increases a mere 5% the following year, you've made a whopping 50% return on your investment. Even for someone carrying a mortgage balance equal to 50% of the home's value, a 5% increase in the house price generates a 10% return on investment. That's not bad either.

You didn't even need to buy a new house to take advantage of this investment math. Many people invested in the homes they already lived in, simply by borrowing against them and using the cash to finance an improvement project or addition. Home equity borrowing surged, as did cash-out refinancing. This occurred when a homeowner took out a larger mortgage, paid off the previous one, and pocketed the difference. With mortgage rates low and falling, homeowners could increase the size of a loan without increasing the monthly payment. Millions of homeowners jumped on this bandwagon, withdrawing nearly $1 trillion a year in equity from their houses collectively at the peak of the boom. Approximately one-third of this went back into homes as additional investment.[11]

Older, wealthier households also invested in housing by purchasing second and vacation homes. The number of second-home purchases rose from a couple hundred thousand a year to nearly half a million at the height of the boom. The typical second-home buyer did not expect a quick profit; a second house could be used occasionally, rented out, or both. Meanwhile, the value would rise, producing a healthy investment gain for the future.

Flippers

It didn't take long for such long-term housing investors to be overwhelmed by flippers, speculators who aim to buy and sell properties quickly for a profit. Such speculation is rarely based on investment fundamentals such as long-term supply and demand. Instead, it is "forecasting with a ruler"—leaping to the assumption that because prices have been rising quickly, they will continue to do so.

Speculation is not uncommon in financial markets, but it had been rare in housing. It might have happened in South Florida and Texas in the late 1970s, and in California and New England in the late 1980s, but this is difficult to document. Buying and selling houses involves transaction costs—fees, interest, and so on—which normally make it hard to turn a quick profit this way. But not during the recent housing boom. At the height of the frenzy, flippers flooded large parts of the housing market, and their own speculation helped drive the price boom they were betting on. As flippers bid up prices, it raised the appraised values on neighboring properties, which induced still more flipping and even higher prices.

The worst flipping occurred in California, coastal areas of the East, Florida, and much of the Mountain West. Not surprisingly, flippers were aggressive users of loans with low or no down payments; the high leverage of those loans juiced their returns. Here's how it worked: A flipper might purchase a new condominium for $200,000 and put down $10,000, only to sell it three months later for $225,000. Even after expenses of $5,000, the flipper would end up $10,000 richer. The annualized return on such a transaction is an incredible 400%—that is a $20,000 profit on a $10,000 investment in only three months.

The lure of such windfalls made flipping surge. The share of mortgages issued to investors, as opposed to people buying homes to live in, doubled between 2001 and 2005, going from 8% to 16%.[12] And this statistic certainly understates the increase because many flippers fudged their intentions when they applied for loans, to obtain the better credit terms given for owner-occupied houses.

Flippers were most active in the hottest markets. In Miami, Florida; Myrtle Beach, South Carolina; Phoenix, Arizona; and Las Vegas, Nevada, the reported investor share of mortgage originations and house sales topped out at more than a third (see Figure 3.5). But flipping occurred even in relatively staid places such as the condo market in downtown Philadelphia, and even in homes by a lake in Lansing, Michigan.

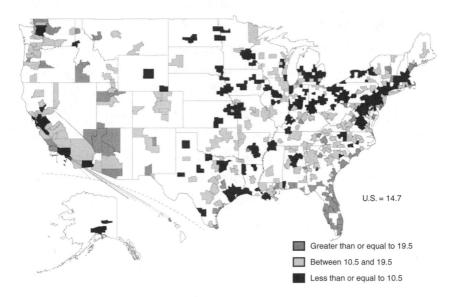

U.S. = 14.7

■ Greater than or equal to 19.5
□ Between 10.5 and 19.5
■ Less than or equal to 10.5

Figure 3.5   Where was the flipper? Investor share of home purchase originations, % of $, 2006

Flippers operated in a gray area of the housing market. Many home builders, particularly the large national firms, publicly disapproved of flipping and instituted policies to stop it. But this had little effect. In some cases, the policies weren't strictly enforced; in others, the builders knowingly looked the other way; and in still others, flippers devised clever ways to avoid detection. In hindsight, it became clear that entire tracts of new homes were built and bought by speculators who never intended to live there. Those developments stood vacant long after the boom subsided.

At the Peak

It's fair to say that, by the middle of the decade, a vast number of Americans had become housing speculators of some kind. Flippers were the most overt, but millions of others also believed that home prices would stay high permanently. Not that annual double-digit gains would go on forever, but prices would surely not fall, at least not for very long and certainly not very far.

This belief persuaded first-time home buyers that it was okay to stretch their finances to achieve home ownership. Trade-up buyers used the power of positive thinking to dream big, particularly because they planned to spend more of their leisure time at home. Even home-owners who didn't plan to move accepted the idea of housing as a good investment, especially compared with stocks and bonds. Others thought it was a perfect time to buy a second home. The flipper took this faith to the extreme. Lenders might have empowered us to act on our impulses, and regulators might have failed to adequately warn us of the dangers. But at the peak of the boom, we were all believers.

4

Chairman Greenspan Counts on Housing

For most Americans, owning a home is a deep-seated and long-standing desire. The quest for home ownership has arguably motivated households' financial decision making since the nation's founding. Yet why, in the middle of the century's first decade, did so many of us decide to buy houses all at once? During the peak of the housing boom in 2005, an astounding proportion—more than one-tenth—of the nation's homes were bought and sold.

Many factors drove this home-buying binge, but the biggest was easy credit—more specifically, the period's record-low mortgage rates. In a normal year, more than three-fourths of all home sales require a mortgage loan, and, on average, about three-fourths of a home's purchase price is paid for with borrowed money. The cost of borrowing money is critical for home sales; nothing else we buy as consumers depends so much on it.

Houses seemed a once-in-a-lifetime buy at the start of this decade. A fixed-rate loan to a prime borrower carried an interest rate of slightly more than 5%; rates on adjustable mortgage loans were well below 4%. Fixed-rate loans had not been so cheap since just after World War II, and ARM rates had never been lower. These rates were even more enticing because only a few years earlier, fixed-loan rates were above 8% and ARM rates more than 7%.

Behind the bargain-basement interest rates was a Federal Reserve on high alert. An unending string of calamities, beginning with the bursting of the Internet stock bubble and extending through 9/11 and the invasions of Afghanistan and Iraq, weighed heavily on the economy. Even the massive Bush tax cuts weren't providing much of an economic boost. China's rapid emergence on the global scene was also creating an economic upheaval. Thanks to China's ultra-low-cost production, prices for manufactured goods were falling all around the world. The Fed's overriding concern quickly became not inflation, but deflation—the kind of broad price decline that the United States hadn't seen since the Great Depression.

Fed Chairman Alan Greenspan responded with an unprecedented reduction in interest rates. Greenspan had refused to use the powers of the Fed to prick the tech-stock bubble of the late 1990s, arguing that it wasn't the central bank's place to second-guess investors. But he believed the Fed had a duty to step in aggressively *after* bubbles burst if their fallout threatened the real, outside-of-Wall Street economy. And if the economy was at risk of falling into a deflationary trap, the Fed had to ride to its rescue.

Greenspan believed that if interest rates were quickly brought low enough, they would ignite a surge in housing activity. He was correct; home sales, construction, and housing prices all took off. The housing boom had begun. As people noticed their neighbors' house prices rising, they began to feel wealthier themselves. They also discovered that lenders were eager to help them take some of that wealth out of their homes, via refinancing, home-equity loans, and other newly popular financial schemes. In effect, homes were being turned into cash machines, helping fuel a consumer buying binge.

Some saw danger in this; Greenspan did not. The Fed chairman believed that although stocks and other financial assets might be prone to bubbles, housing was immune. He argued that the costs involved in buying and selling homes were too high for speculation to take root. Moreover, even if some local housing markets became overheated, the danger to the wider economy was limited because housing was inherently a local market, not a national one.

Greenspan was partly correct; the housing boom lifted the economy out of its post–9/11 malaise. But he was dead wrong about the impact of a housing bubble. When it burst, it set off the subprime financial shock.

Lower Rates, Bigger Homes

Nothing matters more to a potential home buyer than the prevailing mortgage rate. This rate determines how large a home, if any, a household can afford. Other things matter, too—such as employment, credit history, and whether the buyer can come up with a down payment—but the principal hurdle between a household and a home is the mortgage rate.

During the past quarter-century, this hurdle has grown steadily smaller, and it all but disappeared in the housing boom. It was hard to even remember how high mortgage rates had once been. In the early 1980s, annual interest on a 30-year fixed mortgage exceeded 18%. A decade later, it had fallen to a more manageable 10%, and by 2000, it was even lower, at 8%. As recession and deflation fears took hold after 9/11 and during the invasion of Iraq, fixed rates briefly touched 5.25%. They moved higher during the decade but rarely stayed much higher than 6% for long (see Figure 4.1).

%

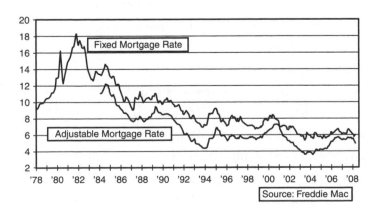

Figure 4.1   **Steadily falling mortgage rates**

The decline in rates translated into much smaller monthly mortgage payments. The average home buyer in 2000 took out a $150,000 mortgage. At the 18% mortgage rates of two decades earlier, such a loan would have required a $2,400 monthly payment,[1] half the average household's after-tax income. At 8%, the payment would be $1,250; at 6%, the cost drops to a very manageable $1,050 per month.

You can best see the difference between the housing market of the early 1980s compared to the market early this decade through the experience of a first-time home buyer. A first-timer 25 years ago couldn't afford to purchase the home he grew up in—the home his parents had bought when they were about the same age. In contrast, a first-timer early in this decade, just before the housing boom, could not only buy the home he grew up in, but could also afford to add a pool or another bedroom.

A Call to ARMs

A quarter-century of falling interest rates helped make housing much more affordable to more Americans. The rise of the adjustable-rate mortgage (ARM) further magnified this process. ARMs had been around since the late 1960s in a few California communities, but they went nationwide during the period of high and volatile interest rates in the early 1980s.[2] Lenders liked ARMs not because they were cheaper for borrowers—although that was a plus for marketing—but because they reduced the lenders' own interest-rate risk. Banks make a profit only when the rates they charge for loans exceed the rates they pay to depositors. When mortgage rates are fixed for 30 years, banks run a risk that deposit rates might rise in the interim and wipe out their earnings. This happened in the early 1990s; thousands of savings and loan institutions became insolvent as a result.[3]

Enter the adjustable-rate mortgage. Because ARM rates move periodically, lenders can more easily match ARM rates with the rates they pay depositors. The initial rate on an ARM is much lower than that on a fixed-rate loan, largely because the borrower is taking on the interest-rate risk the lender wants to avoid. If deposit rates rise— which they generally do if rates in money markets or for securities such as Treasury bills rise—borrowers' ARM payments rise soon thereafter. But a borrower who is willing to take this risk can start out with a much cheaper mortgage. During the past quarter-century, ARM rates have averaged almost 2 percentage points below rates on fixed-rate loans. For a $200,000 loan—about the average size of a mortgage in 2008—this translates into a monthly saving of $275, a large difference for a household stretching its budget to buy a home.

Many homeowners who don't plan to stay put for long also find ARM loans attractive. The average American moves at least once every seven years; for these people, the industry invented a hybrid version of the ARM in which the initial interest rate can remain fixed for up to seven years before adjusting. Such loans are less costly than fixed-rate mortgages because the ARMs are linked to short- and inter-mediate-term interest rates, which typically are lower than the long-term rates that govern fixed-interest mortgages.

Shifting interest-rate risk from lenders to borrowers was thought to be a win-win proposition: The chance of another S&L-style debacle would diminish, and home buyers would have new choices, potentially saving them money if they chose wisely. Even Fed Chairman Alan Greenspan was an avid fan of ARMs. In a speech to a credit union trade group in early 2004, Greenspan argued, "[R]ecent research within the Federal Reserve suggests that many homeowners might have saved tens of thousands of dollars had they held adjustable-rate mortgages rather than fixed-rate mortgages during the past decade, though this would not have been the case, of course, had interest rates trended sharply upward."[4]

Greenspan urged mortgage lenders to provide "greater mortgage product alternatives to the traditional fixed-rate mortgage. To the degree that households are driven by fears of payment shocks but are willing to manage their own interest rate risks, the traditional fixed-rate mortgage may be an expensive method of financing a home."

Lenders responded to Greenspan's "call to ARMs" aggressively, developing a new, wider array of adjustable loans. Originally, ARMs had been designed relatively simply, with rates that adjusted based on the one-year Treasury note or an S&L's cost of funds—mostly short-term deposits.[5] Perhaps it was just coincidence, but soon after Greenspan's speech, lenders began aggressively marketing a plethora of ARM products, ranging from the hybrid ARM, to the option ARM, to the teaser-rate subprime ARM.

The steady decline in interest rates and smorgasbord of loan products provided a lift to housing that became magnified several times over during the housing boom. Most households hunting for a home begin by meeting with a real estate agent. Realtors are adept at quickly sizing up the prospective buyer's financial circumstances. Based on those, the agent determines the lowest mortgage rate available and, therefore, just how much the buyer can spend on a house. Often the first home shown is priced just above what the agent has determined the buyer can afford. For all but the most disciplined buyers—and there weren't many in the housing boom—you psychologically can't go back. Buyers are primed to buy as much home as they can possibly afford.

Home sellers can sense this, of course, and as agents and buyers show up at the door more frequently, asking prices begin to rise. It doesn't take long for lower mortgage rates to result in higher house prices. Rising prices don't necessarily dissuade prospective buyers—at least, they didn't during the housing boom—as buyers begin to factor future house-price gains into their decision making. The higher the expected future profit, the more willing a buyer will be to buy a bigger home and take on a bigger mortgage. Moreover, if the value of a home appreciates faster than the interest rate on its mortgage, then the bigger the mortgage, the bigger the gains for the homeowner.

Under such conditions, it makes sense to buy as much house as a lender will allow.[6]

Greenspan's "Put"

Interest rates fell steadily through the 1980s and 1990s, but they plunged in the early 2000s to lows rarely experienced, igniting the housing boom and setting the stage for the subprime financial shock. Driving interest rates lower was the Greenspan-led Federal Reserve Board. Between New Year's Day 2001 and Memorial Day 2003, the Fed engineered a dramatic decline in the benchmark lending rate for banks, taking it from 6.5% all the way to 1%. Not since John F. Kennedy was president had the Fed funds rate been so low.[7]

The Fed drove rates down as the collapse of Silicon Valley's tech-stock bubble in early 2001 began to ripple through the economy far beyond California. Stock prices had surged nearly five-fold during the 1990s, and prices for the shares of technology companies—particularly those exploiting the amazing new Internet—had sky rocketed by some ten times, as measured on the NASDAQ exchange (see Figure 4.2). Speculation fueled this bubble; investors bought stock assuming that because their prices had been rising rapidly, they would continue to do so, using borrowed money—leverage—to multiply their bets. Margin debt—money borrowed from stockbrokers and used to purchase extra shares—piled up in record amounts.[8]

The bubble began to burst only days after stock prices hit their peak, in the weeks just after the turn of the decade. By the end of 2000, investors were completely panicked. The value of the NASDAQ was slashed in half. Other, broader measures of stock prices held up better, at least for a while, but more than $2 trillion in household stock wealth eventually disappeared. The economic fallout was substantial. By Christmas 2000, consumer confidence was plunging, hiring had come to a standstill, and businesses were cutting back on investment

Nasdaq Stock Index, 03-05-71 = 100

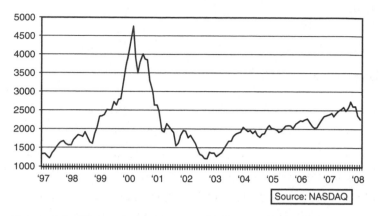

Figure 4.2   **The technology stock bubble: NASDAQ Stock Index,**
03-05-71 = 100

spending, even for new high-tech equipment. The economy was head-
ing fast into the 2001 recession.

The Fed began to aggressively lower interest rates. This was precisely how Chairman Greenspan said the Fed should respond to a
bursting investment bubble. Greenspan had laid out his position in a
June 1999 appearance before Congress's Joint Economic Committee.
He argued that policymakers could not accurately identify bubbles
until after they had burst and, thus, should not try in advance to de-
flate them: "[B]ubbles generally are perceptible only after the fact. To
spot a bubble in advance requires a judgment that hundreds of thousands of informed investors have it all wrong. Betting against markets
is usually precarious at best."

Greenspan believed the Fed should respond aggressively after the
fact, lowering rates only when a bursting bubble appears to threaten
the economy. "While bubbles that burst are scarcely benign, the consequences need not be catastrophic," Greenspan said. Japan's bubble
economy burst in the late 1980s, but that country's failure to react
promptly, not the bubble itself, caused the decade-long recession that
followed. Similarly, the Great Depression of the 1930s arose not from

the stock market crash of 1929, but from the government's failure to manage the aftermath.

Greenspan argued that his decision to lower rates aggressively in the wake of the October 1987 stock market crash had kept that financial crisis from ending the economic expansion of the 1980s. Similarly, dramatic rate cuts in 1998 seemed to have successfully limited the fallout from the collapse of hedge fund Long-Term Capital Management. These experiences had shaped his thinking about how to handle the tech-stock bust.

These words and actions strongly suggested to Wall Street that the Fed would stop any future market mishap from becoming a complete financial meltdown—that, in effect, the chairman had their proverbial financial backsides covered. Commentators called this notion "the Greenspan put,"[9] using a term from the options market. A "put" option gives its owner the right to sell a stock or bond at a preset price, offering protection against future drops in the market. Greenspan's "put" was an implied promise that if things ever went badly awry for Wall Street, the Fed would step in and cut rates enough to cushion the fall. It wasn't a guarantee that investors couldn't lose money, but it did suggest that they wouldn't lose their shirts.

Greenspan's conviction that the Fed should not prick bubbles, but rather should wait to clean up the economic mess after they burst, contributed significantly to the subprime financial shock. So did his belief that housing markets, unlike stock markets, were largely bubble proof. He spelled this out in a March 2003 speech:[10]

> It is, of course, possible for home prices to fall as they did in a couple of quarters in 1990. But any analogy to stock market pricing behavior and bubbles is a rather large stretch. First, to sell a home, one almost invariably must move out and in the process confront the substantial transaction costs in the form of brokerage fees and taxes. These transaction costs greatly discourage the type of buying and selling frenzy that often characterizes bubbles in financial markets. Second, there is no national housing market in the United States. Local conditions

dominate, even though mortgage interest rates are similar throughout the country. Home prices in Portland, Maine, do not arbitrage those in Portland, Oregon. Thus, any bubbles that might emerge would tend to be local, not national, in scope.

Deflation Fears

Greenspan's position on house price bubbles was not simply an academic debate; it was part of the intellectual foundation of his strategy for handling the apparent trend toward deflation in the wake of 9/11. The turmoil that followed 9/11 gave the Fed no option but to lower rates aggressively. Yet despite this aggressive response and the massive Bush tax cuts, the economy continued to sputter. As American forces were preparing to invade Iraq in spring 2003, deflation was Greenspan's predominant worry.

He described the economic pain of deflation in a late 2002 speech before the Economic Club of New York.[11] Deflation, he feared, would undermine incomes and profits, making household and business debt loads financially overwhelming. The resulting credit problems and bankruptcies would feed further deflation, launching a vicious cycle. The Fed chairman calculated that the economy's only chance of avoiding such a deflationary trap was an unprecedented 1% funds rate.[12] This, he reasoned, would ignite a housing boom without creating a housing bubble.

Greenspan's strategy worked. As interest rates fell, the housing market took off and lifted the economy into a self-sustaining economic expansion. By 2004, home sales, housing starts, and housing prices were surging. Thousands of jobs were being created in housing-related industries, and other industries were adding to payrolls as well. Deflation quickly faded from the economic lexicon.

The irony is that deflation wasn't the grave threat Greenspan feared. His worries were based on data from surveys that are subject to revisions—sometimes large revisions. It turned out that inflation did slow during this period, but as the revised data later showed, it slowed not nearly as much as Greenspan and others thought (see Figure 4.3).[13] Perhaps it is just as difficult to know how the economy and inflation are performing as it is to know if a bubble is forming. Equally ironic is that Greenspan thought dispelling deflation was necessary to ensure that debt loads wouldn't crush overextended households and businesses. As it turned out, the borrowing boom that Greenspan ignited created its own, perhaps equally damaging, credit debacle.

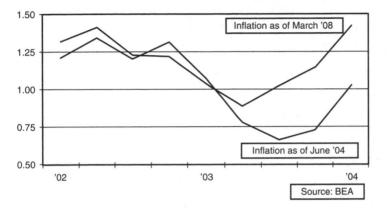

Figure 4.3   Deflation wasn't the threat feared: Inflation, % change year ago, core consumer deflator

Households on a Buying Binge

Greenspan was counting not only on an interest-rate-juiced housing market to pull the economy out of its post–9/11 malaise, but also on the hedonism of the American consumer. With housing prices and housing wealth rising quickly, and homeowners able to cheaply tap that wealth for ready cash, his expectations turned out to be well founded.

A well-established economic theory known as "the wealth effect" states that as your wealth increases, you will spend more and save less. The more your assets—a house, a retirement fund, a child's college fund—appreciate in value, the more willing and able you will be to spend your current income. Not only does the theory make intuitive sense, but it also has proved true in practice. And once again in the 2000s, as housing prices and housing wealth soared, homeowners became more avid spenders.

Although economists accept that the wealth effect exists, they do debate its size. How much does increased housing wealth add to spending? Estimates vary, but given more than $8 trillion in increased housing wealth during the boom, even a very small wealth effect implies a lot more spending.[14] Suppose that for every $1 increase in housing wealth, consumer spending subsequently increased by only a nickel—a conservative estimate of the effect. The housing boom then added more than $75 billion a year to consumer spending—enough to raise the economy's overall rate of growth by half a percentage point every year.

It's actually likely that the housing wealth effect was measurably greater than 5¢ per dollar and that the traditional pattern was supercharged as homeowners withdrew massive amounts of cash from their homes. For many, their house became another ATM. Greenspan thought the topic was so important that he personally conducted research published in Federal Reserve working papers.[15]

Homeowner cash withdrawals began to rise early in the decade via an unprecedented wave of mortgage refinancing. As fixed mortgage rates plunged from more than 8% to less than 6%, nearly anyone with a mortgage could profitably refinance it; they could quickly make up the transaction costs of the refinancing by saving the interest on the new mortgage.[16] These transaction costs were also falling fast, thanks to roaring competition among mortgage lenders and the spreading use of the Internet to reduce loan processing costs. In 2000, the value of all U.S. home-refinancing deals totaled less than $300 billion; as the refinance (refi) boom peaked three years later, the annual pace of such deals topped $4 trillion (see Figure 4.4).

The cost saving to homeowners was enormous. On the mortgage loans refinanced in 2003 alone, homeowners were cutting their interest expenses by more than $50 billion a year. Homeowners were also

Value of Mortgage Refinancings, Billions $

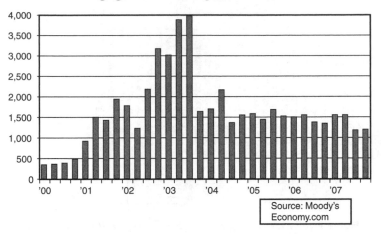

Source: Moody's
Economy.com

Figure 4.4   Mortgage refinancing activity booms: Value of mortgage refinancings, billions ($)

using their refis to raise cash. In a cash-out refi, the homeowner takes a new and bigger loan, pays off the original mortgage, and gets a check for the difference. Because mortgage interest rates were falling, the new, larger mortgage didn't necessarily require a larger monthly payment. Homeowners cashed out an estimated $100 billion in the 2003 refi boom. This was a bonanza for consumers, who used some of the cash to pay down higher-cost credit card debt and finance other investments, but spent most of it on home improvements, cars, or anything else they could shop for.

Homeowners also raised hundreds of billions via increased home equity borrowing. With interest rates low, homeowners could cheaply borrow against the value of their homes, either taking a lump-sum check with a second mortgage or setting up a home-equity line of credit up to a set amount—the average was $20,000.[17] The amount of home equity debt surged four-fold during the first half of the decade, from $200 billion to $800 billion, with homeowners tapping their houses for cash as they did through cash-out refinancing (see Figure 4.5).[18]

Home Equity Lines Outstanding, Billions $

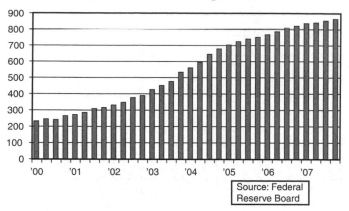

Figure 4.5   Home equity borrowing soars: home equity lines outstanding, billions ($)

The housing boom also prompted many homeowners to cash out by trading down—selling their homes at a high price and buying smaller places or even renting. Empty nesters, in particular, saw this as an opportune time to take a capital gain. In resort communities, some homeowners seized the opportunity to sell their properties to developers or investors for large profits. Some long-term residents of New Jersey beach towns, for example, moved to less expensive homes inland. They reinvested much of the resulting profits, creating comfortable family nest eggs—but they also spent some.

The Federal Reserve's dramatic interest-rate cuts had worked. Instead of remaining in a slump after 9/11, and the Afghan and Iraq invasions, the U.S. economy recovered. But that growth was built on a housing boom—a boom that ultimately became a bubble. Chairman Greenspan had expected the boom, but he had not counted on the bubble—and he certainly didn't expect what came afterward.

To this day, Chairman Greenspan rejects the notion that his aggressive lowering of interest rates earlier in the decade helped contribute to the subprime financial crisis. Indeed, it is reasonable to argue that based on the apparent threat of deflation at the time it was necessary for the Federal Reserve to act forcefully. It is even understandable why he felt that the most efficacious way to lift the broader economy was through a booming housing market. It is wrong to argue that these policies did not contribute to the crisis that subsequently ensued. They did.

5

Global Money Men Want a Piece

The Greenspan-led Federal Reserve wasn't the only source of easy money powering the housing boom and inflating the bubble. A flood of capital also poured in from around the world. Global investors thought U.S. housing was a great investment. Their funds drove mortgage rates lower and empowered lenders to offer increasingly aggressive—and ultimately unmanageable—mortgage loans.

International investors were flush with dollars the swollen U.S. trade deficit generated. Hundreds of billions of dollars flowed overseas each year in exchange for the imported goods Americans craved. U.S. consumers had been on a buying binge, fueled by the Federal Reserve's rate cuts, the massive Bush tax cuts, and all the credit they needed. Imports, in particular, were bargains, thanks to an explosion of low-cost Chinese production and the high-flying U.S. dollar. Surging prices for oil and other commodities, driven in part by booming Chinese demand, also added to the import bill. As a result, investors in places from China and India to Russia and Brazil were collecting huge pools of dollars.

For these newly flush global money men (and women), the bonds and other credit market securities Wall Street devised seemed to be perfect investments. Global investors could match the amount of risk they were willing to take with an instrument tailored to provide it—or, at least, that's what they thought. And the U.S. bond market was huge, liquid, and historically safe. Liquidity showered U.S. credit markets, pushing interest rates lower.[1]

It didn't take long for global investors to become especially enamored of mortgage-backed bonds. Foreigners had historically been buyers of risk-free U.S. Treasuries, and the bonds government-tied institutions such as Fannie Mae and Freddie Mac issued and insured were only a small step removed. It wasn't much of a leap to invest in mortgage securities whose ties were to Wall Street instead of to the U.S. government.

A self-reinforcing cycle developed: American consumers were eager to buy and the rest of the world was happy to sell, producing the goods Americans wanted and collecting their dollars. But those dollars didn't stay overseas; they reentered the U.S. economy as investments in a broad array of financial securities—none more popular than mortgage-backed bonds. As foreign investors bid up the prices of those bonds, they pushed interest rates lower, following the rule of all debt securities that price and yield move in opposite directions. The lower interest rates were passed along to mortgage borrowers, and competition among lenders led to easier lending terms as well. Cheap and easy credit spurred more home purchases and still more borrowing and spending. The cycle was complete.

The easy-money policies of most central banks also revved up the global cash engine. Most economies had struggled in the wake of 9/11 and the U.S. invasion of Afghanistan and Iraq, and their manufacturers were withering under the onslaught of Chinese competition. With inflation giving way to deflation, they had a green light to slash interest rates. The Japanese were particularly panicked after more than ten years of economic malaise; they pushed their interest rates literally to zero.

Cash was everywhere. At first, investors were skittish about the U.S. stock market after the technology-stock bust. They also had qualms about investing in emerging economies, remembering the late-1990s Asian financial crisis and Russian bond default. But these concerns quickly faded. By the mid-2000s, investors acted as if the stock, bond, and real estate markets were full of screaming buys. The enthusiasm was even greater if they could be bought with borrowed money.

By early summer 2007, risk taking in global financial markets had reached unprecedented levels. Global investors were taking huge gambles and paying premiums for the privilege. All the preconditions for a major financial upheaval were in place.

China Muscles In

Where did all this global capital come from, and why did so much of it end up in the U.S. housing market? The answer begins in China at the turn of the millennium, just as the new Chinese economy was bursting onto the global stage.

The catalyst for China's stunning economic ascent was its entry into the World Trade Organization (WTO). Membership in the international organization that sets the rule for trade among its members conferred economic advantages of lowering barriers and opening doors. It also signaled that a country mattered—that it had a seat at the table of global commerce. The Chinese leadership had long lobbied to join the WTO, and it finally happened in 2001.

Entry into the WTO significantly opened up global markets for China's goods. For increasingly footloose global manufacturers, it meant new or expanded opportunities to hire hundreds of millions of Chinese workers on better terms than could be obtained anywhere else on the planet. Combined with a fixed and increasingly undervalued currency, the yuan, this made China the lowest-cost location to produce goods for the rest of the world.[2]

China's manufacturers received another big lift in 2005, when the 20-year-old multifiber trade agreement expired. This trade treaty had limited the exports of textiles and other garments from developing economies such as China to the United States and other developed economies. With its expiration, shipments from low-cost Chinese producers surged.[3]

In the mid-1990s, China was a small player in the global economy, but within ten years, it was producing more than a tenth of the globe's manufactured goods (see Figure 5.1). China's gains came at the expense of manufacturers everywhere else: Apparel, textile, and furniture producers in the Southeastern United States were hit hard, as were lower-end producers in Mexico and Central America. Even Italian producers of fine consumer goods struggled. Because manufacturing is so important to most global economies, China's rapid grab of global market share caused wrenching adjustments in many places around the world.

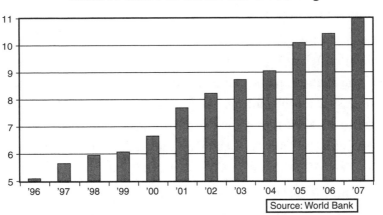

Chinese Share of Global Manufacturing

Source: World Bank

Figure 5.1   China blows onto the economic scene.

Outside of China itself, the principal beneficiaries of the country's ascent were American consumers. No other nation produced more items for U.S. store shelves than China; by 2008, more than a tenth of America's imported consumer goods were crossing the Pacific and through the ports of Los Angeles or Seattle.[4] Big U.S. retailers—most notably Wal-Mart—showed themselves extraordinarily adept at setting up efficient supply chains: from Chinese factories, to container ships, to U.S. shopping malls or Internet catalog sites. Prices plunged. The cost of Chinese-made products from sweaters to computers plunged by 20% during the first half of the decade, enabling U.S. retailers to actually lower the prices on the goods they sold to consumers. Inflation had given way to deflation—outright declining prices—in most stores.

These bargains were too good to pass up. As consumers scarfed up the deals, the nation's import bill and trade deficit ballooned. The red ink in U.S. trade with China was $50 billion when 2000 began; by 2008, it totaled a whopping $250 billion. Trade with China alone now accounts for almost a third of the total U.S. trade imbalance.

The Chinese were initially unsure of what to do with their new riches. Investment had been anathema under Mao, and few mainland residents, even among the government elite, had any idea how to go about it. The easiest and most obvious place to put U.S. dollars was in U.S. Treasury bonds. They were safe and liquid, and didn't require much financial sophistication to understand. The Chinese were similar to any young person earning a salary for the first time; they wanted to make sure they had cash socked away for a rainy day. In a sense, U.S. Treasury bonds became China's certificates of deposit. And before long, China had a lot of them—some $500 billion worth, or about a tenth of all the Treasury bonds in circulation.[5] Only the Japanese owned more, although that would change as the Chinese stake continued to rise while the Japanese were selling theirs off (see Table 5.1).[6]

TABLE 5.1   Foreign Holdings of U.S. Treasury Securities (Billions $)

Country	Jan 2008	Dec 2006	Dec 2004	Dec 2000
Japan	587	623	690	318
China, Mainland	493	397	223	60
United Kingdom	160	92	96	50
Brazil	142	52	15	-
Oil Exporters	141	110	62	48
Caribbean Banking Centers	108	72	51	37
Luxembourg	68	60	41	-

TABLE 5.1   Foreign Holdings of U.S. Treasury Securities (Billions $)

Country	Jan 2008	Dec 2006	Dec 2004	Dec 2000
Hong Kong	55	54	45	39
Germany	43	46	50	49
Korea	42	67	55	30
Switzerland	39	34	42	16
Taiwan	39	59	68	33
Singapore	38	31	30	28
Mexico	36	35	33	15
Russia	35	-	-	-
Norway	34	32		
Thailand	29	17	13	14
Turkey	28	23	12	-
Canada	24	27	33	14
Netherlands	16	21	16	11
Total	**2,403**	**2,115**	**1,814**	**1,021**

Source: U.S. Treasury Department

As China's nest egg grew larger, its financial expertise and infrastructure grew, enabling it to make bigger and bolder investments. A ten-year Treasury bond yielding 4% is fine when all you want is safety, but a 4% return looks paltry when you are rolling in cash and your own economy is growing at more than twice that pace. The Chinese began to expand their portfolios to include U.S. agency bonds—debt issued by Fannie Mae, Freddie Mac, and the Federal Housing Finance Board—to fund their own purchases of U.S. mortgage loans and securities. Although the U.S. government did not officially back these bonds, they were all but guaranteed. However, the return on agency bonds soon began to look lame to the Chinese. They began to pay attention when Wall Street's emissaries came calling to pitch other investments: corporate bonds, residential mortgage securities, and eventually even exotic derivatives such as collateralized debt obligations.

When it came to residential mortgage securities and their derivatives, Wall Street's story line was particularly convincing to the Chinese: Trillions in dollars of residential mortgage loans had been made to U.S. homeowners during the previous half-century, and the losses on those loans could be counted in basis points—in hundredths of a percentage point. Yes, home prices had declined in some parts of the country, but only briefly and temporarily; since the Great Depression, nationwide price declines had never existed. And the securities the Chinese were buying had been structured so that they would always get their money back, according to the rating agencies so revered by international investors.

Emerging Investors

The Chinese weren't the only global investors piling into U.S. credit markets. Other emerging economies—nations whose populations were still poor but whose living standards were rising fast—were also suddenly flush. Globalization had been good to them; about half of global production was now coming from emerging economies such as Brazil, India, Poland, and Russia.[7]

Soaring prices for the oil and other commodities they produced also lifted these economies.[8] The average cost of crude oil quintupled in the 2000s, from $20 per barrel to more than $100; other raw-materials prices, from copper to soybeans, also jumped. This was due to booming Chinese demand; China needed commodities to drive its factories and feed its expanding middle class. Because international buying and selling of commodities was mostly done in U.S. dollars, emerging economies were showered with greenbacks, and as with the Chinese, they thought a U.S. bond was a great investment.

The sums earned in trade were massive. The U.S. trade deficit with emerging economies swelled from $150 billion a year in 2000 to more than $350 billion in 2008. Half this increase was with OPEC nations—the big oil-exporting countries upon which the globe relies for much of its energy—whose Treasury bond purchases increased in lockstep with the dollars they raked in as the price of oil rose. The other half was with oil and natural gas producers such as Russia, copper producers such as Chile, coffee exporters such as Columbia, plywood producers such as Indonesia, and so on.

Developed economies weren't left out of the action; they, too, were taking in large amounts of dollars in trade with the United States. Only a few years earlier, the dollar had been trading near record highs against the euro, the British pound, the Canadian looney, and the Japanese yen. The lopsided exchange rate had made these nations a bargain for U.S. tourists and U.S. importers alike. Dollars flew from American pockets to British, Canadian, and Japanese cash registers; the U.S. trade deficit with these economies doubled to $200 billion annually during the first half of the decade. Investors in London, Frankfurt, and Tokyo are wealthy and experienced, and they were more interested in investments offering high returns than safe investments. Treasury bonds wouldn't suffice; their yields were much too low. More complicated U.S. credit instruments, such as mortgage-backed bonds and their derivatives, filled the bill.

If we add up the hundreds of billions of dollars that flowed out of the United States in trade and then back in as investments in U.S. credit markets, we can clearly see the magnitude of global investors' contribution to the housing bubble. The U.S. trade imbalance was without historical comparison; the deficits doubled during the first half of the decade, reaching a record $800 billion in 2006. All those billions flowing overseas each year financed a three-fold surge in the foreign holdings of bonds, to an astonishing $6 trillion (see Figure 5.2). Overseas investors' Treasury holdings more than doubled and were on pace to become the majority owner of all publicly traded U.S. Treasury debt. The foreign appetite for mortgage-backed bonds was even larger; overseas holdings of agency-related debt and Wall Street–issued mortgage securities swelled. At the peak of the housing boom in 2006, international investors owned nearly a third of all U.S. mortgages.

Credit Market Instruments Held by Foreigners, Billions $

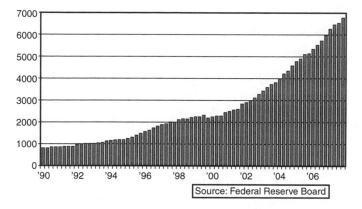

Figure 5.2   International investor holdings soar.

Central Banks Pump It Up

The extraordinarily easy money policies pursued by most of the globe's central banks also helped pump up the U.S. credit and housing market. Fallout from 9/11 and the U.S. invasions of Afghanistan and Iraq had hit the global economy hard early in the decade. Europeans were still absorbing the formerly Communist states of the East into their economic community and adjusting to their newly adopted currency, the euro. Much of Central and South America had recently reformed those national economies, and Southeast Asia was still recovering from its late-1990s financial crisis.

China's rapid economic ascent created new challenges for nearly everyone. Although the burgeoning mainland economy lowered prices for global consumers, it also destroyed the profits and jobs of its competitors. Not only were higher-cost developed economies such as the U.S. and Germany losing market share to China, but so were developing economies such as Mexico or Poland, where production costs were low—but not as low as in China.

Central bankers tried to ease the pain of all these adjustments by cutting rates. With a flood of cheap Chinese goods helping to lower inflation, policymakers had the latitude to reduce borrowing costs dramatically. The U.S. Federal Reserve led the way, but most other central banks soon followed. The Bank of England, the fledgling European Central Bank, the Mexican Central Bank, and the Bank of Canada all lowered rates. The average global central bank target interest rate declined from a peak of 5% in late 2000 to a low of 1.5% in 2003, where it stayed throughout much of 2004 (see Figure 5.3).[9] Even more telling was the negative *real* central bank target rate—the difference between the stated rate and inflation. (If the benchmark interest rate is 1.5% but inflation is 2.5%, the real rate is –1%—a condition at least theoretically attractive to borrowers.) Central bankers have historically reserved negative real rates for times of economic crisis or recession. The global real rate went negative in 2002, and it didn't turn positive again until well into 2006.

Average Central Bank Target Rate

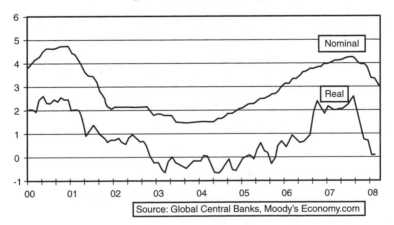

Source: Global Central Banks, Moody's Economy.com

Figure 5.3   Global central banks pump it up.

No central bank was pumping out more cash than the Bank of Japan. China's success rocked the Japanese economy. Japan had been the global export powerhouse in the 1970s and 1980s, but its bigger problems stemmed from the collapse of Japan's real estate and stock markets. A speculative bubble had developed in Japanese asset markets in the 1980s; as it unraveled during the 1990s, bad loans piled up in the country's banks. The banks took years to recognize their mistakes, refusing to write off their bad loans and tying up what capital they had. A long, painful credit crunch ensued, making it hard for even healthy businesses to expand their operations or for households to spend. With the Japanese economy moving sideways and deflation a persistent fact of life, the Bank of Japan steadily lowered rates. By the early 2000s, the rate targeted by the Japanese central bank was nearly zero—0.10%, to be more precise—and Japanese policymakers insisted it would stay that way for as long as it took to revive their economy and rid themselves of deflation.[10]

Global investors quickly devised a way to take advantage of Japan's zero-interest-rate policy: They borrowed yen in Japan and then traded the yen for dollars, euros, or Australian dollars—any other currency that seemed safe and offered better returns when invested. This became known as the yen carry trade. The trade was profitable as long as the yen stayed weak; investors could trade their higher-yielding dollars or euros back into yen, repay their loans, and pocket the difference. The Bank of Japan's steadfast promise not to change its monetary policy made a weak yen a safe bet. Trillions of yen poured out of Japan and into investments across the globe; U.S. credit markets and housing received a fair share.

A Global Sea of Liquidity

By mid-decade, a sea of cash was washing over global asset markets. Investors couldn't get enough of whatever was for sale, wherever it was. Stocks, bonds, and real estate, in Moscow, Beijing, or Los Angeles all seemed to offer buying opportunities, and prices rose sharply.

Even the professional investors who managed global pension funds, insurance companies, and hedge funds were swept up in the excitement. Initially, skeptics argued that markets were becoming overpriced, and for a time they were heeded; the financial pain of the tech-stock bust and the Asian financial crisis had not been forgotten, and most of the signals used to value investments were flashing red. However, as asset prices continued to march higher, those arguing that something was askew in global asset markets steadily lost credibility. Eventually they either changed their minds—skepticism could be bad for your career—or their views were dismissed as simplistic and impractical.

A few academics and policymakers—mostly at central banks—continued to warn that investors were taking on too much risk and that global markets were overheating. But the realities of the investment world dictated: If a manager is given money to deploy, he must deploy it or the money will go elsewhere. Managers are evaluated based on the returns they bring relative to their peers, not over several years or even over a single year, but over the space of a quarter—three short months. Life can get very lonely for a cautious investment manager in a runaway market.

Some hand wringing at investor conferences about rising global asset prices and aggressive risk taking did occur. Professional investors had a general sense that someday a market correction would bring asset prices back down modestly. But as time went on, those discussions grew increasingly theoretical and less relevant to the actual investment decisions being made.

A mounting intellectual defense of lofty global asset prices existed among managers searching to make sense of their investment decisions. This time it was different—or so the argument went. Never before had the global economy been this stable or this open. In the new economic world, business cycles might be milder and briefer than they had been historically. Ups and downs in employment and income, corporate profits, landlords' rents—conditions that determined the value of mortgage-backed bonds, corporate shares, or the price of an office tower—were growing progressively less volatile.

What some called the Great Moderation was driven by a shift in economic activity to more stable industries, such as information and health services, and away from businesses that suffer bigger swings, such as manufacturing. Better and timelier business decisions, resulting from the use of new information technologies, made it less likely that firms would misjudge their sales and get stuck with excess inventories, forcing production and job cuts. A more globally integrated economy ensured that countries suffering an economic setback could sell their wares to stronger ones, thereby cushioning their problems. Public policy was also smarter; governments and planners were better at managing their economies. As an example, most central banks had been granted enough political independence to pursue what could be unpopular efforts to achieve the explicit inflation targets they had adopted.

Global investors also took comfort in the cornucopia of new investments now available—collateralized debt obligations, collateralized loan obligations, leveraged loans, credit default swaps, auction-rate securities, and so on. These Wall Street concoctions were thought to more finely parse the risks of investing than a plain-vanilla stock, bond, or parcel of real estate could do. Risk could be more easily hedged, matched with other investments that would rise or fall in value in roughly the opposite direction. Hedging could limit gains on an investment, but it would also limit losses—or so money managers thought. Investors believed they could sign up for precisely as much risk as they wanted—no less and, importantly, no more.

Investors were emboldened. A more stable global economy meant more stable returns, and the new designer investments enabled them to fit their needs with precision. Feeling secure, their inclination was to magnify their returns through leverage—they borrowed money to buy even more of whatever they were investing in. Leverage can generate extraordinary returns if the bet works out, but it can be financially devastating if it doesn't.

The typical money manager acted similar to the owner of an over-sized SUV with a five-star safety rating. He felt safe not only driving fast, but also chatting on his cell phone at the same time. More crashes might occur, yet the SUV driver suffers no more bodily injury than if he had driven more carefully in a smaller car with only a three-star rating. For other drivers, however, the damage is substantially worse.

The liquidity sea also filled with new money—savings that had been locked away in different corners of the world and only now was finding its way into the global financial system. Similar to others, the owners of these funds were attracted by rising asset prices, the stable economy, and the risk matching afforded by designer investments. Many nations also began to remove the limits on their citizens' ability to invest outside their borders. For the first time, a Japanese or Finish saver could invest in Irish stock or a Fannie Mae bond.[11]

Euphoria in global asset markets reached an apex in the weeks leading up to the subprime financial shock in summer 2007. In most countries, stock prices, commercial property values, and prices for most bonds had risen to record highs. Investors had never been willing to pay so much to get so little. The tie between stock prices and corporate earnings—called the price-earnings (PE) ratio—went skyward in most emerging economies.[12] The ratio of rental income to commercial real estate prices—called the capitalization rate—hit record lows in most developed economies. The yields on most bonds compared with yields on risk-free Treasuries—known as the yield spread or the risk premium—was wafer thin, particularly in the United States (see Figure 5.4).

By the time the financial shock hit, global asset markets were awash, even drowning, in a sea of liquidity. Investors had driven up prices for all assets, had taken on leverage, and were still desperate for something to invest in that would generate a sufficient return. U.S. credit markets—in particular, securities backed by residential mort-gages—were attracting more than their share of investors. All the pre-conditions for a financial shock were in place, with American homeowners in the middle.

Yield Spread Between Junk Corporate Bonds and Treasures

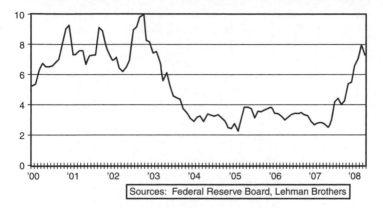

Sources: Federal Reserve Board, Lehman Brothers

Figure 5.4   Investors ask for little compensation.

6

Bad Lenders Drive Out the Good

Residential mortgage lending was previously a very staid business. Lenders meticulously considered the merits of making loans: They obtained careful appraisals, required sizable down payments, and made sure each borrower had a stable job and reliable income. Lenders knew their institutions would take substantial financial hits if borrowers failed to make good on their loans. They also knew regulators were watching, checking to make sure each loan was sound.

Staid was the last thing you could call mortgage lending during the housing boom. *Frenzied* might be a better term; and as the boom became a bubble, *out of control* would be even more appropriate. The mortgage business had been completely transformed. Lenders now made their money solely on volume; the more loans they originated, the greater their profits. Whether borrowers would be reliable payers was, at best, a secondary concern; Wall Street was buying the loans and, it was thought, using its financial alchemy to ensure that everyone made out. Regulators still cared, but they took comfort in the fact that the lenders they oversaw weren't on the hook if things turned out badly. The institutions most exposed were nonregulated private mortgage lenders and investment banks, ranging from New Century Financial to Bear Stearns. And although they were growing in size and number, they weren't the regulators' responsibility.

Wall Street drove the changes in the mortgage lending business. Making a loan and maintaining ownership of it was no longer as profitable as making the loan and selling it to an investment bank. The investment banks had connections to yield-hungry investors all over the world who were willing to pay fat premiums for anything lenders could originate.

Lenders obliged en masse. They had been making subprime loans for some time, but these originally required large down payments and careful scrutiny of subprime borrowers' income and savings. Lenders also demanded compensation for the extra risk of making a subprime loan; under the so-called "risk-based pricing" model, the greater the chance of default, the higher the interest rate and the bigger the fees a borrower would need to pay. However, as the market heated up, down payment requirements shrank and documenting a borrower's income slid from a requirement to a recommendation. Risks were rising, but in the hypercompetitive environment, interest rates and fees could not.

Lenders let their standards slip because if they didn't make a loan, their competitors would. No industry had more avidly embraced the Internet than mortgage lending, and the effect had been intoxicating for both consumers and lenders. Borrowers previously had few choices; if they needed a loan to buy a house, they could apply at their neighborhood bank branch. Now a horde of eager prospective lenders was only a mouse click or two away. The Internet was a boon for lenders as well, offering any storefront or basement-based operation access to customers across the country, and dramatically cutting the overhead costs involved in making loans. But the net effect was a competitive frenzy, with lenders furiously undercutting each other to gain customers. Everyone, it seemed, was in the mortgage business. Alongside traditional banks and thrifts were largely unregulated real estate investment trusts, Wall Street investment banks, and even home builders trying to move their unsold units. In this atmosphere, a lender demanding strict, old-fashioned credit standards would soon be out of business.

A few old-time mortgage lenders worried that the tried-and-true rules were being abandoned, but most were swept up in the hubris of the time. The housing boom was built on a solid foundation, or so they reasoned. Loans with no down payment were a problem only if housing prices weren't rising, and prices were rising rapidly. Certainly, they would eventually slow down and level off, but no one expected prices to actually decline. And the lenders' math-whiz consultants had devised new, sophisticated models of borrower behavior. Applying their algorithms and formulas to past performance, they were confident they could separate the good borrowers from the deadbeats.

As the housing bubble expanded, mortgage lending moved from merely aggressive to increasingly reckless and, in some cases, disingenuous and predatory. On TV, over the Internet, and through the mail, lenders hawked an array of loans with questionable-sounding names: "stated-income," "piggy-back," "interest-only," "pay-option," and "negative amortization" loans. All were designed to squeeze borrowers with sketchy incomes and no down payment money into homes they couldn't afford, except under the very best of circumstances. Much of this seemed obvious in retrospect: For example, the ubiquitous so-called "2-28" subprime ARM loan was financially tenable only if a borrower could count on refinancing before the two-year fixed-rate term of the loan expired and the monthly payments shot up. And even if they could refinance in time, borrowers were nailed with a hefty penalty for paying off the loan early.

Many new homeowners were aware of the financial obligations they were taking on, but many clearly were not. And as time went on, chances declined that they would receive much guidance from their lenders. Most lenders feel they have a fiduciary responsibility—if not a legal one—to match borrowers with loans that are appropriate for their financial circumstances. But during the housing bubble, an increasing number didn't appear to care. A borrower who takes on a loan that ultimately proves unaffordable is culpable for his predicament, but the lender first determines whether to grant the loan.

Mortgage Monkey Business

Given the financial stakes involved, getting a mortgage was surprisingly easy. During the mid-2000s, all it took was a visit to the local bank branch or mortgage broker, either of which a borrower could find in the nearest strip mall. The process took only a short time—the loan officer did a few calculations, pulled a credit report, and requested some additional financial information. When the deal closed, the borrower needed to sign a handful of documents, and the money and property title were transferred.

All this is a breeze when times are good and credit is easy, but even when things tighten up, such as in the current period, the mortgage lending business is very efficient. It has to be; profit margins are paper thin and volume is necessary to make any kind of money. With thousands of brokers working on commission, they needed to make a lot of loans to earn a good living.

For a home buyer seeking a loan, the most important contact was often either a mortgage banker or a mortgage broker. These professionals' jobs involve examining the borrower's financial situation, working out the math to determine the appropriate size and type of loan, collecting the relevant documents, and securing the funds necessary to make the loan. Similar to independent insurance agents, who provide a broader distribution channel for the large insurance carriers, mortgage bankers and brokers provide a similar service for the big financial institutions with the cash to originate loans.

Mortgage banks and brokerages are generally small businesses; at the peak of the housing boom, 75,000 of them were scattered across the country, employing 350,000 workers (see Figure 6.1). They are low-cost operations that often appear and disappear quickly, depending on origination volumes and business conditions in a particular region. Their competitive advantage is choice; they offer borrowers a variety of potential deals, from government-backed loans to those offered by major depository institutions.[1]

Employment in Mortgage Banking/Brokerage, Thousands

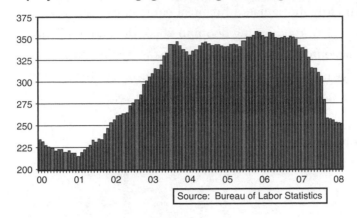

Source: Bureau of Labor Statistics

Figure 6.1   Mortgage banking booms

Mortgage bankers and brokers had historically been lightly regulated; states set the rules that applied to them, which varied substantially across the country.[2] This enabled these originators to become major players in subprime lending; during the housing boom, they accounted for more than half of subprime lending. But after a mortgage deal closed, the broker's role ended. Only if homeowners came back to refinance or buy another home would they ever encounter a broker twice—assuming that the same broker was still in business.

Most borrowers never meet the other professionals involved in making and managing their loans. These include appraisers, inspectors, and title agents—people who are supposed to make sure the house being purchased is worth its agreed-upon price. Mortgage underwriters evaluate the lender's risk in making a loan. The underwriters' models compare information about a borrower to details about others in similar circumstances, to determine the chance that a loan will be paid back regularly and on time. Mortgage insurers provide a backup in case the models are wrong and the borrower defaults. Mortgage servicers collect monthly payments and pass along the proceeds to the owners of a mortgage, and they are also responsible for working with borrowers who are struggling to make their payments.

The financial institutions that put up the funds for home buyers—banks or primarily unregulated financial companies—are very large. During the peak of the housing boom in 2005, the nation's 30 largest institutions accounted for half of all the loans originated (see Table 6.1). Countrywide topped the list, originating more than 1 million loans worth almost a quarter-trillion dollars that year.[3]

TABLE 6.1   Top Mortgage Lenders at the Peak of the Housing Boom in 2005

Mortgage Originations	#	% of Market	$ Volume	% of Market	Current Status
Countrywide FC	1,017,752	6.5	222,860,047	7.9	Acquired by Bank of America
Wells Fargo & Co	914,234	5.9	197,138,611	7.0	—
Washington Mutual BK FA	403,285	2.6	118,285,145	4.2	Capital infusion by private equity firm TPG
Bank of America Corp.	419,120	2.7	85,789,951	3.0	—
Chase Manhattan Mortgage Corp.	367,831	2.4	72,545,438	2.6	—
National City Corp.	423,668	2.7	72,223,807	2.6	Capital infusion: senior notes issued to shore up Tier 1 capital ratio
Citigroup	305,809	2.0	51,248,743	1.8	—
World SVG BK FSB	171,198	1.1	49,554,657	1.8	Acquired by Wachovia
GMAC Mortgage Corp.	255,861	1.6	43,863,220	1.6	ResCap unit is being supported by parent GMAC; Cerberus owns GMAC, but the private equity firm has not injected fresh outside capital yet

TABLE 6.1 Top Mortgage Lenders at the Peak of the Housing Boom in 2005

Mortgage Originations	#	% of Market	$ Volume	% of Market	Current Status
Argent Mortgage Company LLC	254,398	1.6	43,701,933	1.6	*Wholesale lender bought by Citi during the summer of 2007 from ACC Capital Holdings*
American Home Mortgage Corp.	207,427	1.3	42,044,067	1.5	*Bankrupt; Wilbur Ross bought it in bankruptcy*
New Century Mortgage Corp.	221,829	1.4	40,838,123	1.4	*Bankrupt*
Suntrust BK	214,472	1.4	38,287,405	1.4	—
Fremont INV & LOAN	193,564	1.2	36,144,403	1.3	*Bankrupt*
Option One Mortgage Corp.	203,279	1.3	35,883,131	1.3	*Wilbur Ross bought it from H&R Block*
First Horizon Home Loan Corp.	195,121	1.3	34,567,932	1.2	—
Greenpoint Mortgage Funding	118,098	0.8	33,399,038	1.2	*Does not originate any new loans; Capital One owns it*
ABN Amro Mortgage Group, Inc.	176,504	1.1	33,295,165	1.2	—
Indymac BK FSB	126,119	0.8	31,895,022	1.1	—
HSBC Holdings Plc.	267,355	1.7	30,601,979	1.1	—
Washington Mutual BK FSB	171,896	1.1	28,410,818	1.0	*Capital infusion by private equity investors lead by TPG*
Ameriquest Mortgage Co.	161,472	1.0	27,456,887	1.0	*Shut down after Citi bought Argent from ACC Capital Holdings; ACC owned both Ameriquest and Argent; the former is a retail lender and the latter is a wholesale lender*

TABLE 6.1   Top Mortgage Lenders at the Peak of the Housing Boom in 2005

Mortgage Originations	#	% of Market	$ Volume	% of Market	Current Status
WMC Mortgage Corp.	142,201	0.9	27,300,288	1.0	*GE sold it during the summer 2007*
Wachovia Corp.	174,429	1.1	25,802,339	0.9	—
Flagstar BK FSB	149,366	1.0	24,922,760	0.9	—
First Magnus Financial Corp.	133,567	0.9	23,085,302	0.8	*Bankrupt*
Ohio SVB BK	109,352	0.7	21,440,298	0.8	—
MortgageIT, Inc.	90,910	0.6	20,439,166	0.7	—
PHH Mortgage Corp.	111,079	0.7	19,948,314	0.7	—
Wachovia Mortgage	89,725	0.6	18,831,044	0.7	—
All other lenders	7,785,931	50	1,265,547,260	44.9	
Total	**15,576,852**	**100**	**2,817,352,293**	**100**	

Sources: Mortgage Bankers' Association, Moody's Economy.com

These institutions aren't necessarily the ultimate owners of the mortgage loan. Owners include depositories—a commercial bank or savings and loan—or an investor who bought an interest in the loan via a mortgage-backed security. Investors can reside anywhere in the world, and might be an individual or an institution—a pension fund, hedge fund, investment bank, or any of the other players in the global capital markets. Depositories own about half of all residential mortgage loans, and investors own the other half. Whoever or whatever they are, mortgage owners are often far removed from the mortgage-making process. They've never met the brokers who originated the loans they own, and they will meet the loan servicer only if a loan goes bad and the party at the other end of the chain—the borrower—stops making monthly payments.

The housing boom was a heady time for the mortgage business. The entire industry—from brokers to servicers—was humming, with many mortgage professionals working long hours, nights, and weekends. The volumes were astounding; between 2004 and 2006, more than $9 trillion in loans was originated, accounting for half of all U.S. first mortgages in effect in 2008 (see Figure 6.2).

Mortgage Originations, Trillions $

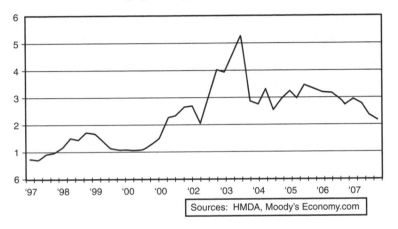

Figure 6.2   Mortgage lending soars.

With soaring volumes came soaring profits, but the mortgage business remained fiercely competitive and margins remained thin. Lenders were driven to keep volumes up and the cash coming in—and they became increasingly creative in finding ways to put households with shaky finances into homes.

Gresham's Law at Work

Starting a mortgage brokerage firm in the early 2000s was easy; there were few barriers to entry and even fewer to shutting down and leaving the business. Brokerages appeared quickly whenever home buying picked up, and they vanished just as quickly when activity cooled. Costs were low: office rent, a few desks and computers, and some commissioned agents. Relationships with real estate agents and home builders helped but weren't necessary for success. The key was offering the best interest rate, the lowest origination fees, and—particularly during the housing boom—the easiest loan terms.

But gaining a competitive edge just by offering low interest rates and origination fees grew difficult early in the decade. Rates were already about as low as they had ever been, and lenders were offering rates not much higher than their own cost of funds—in effect, offering borrowers the wholesale price of money. Fees and points on mortgage loans—what lenders charge for their costs and their time—had also fallen sharply. The average fee on a mortgage loan in the midst of the housing boom was 0.35% of the loan amount—a rock-bottom rate.[4] Only a decade earlier, such fees had amounted to more than a percentage point (see Figure 6.3).

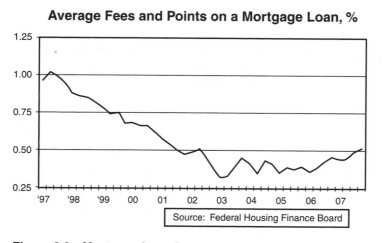

Average Fees and Points on a Mortgage Loan, %

Source: Federal Housing Finance Board

Figure 6.3   Mortgage fees plunge.

The mortgage industry's quick adoption of the Internet also pumped up competition during this period. The web seemed custom-built for a business that had been drowning in documents—simply managing it all had required a substantial back-office bureaucracy to review, organize, and file. With the Internet, obtaining needed information from a credit bureau, appraiser, or title company required only a few clicks.

The Internet also empowered consumers; home buyers could now shop for the best or cheapest mortgages. The local neighborhood bank was no longer the only effective choice. Lenders saw an enormous opportunity to reach borrowers in far-flung places; beginning in the late 1990s, lenders poured resources into developing web sites and other Internet-based marketing tools. As it happened, Congress had just recently given lenders the legal go-ahead to seek customers nationwide.[5] With the growth of online marketing, borrowers could immediately match up offers from lenders across the country and see how tweaking their own financial information—the size of their down payment, the credit score, and so on—affected the interest rates and terms available.

Borrowers were becoming much savvier loan shoppers for other reasons. Tens of millions of homeowners had refinanced their loans at least once to take advantage of the period's falling interest rates, and they had gained an understanding of the lending process.[6] They were much more willing to challenge lenders' origination fees and to move on to the next lender if they weren't satisfied.

Barriers to competition were also being ripped down as cheap (low interest rate) money became available to lenders of all stripes. Previously, depositors in commercial banks and savings and loans provided the only source of funds to make mortgage loans. However, as Wall Street figured out how to securitize loans, funds began coming in from all corners of the globe, and having deposits was no longer an advantage. Moreover, the investment bankers who sliced, packaged, and sold mortgage loans to investors wanted a full pipeline; the more lenders were out there signing up borrowers, the more there was to securitize. In fact, some investment banks grew frustrated that they couldn't get enough and began setting up their own mortgage-lending subsidiaries. Bear Stearns, Lehman Brothers, Credit Suisse, and others quickly became among the industry's most aggressive lenders.

Competition was also taking new forms. Mortgage-lending companies were being set up not as traditional depositories or brokers, but as real estate investment trusts (REITs). In the 1990s, REITs became the favored corporate form for developers as a way of avoiding corporate income taxes. Technically, all REIT profits were paid out to shareholders, who then paid personal taxes on them.[7] But REITs also avoided the watchful eyes of bank regulators; because they were publicly traded, they fell under the umbrella of the Securities and Exchange Commission (SEC). The SEC regulates the stock market, with its main focus on issues such as insider trading and corporate transparency—not the ins and outs of mortgage lending. Mortgage-lending REITs literally fell through the regulatory cracks, and their sponsors took full advantage of the status. Some of the most egregious, aggressive, and ultimately failed players in the housing bubble were REITs, including American Home Mortgage, New Century Financial, and NovaStar.

As the Federal Reserve slowly raised interest rates between summer 2004 and summer 2006, competition among lenders boiled over. To keep generating new mortgages, even as higher rates made homes less affordable, lenders had to lower their underwriting standards. The REITs and investment banks led the way. A form of Gresham's law took hold, in which the most aggressive lenders forced the rest—even the more cautious among them—to either lower their standards or lose their market share.[8] A lender could keep going only by making loans on terms they would have considered unimaginable only a few months earlier. The bad lenders were driving out the good ones, as even well-established, conservative lenders gave in to the pressure.

Policymakers Change the Rules

The nation's financial policymakers encouraged both the burgeoning competition in the mortgage industry and the rapid expansion in lending that resulted. Officials' motivations ranged from altruistic to crassly political. For both ideological and partisan reasons, the Bush administration had long disdained government-supported mortgage lenders such as the FHA, Fannie Mae, and Freddie Mac. These institutions had been plagued by management problems and accounting irregularities. In the case of Fannie and Freddie, even the Federal Reserve Board thought they were too large and insufficiently funded. The administration believed that the private market could provide all the mortgages Americans needed, more efficiently and at less cost than government-sponsored lenders.

With administration support, regulators began putting fetters on the government-related lenders just as they were easing up on private lenders—at precisely the moment when regulatory oversight was most needed. Even under normal circumstances, regulators have a difficult time encouraging lenders to be prudent. When times are flush and borrowers are paying on their loans, lenders resist any suggestion that they might be overdoing it—extending too much credit and not properly accounting for the risks. But this is precisely when lenders tend to make mistakes and, therefore, when regulators need to be most vigilant. But cracking down wasn't a politically popular idea during the housing boom; legislators and the White House were looking for less oversight, not more.

Model Hubris

If mortgage lenders were nervous about their falling loan standards, they could always take confidence in their models. Lenders believed deeply that, whatever their guts told them, their statistically based, computer-driven models could reliably determine whom they should lend to, what kinds of loans they could offer, and how much interest they should charge. The models were brilliant; using the available information on the borrower and the property, they would forecast the odds of the borrower paying regularly and on time. Fannie Mae and Freddie Mac had long been champions of these so-called automated underwriting (AU) models, and now other lenders became converts as well.[9] Lenders felt sure that their AU models could accurately judge a borrower's creditworthiness.[10]

One essential input into every lender's model is a borrower's credit score.[11] This is a number, typically ranging from 350 to 850, indicating the risk that a borrower will eventually face a credit problem. The lower the score, the more problem-prone the borrower is. A score below 620 generally marks a borrower as subprime. Scores are constructed from credit files—information that lenders report regularly to credit bureaus. Scores reflect not only past payment history, but also how a person uses credit. For example, the more credit cards in your wallet and the closer you are to your credit limits, the greater the risk is of lending you more money and, therefore, the lower your score.

Another essential input into all mortgage-lender models is the value of the house being purchased. Lenders use old-fashioned appraisals, but they also rely on so-called automated valuation models (AVM) for this. An AVM is automated because it doesn't require an actual human being to look at the property; instead it uses statistics and computing power to estimate a home's value: recent sales of comparable homes, tax assessments, other characteristics of the property, and price trends in the immediate area. AVMs are much less costly than human appraisals and require no waiting for an appraiser to visit a home.

Lenders had little choice but to believe in their models during the housing boom. Loan applications were coming thick and fast; without models that could spit out answers instantaneously, the applications couldn't be processed quickly enough to meet the competition among lenders. Automated underwriting models, credit scores, and AVM-produced house values are, in most circumstances, effective and promising tools, but lenders were much too comfortable with the results and had come to totally rely on them.

Models are only as good as the information that goes into them, and by 2007, the information going into many models was increasingly suspect. Borrowers had figured out how to manipulate their own credit scores, not by improving their habits, but by making a few simple adjustments in how they managed their debts. For instance, some borrowers paid a fee to be added as an "authorized user" on the credit-card accounts of people with higher scores. The positive payment information from the good cardholder improved the additional user's credit score. Such transplanting of credit DNA wasn't widespread, but it shows how borrowers were able to game the system and affect lenders' models.[12]

Another serious problem with AVMs was that they could fall significantly behind market conditions, particularly at times when those conditions were changing rapidly. For months after housing prices began to bust, automated valuation models were still showing values that reflected a much stronger market. Lenders were making decisions as if the good times were still rolling, long after they had ended. AVMs also had trouble capturing the real prices being paid for homes at a time when sellers were offering back-door discounts in the form of seller financing or other nonprice concessions. Such off-the-books discounting became common as housing markets weakened; sellers were offering to fix decks or repave driveways to close a sale instead of dropping their official prices. (In fact, a weakness of automated valuations is that they can't quantify all the small and intangible characteristics that determine a home's market value. A model might capture the price of a pool or built-out basement, but not the value of the view from the front porch or a troublesome neighbor.)

Lenders' models depend fundamentally on the premise that history is an accurate guide to the future. Most times this is a reasonable assumption and models will predict the behavior of borrowers reasonably accurately. But at times—such as during the housing boom—conditions don't match anything experienced historically, and then the models no longer work. In the housing boom, lenders failed to recognize this. Their belief in the predictive prowess of their models emboldened many of them to throw aside philosophical concerns and make what proved to be colossally bad decisions.

The quality of lenders' underwriting inexorably eroded. At its most crazed point at the apex of the housing bubble, disingenuous, predatory, and even fraudulent lending corrupted significant parts of the mortgage market. The mortgage industry's dramatic transformation from a staid business to a financial Wild West created the fodder for the subprime financial shock.

7

Financial Engineers and Their Creations

The Italians make designer sunglasses; the Japanese manufacture precision vehicles. Russian vodka has no comparison, and until the subprime financial shock, everyone wanted some of America's financial ingenuity. It was our comparative advantage. The efficiency of the U.S. financial system was the envy of the world; it could take the nation's paltry savings and direct it to financing investments that reaped big returns. Why save 50% of your income—as they do in China—or even 10%, as the Germans do, if you could put aside close to nothing and get the same returns or better, simply by making the right kind of investments? The U.S. financial system was better at this than anyone; the wizardry of America's financial engineers seemed unparalleled.

Despite the complexity of the American financial system, its basic function is quite simple: Take what we save and lend it to others who can do something productive with it. In times past, this was done entirely by banks.[1] Making a loan was very straightforward. A bank would take cash from depositors and lend it to a household or business. The bank would pay the depositor some interest and make a profit by charging a little more in interest from the borrower. The bank owned the loan until it was repaid and took the loss if the borrower fell into unhappy circumstances and defaulted. Because the banks' deposits were insured by the government, regulators required them to hold some cash—capital—aside in case too many borrowers defaulted. Regulators also monitored the banks' lending to make sure it was prudent; if a bank made too many bad loans it could fail, putting the government on the hook to repay depositors' money.

The banks lost their tight grip on the financial system beginning in the 1970s and 80s. These were tough times for banking; volatile inflation and high interest rates made it difficult to make a profit.[2] The high rates crimped lending and sent deposits fleeing to newly established money market funds, which offered higher returns to savers. Many banks also stumbled badly in the early 1980s by lending too aggressively to Latin American nations who mismanaged their debts and ultimately defaulted on billions.[3] The collapse of the savings and loan (S&L) industry was even more devastating, with more than 1,000 institutions failing between the mid-1980s and early 1990s. The massive financial debacle left regulators to sort out hundreds of billions of dollars of loans from the defunct S&Ls.

The vicissitudes of financial markets and the financial chicanery of unscrupulous S&L owners created the S&L mess, and eventually high finance resolved it. The Resolution Trust Corporation (RTC), established by policymakers to dispose of the S&L's assets, gracefully employed a financial technique known as securitization. In a securitization, loans are combined or pooled, and their collective interest and principal payments are used to back a tradable security that is sold to investors. As a group, the investors become owners of the loans and are entitled to receive its interest and principal payments. The RTC securitized everything from auto loans to commercial mortgages, sold them to investors, and resolved the S&L crisis at a surprisingly low cost to taxpayers.[4]

Securitization wasn't born at the RTC—that honor goes to mortgage lenders Fannie Mae, Freddie Mac, and the FHA in the 1970s—but the RTC demonstrated that the technique could be used commercially for all types of loans. The RTC also helped create the legal and accounting rules necessary for securitization to work, as well as the trading infrastructure needed for investors to buy and sell the securities. As the RTC wound down its operations in the mid-1990s, Wall Street happily took the wheel of the securitization machine.

Investment bankers first applied securitization to the mass market via credit cards. Using borrowers' credit scores and targeted direct-marketing techniques, banks had already figured out how to put cards in the hands of millions of average-income or even low-income households. The only limit on the banks' growth in this area came from their own balance sheets—banks lacked sufficient deposits or capital to grow freely. Securitization lifted both constraints. When a credit card was securitized, banks didn't need deposits; the investors buying the credit card-backed securities provided the money. Capital wasn't an issue, either, because the investors—not the card-issuing banks—owned the loans. Credit-card lending soared, with receivables doubling in the mid-1990s.

Securitization also powered a boom in home equity and manufactured housing lending. Second mortgage loans had received a big lift in the late 1980s, when Congress eliminated the tax deductibility of interest payments on nonmortgage debt.[5] Interest on a home equity line of credit was still deductible, however, giving homeowners a cheap and easy way of borrowing against their houses. Manufactured homes took off as house prices rose, making it harder for prospective first-time home buyers to come up with down payments on traditional dwellings. Creative marketing also made manufactured homes seem attractive alternatives to apartment living. The amount of outstanding home-equity and manufactured-home loans almost tripled during the mid-1990s.

Many of the most active credit-card, home-equity, and manufactured-housing lenders were not banks at all, but finance companies. These institutions didn't collect deposits—they didn't need to because the loans they originated were securitized. And since they didn't collect deposits, finance companies weren't subject to the same regulatory oversight as banks. Taxpayers weren't on the hook if they went belly up, only their shareholders and other creditors. Finance companies thus had little to discourage them from growing as aggressively as possible, even if that meant lowering or winking at traditional lending standards.

The banks' long-standing "originate-to-hold" model of lending, in which they kept the loans they made on their own balance sheets, was rapidly giving way to a new "originate-to-distribute" model, in which loans were securitized and sold to a wide array of investors. This change in the banking business model was roundly endorsed by regulators. Because banks didn't own the loans, they didn't bear the risk, diminishing the odds of another S&L-type crisis. Regulators felt anything banks could get off their balance sheet was fine by them. Of course the risk involved in making these loans didn't go away; it simply shifted to investors and by extension to the broader financial system.

What happened next should have sounded an alarm about the limitations of securitization. Delinquencies, defaults, and personal bankruptcies ballooned, as households that shouldn't have gotten a credit card or home equity line in the first place ran into trouble. The securities backed by these loans were also hit hard and contributed to the global financial crises of 1997-98. That episode began among the indebted economies of Southeast Asia, extended to Russia (which defaulted on its debt), and ended with the collapse of hedge fund Long Term Capital Management. Less remembered is the freezing up of the asset-backed securities market, in which credit-card, home-equity, and manufactured-housing securities were traded. For several days during the fall of 1998, no trading at all took place in these markets. The panic was quickly quelled when the Federal Reserve slashed interest rates and Fannie and Freddie stepped in to buy a lot of mortgage securities, providing much-needed liquidity to the markets. But it wasn't enough for many finance companies, which either failed or were acquired—in many cases by banks. The dollar amounts involved in that crisis were dwarfed a decade later by the subprime financial shock, but much of what happened later seemed all too familiar.

Securitization Dissected

At bottom, securitization is not very complicated. The interest and principal payments paid on the pooled loans are paid to investors in a specific order, which is spelled out by the securities' "tranches"— French for slices. Those investors who are particularly averse to risk buy the tranches viewed as most secure by the credit rating agencies. Investors in these senior tranches get paid first, before all other investors. To add more protection, a pot of money from the loan payments is set aside just in case a large number of borrowers default.[6] The tradeoff for all this protection is a lower return—investors in senior tranches receive lower rates of interest on their investment. Senior tranches make up the bulk of most securitizations; in the average residential mortgage-backed security (RMBS), for example, senior tranches account for 80% of the face value—also called the capital structure—of the security (see Figure 7.1).

Capital Structure of a Typical Mortgage Security

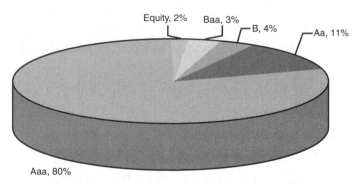

Equity, 2%   Baa, 3%   B, 4%   Aa, 11%

Aaa, 80%

Figure 7.1   Most mortgage securities are mainly Aaa.

After senior investors get their money, investors in the middle-rated or mezzanine tranches receive theirs. Investors in these tranches are assured of payment under most circumstances, but if the economy suffers a recession or housing experiences a cyclical downturn, things could get dicey, and mezzanine investors might not get all their money back. Mezzanine tranches account for 18% of the average security's capital structure.

The remaining 2% is the riskiest slice of the security, known as the equity tranche. This portion isn't even rated by the credit-rating agencies. Investors in the equity tranche are the last to be paid, and thus may not get all their money back if too many borrowers default. Because of the obviously high risks, the returns can be large if all goes well.

Wall Street's securitization machine went into overdrive during the housing boom, producing a frenzy in the mortgage securities market. At its peak in 2005, more than $1.1 trillion in RMBS were issued and sold to investors. Another $1 trillion was sold in 2006. In the first half of 2007, leading up to the subprime financial shock of that summer, RMBS sales came in not far off the $1 trillion mark.

For any securitization to succeed, investors must be willing to buy each of the tranches. Banks themselves were first in line, picking up most of the senior-rated segments. Returns on these were low, but greater than the banks' were paying to their own depositors. Just as important, regulators required banks to hold very little capital in reserve against the chance these high-rated securities would default. The high rating meant there was very little risk—or so regulators thought. Insurance companies and various types of asset managers bought the bulk of the mezzanine tranches. These firms were searching for higher returns than the senior tranches offered and they didn't have the same regulatory constraints as the banks. Besides, the mezzanine pieces were still A-rated securities and the chance of default was thought to be relatively low. The biggest buyers of the equity tranches were hedge funds. The managers of these investment pools knew they were taking bigger risks, but their clients demanded extraordinary returns, which are tough to generate without substantial risk and lots of leverage (borrowed money).

Financial Alphabet Soup

Securitization didn't stop with plain-vanilla RMBS. It evolved rather into a dizzying, mind-numbing alphabet soup of financial products. The most notorious was called a collateralized debt obligation (CDO). This was essentially just a mutual fund for bonds and loans. Like a stock mutual fund, which holds stocks from many different companies, a CDO buys bonds; these can be straight-up corporate bonds, or securitizations backed by mortgage loans, credit cards, auto loans, and so on. One key benefit of stock mutual funds is diversification; they enable investors to avoid the risk of keeping too many eggs in one basket. In theory, the same benefit applies to a CDO. If the CDO invests in a wide enough variety of bonds, it should be less risky.[7]

The CDO's lineage can be traced back to the late 1980s, but it came into its own in the early 2000s.[8] CDOs were backed initially by investment-grade corporate loans and bonds and were particularly attractive in the wake of the tech-stock bust, when businesses had to offer high interest rates to attract nervous investors to buy their debt. CDO managers could make good money by simply collecting these interest and principal payments, passing most of it along to CDO investors and keeping a cut for themselves.

But this simple scheme became increasingly difficult as the economy improved; financial pressure on firms receded, as did bankruptcies, and corporate bond yields declined. CDO originators—mostly investment banks—quickly focused their attention on higher-yielding credit-card and auto-loan-backed securities, and ultimately on mortgage securities, including those backed by subprime loans. The product they created was referred to as an ABS CDO (because "asset-backed security collateralized debt obligation" was quite a mouthful), and it exploded onto financial markets. ABS CDO issuance soared from virtually nothing in 2002 to what would have likely been $300 billion in 2007, if not for the subprime financial shock (see Figure 7.2).

ABS CDO Issuance, Billions $

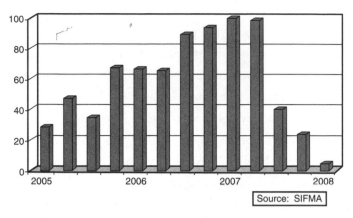

Figure 7.2   CDO issuance soars in the housing hoom.

ABS CDOs were overwhelmingly popular; they seemed to offer a win-win proposition for everyone. Investors liked CDOs for their high returns, apparent diversification benefits, and the ability to precisely calibrate the risk they were taking on. CDOs have the same tranching structure as traditional securitization, with payments going first to senior tranches, and then mezzanine tranches, and an equity tranche that shouldered the most risk. CDO managers collected fat fees that were especially attractive if the CDO allowed for active management of the securities in the CDO. Managers could buy and sell securities out of the CDO to enhance its return or lower its risk. CDO originators also earned lucrative fees and solved one of their biggest problems in putting together a securitization—namely finding enough investors for all the tranches. At times, depending on market conditions, investors weren't quite as interested in one or other of the tranches. Mezzanine tranches in particular could be a tough sell. Most investors either wanted the safety of a senior tranche or the high return of the equity tranche, not the stuff in the middle. So-called mezzanine CDOs were created from the mezzanine tranches of traditional securitizations, tranching them up further and creating more of the better-liked senior and equity tranches, but now within a CDO.

If that wasn't confusing enough, it became even more tangled. CDOs were created from tranches of other CDOs. These were called "CDOs-squared" or "CDOs of CDOs". And as the securitization machine spun out of control just prior to the subprime shock, CDOs-of-CDOs-of-CDOs—or "CDOs-cubed"—were being manufactured. There were also synthetic CDOs, as opposed to "real" ones. With most asset-backed securities, including subprime mortgage securities already accounted for in CDOs, originators needed to cook up something else lest the market cool off. A synthetic CDO did not buy tranches of securitized loans or even tranches of other CDOs; it bought credit default swaps (CDS).[9] A CDS is an insurance contract on a bond or loan in which one party pays the other an insurance premium and expects to be compensated in return if there is a default. Most credit default swaps are written on corporate bonds, but there are also plenty of CDS written on residential mortgage securities. With the notional value of CDS—the face value of the bonds being insured—totaling in the tens of trillions of dollars, there seemed to be no limit to what the securitization machine could produce.

Shadow Banking System

By the time the subprime financial shock hit in summer 2007, the machine was tranching and distributing trillions of dollars in securities to investors across the globe. Securitization's financial web was expanding exponentially, as was its dizzying complexity. Yet policymakers thought this was precisely securitization's most significant strength. The risks involved in making a loan were no longer concentrated within any one financial institution; rather, they were spread across the entire global financial system. Loan defaults were less likely to jeopardize the viability of any particular institution, as their financial pain would be diffused widely among many investors and institutions.

Global banking regulators encouraged banks to securitize their loans, pushing the risks off their balance sheets. This attitude was codified in a series of agreements known as the Basel Accords, named for the Swiss city in which they were first hammered out.[10] The most recent of these agreements, called Basel II, imposes global rules on banks regarding the amount of capital they must hold in reserve to cover loan or investment losses. These capital requirements vary based on the expected risk of the investment—if a bank holds relatively safe government bonds, for example, they are required to hold less capital to guard against loss. This is called risk-weighting, and it makes sense as long as the rules reflect the true risks of a particular asset or investment. For years, highly rated residential mortgage-backed securities, collateralized debt obligations, and similar securities were assigned relatively low-risk weights, and regulators thought they were safe.

Banks thus had a strong incentive to avoid making and keeping mortgages and other loans, and to hold mortgage-backed securities instead. Banks were happy to originate loans—processing borrowers and accepting origination fees—but less interested in actually funding the loans, which required them to hold more capital in reserve. Funding for loans thus came increasingly from non-bank institutions. These institutions were a mixed bag; they included investment banks, hedge funds, money-market funds, and finance companies, as well as newly invented entities called "asset-backed conduits" and "structured investment vehicles" (see Figure 7.3). Together they formed a shadow banking system, which was subject to little regulatory oversight and also not required to publicly disclose much, if anything, about itself. By the second quarter of 2007, just prior to the financial shock, the shadow banking system provided an astounding $6 trillion in credit and were rapidly closing in on that provided by traditional banks.

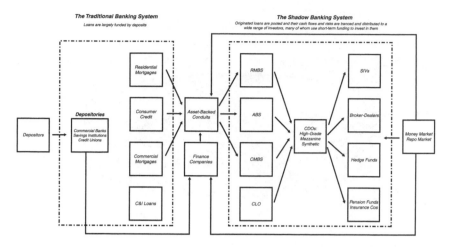

Figure 7.3   The global financial system

It was clear that the banks had off-loaded a substantial amount of risk to the shadow banking system, but it was not at all clear which institutions in this opaque galaxy were bearing those risks, nor exactly how large those risks were. Policymakers took comfort in the notion that risk seemed to be spread widely around the globe and thought that any problem in the shadow banking system wasn't theirs to worry about. Unfortunately, the system didn't work the way they thought.

Liquidity Evaporates

Take the structured investment vehicles (SIVs), for example. Many big global banks established these to make big bets on securitized loans. At their peak in mid-2007, SIVs held $1.4 trillion in subprime RMBS and CDOs (see Figure 7.4). Banks generated handsome profits from their SIVs, earning fees for creating and managing them. Making them particularly attractive, SIVs could be structured so that their investments didn't sit on the banks' balance sheets; thus, banks faced no requirement to hold capital to protect against the SIVs' risks.

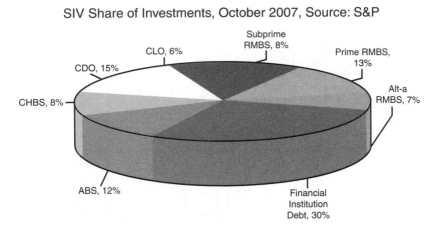

SIV Share of Investments, October 2007, Source: S&P

Figure 7.4   What SIVs invest in.

SIVs took substantial risks, starting with their habit of selling short-term commercial paper—IOUs that came due within a few days or weeks—to finance investments that would mature over much longer periods of time. In banker-speak, they were borrowing short and lending long, much like those doomed S&Ls of the 1980s who were taking deposits on which they had to pay prevailing market rates or risk losing them to finance 30-year mortgage loans. It was a profitable practice as long as money-market funds and others were willing to buy the SIVs' commercial paper. It quickly unraveled when the subprime financial shock caused the SIVs' investments to go sour. Money markets began shunning SIVs' commercial paper, fearing they would never be paid back. In response, the SIVs turned back to the banks that had created them. Most SIVs had credit lines with their parent organizations, set up to tide them over any short-term need for cash. The banks had been happy to set these up, using them to collect additional fees, and never thinking they would really be needed. Now the SIVs were desperate for cash.

At one point in late 2007, it seemed that nearly all SIVs were about to fail, creating a huge forced fire sale of their investments. Such a sale would have meant plunging prices and a much bigger financial shock. Alarmed, the U.S. Treasury Department intervened, brokering a deal among major banks to try and keep this from happening.[11] The deal was never implemented; the SIV-owning big banks chose to resolve their problems individually. Yet as the SIVs' investments flowed back onto the banks' own balance sheets, it became clear that the shadow banking system hadn't spread risk as widely as had been thought. The regulators, moreover, were still on the hook if something went wrong.

Similar short-term funding issues also threatened the asset-backed conduits. Like SIVs, these financial vehicles had been created by big global banks to hold loans that the banks had originated for securitization. The conduits were like warehouses, where loans could reside until pooled into securities. Because the banks never technically owned the loans, they were not required to hold any capital against them. In early 2007, some $400 billion worth of loans sat in such warehouses. Like the SIVs, these were funded with short-term commercial paper; and like the SIVs, by summer 2007 the conduits could no longer sell their commercial paper because the money funds and other investors feared they would never be repaid. As the conduits were forced out of business, the securitization machine ground to a halt.

Leverage Kills

The shadow banking system also amplified risk through leverage. Hedge fund managers were particularly aggressive about investing with borrowed money, even when their investments included the riskiest equity tranches of securitizations. At the peak of the financial frenzy in 2005-2006, many hedge funds were leveraging such investments as much as 15 times—that is, for every dollar of their own money they invested, they borrowed $15. The hedge funds had promised to deliver super-sized returns, and these could only be generated by taking large risks with lots of leverage.

Leverage can indeed turbocharge returns when investors bet right, but it can be financially cataclysmic if they bet wrong. Take the case of a hedge fund buying a subprime mortgage security worth $100. The fund puts down $10 of its own money and $90 it borrowed. If the price of the security rises 10%, the fund's return is 100%—it has doubled its original $10. But if the security's price falls 10%, the fund's equity is wiped out. At that point, it can either put up more of its own money, replenishing its equity; or it will lose the investment to whoever loaned it the $90. Just like a homeowner who gets foreclosed.

Unlike many ordinary homeowners, however, hedge funds were supposed to be sophisticated about risk. They hedged—hence the name—which made them bolder about taking on risk and leverage. They hedged against the risk that an investment's value would fall by making another investment they thought would rise in value in such a circumstance. One popular hedging technique was to balance investments in subprime mortgage securities by short-selling the ABX index.[12] Shorting is a bet that the value of what is being shorted will fall. Like the Dow Jones industrial average or the NASDAQ, the ABX index condenses a lot of market trading into a single number; the trading it tracks reflects the price of credit-default swaps—sophisticated insurance contracts—on subprime securities. When worries about mortgage defaults rise, the cost of insuring against a default on these securities rises and the ABX falls. Long before the subprime financial shock hit, it was evident that conditions were deteriorating because the ABX was falling. Those who shorted the ABX—thus betting it would fall—were making money even as prices for subprime securities were also falling. If, like the hedge funds, they were also buying subprime securities, they were thus at least partially covering their own losses.

Yet investing with leverage can be lethal, even when combined with hedges. This was demonstrated by the implosion of two prominent Bear Stearns hedge funds in July 2007;[13] arguably the proximate catalyst for the subprime financial shock. The hedge funds had invested in CDOs of Aaa-rated subprime mortgage securities. Their investments had been highly leveraged, but to hedge at least some of the risk, the funds used the ABX index. It seemed like a winning formula: Factoring in interest received on the CDOs with the cost of the debt to purchase them and the cost of the credit insurance to hedge them, the funds ended up with a hefty positive rate of return—"positive carry" in hedge fund lingo. Yet it all went badly awry as surging mortgage delinquencies rapidly undermined the price of the funds' subprime securities. The fund managers had not hedged enough to cover their leverage-enlarged losses. The banks that had loaned money to the funds grew nervous as their collateral—the subprime bonds—evaporated. The banks demanded the Bear funds put up more collateral, forcing them to sell their bonds to raise cash. That selling made prices for subprime bonds fall even faster, making the banks even more nervous and sparking more demands for collateral, which caused more selling. It didn't take long before the Bear hedge funds had been wiped out.

Diversification Disintegrates

Regulators were much too confident that diversification would protect the new-fangled securitizations being distributed throughout the shadow banking system. CDOs in particular were supposed to benefit from diversification, by combining securities that weren't alike. If one of the securities in a CDO performed poorly, it would be offset by another, better-performing component in the CDO soup.[14] CDO managers were paid handsomely for their presumed ability to mix securities just right and produce a well-diversified CDO.

CDOs of corporate bonds were able to achieve diversity by including bonds from companies in different industries. Combining bonds from Delta Airlines with ExxonMobil, for instance, was one way to protect a CDO from the impact of big spikes in oil prices. As Delta is hurt by surging fuel costs, Exxon's bonds are soaring for the same reason. Similarly, combining bonds from a homebuilder with those of a healthcare provider would help cushion investors in a downturn; as builders struggle to raise cash, healthcare remains largely unaffected.

CDOs of mortgage securities were supposed to achieve diversity by mixing mortgage securities from different parts of the country. In the past, housing downturns were relatively concentrated; house prices can fall in Los Angeles, Houston, or Boston, but never in too many places all at once (the Great Depression aside). Because a CDO effectively combined mortgages from all over the country, it seemed a good, safe way to invest in housing.

CDO issuers, managers, and investors largely dismissed the idea that a downturn could affect more than a few overvalued local markets; they failed to recognize they were in a national housing bubble. When prices started falling and homeowners stopped paying on their mortgages nearly everywhere, it quickly became clear that the CDO had not diversified risk at all. It had in fact concentrated risk in a highly leveraged investment.

Who's Responsible?

Of the places you can point the finger for the housing bubble and subprime financial shock, perhaps the most deserving is the removal of responsibility from the financial system. Lost in the rapid, wholesale rush to securitization and the shadow banking system was the notion that someone—anyone—should ensure that individual loans are made responsibly, to responsible borrowers. A bank that makes and holds a loan has a clear incentive to be responsible and guard against excess because its own bottom line will suffer if it isn't repaid. Government regulators also have a responsibility to make sure that banks are lending prudently because taxpayers will pay if they don't.

Securitization undermined this incentive for responsibility. No one had enough financial skin in the performance of any single loan to care whether it was good or not. A shaky mortgage would be combined with others, diluting its problems in the larger pool. At every stage along the long securitization chain, there was a belief that someone—someone else—would catch mistakes and preserve the integrity of the process. The mortgage lender counted on the Wall Street investment banker, who counted on the CDO manager, who counted on the ratings analyst or perhaps the regulator.

In the period leading up the subprime financial shock, America's financial ingenuity seemed without parallel. Our best financial minds appeared to have devised a machine to channel the world's savings into productive uses more efficiently and with less risk than ever before. The machine's engineers were reaping unimaginable benefits— billions of dollars a year in compensation were going to just a few thousand individuals. There were a few complaints, but they were faint; households with no prospects for homeownership just a few years earlier were now becoming homeowners.

Yet it turned out the machine was running amok, as all along the chain, everybody assumed someone else was in control.

8

Home Builders Run Aground

Home building is a cyclical business. Few other industries experience the same roller-coaster ride in demand and price. As clear as this seems in retrospect, it was far from conventional wisdom during the housing boom. For an unprecedented fifteen years, beginning in the early 1990s and lasting until the boom's peak in 2005, home building posted steady annual growth in activity, sales, and profits. Even during the 2001 recession, the industry's ascent was interrupted only briefly.

The home-building industry seemed to have gotten its act together in the 1990s. From a fragmented collection of small, privately held and essentially local builders, each putting up a few dozen homes a year, the industry had transformed itself, becoming dominated by a dozen publicly traded national firms who built thousands of homes annually. In 1990, less than one in ten U.S. homes was built by a publicly held firm; by 2005, the proportion was nearly one in three.

The industry's consolidation had been driven by the cost savings that came with scale. Everything from lumber to dry wall was cheaper in bulk. More important than materials, however, was the big builders' ability to acquire large tracts of the most attractive land in the nation's most lucrative housing markets. Because of their heft, large firms were better able to navigate the labyrinth of zoning and permitting restrictions thrown up in many places to thwart development. Builders with large national operations were also more likely to withstand the kinds of regional economic downturns that had done in many of their smaller competitors.

In theory, publicly traded builders' advantage included more and better information about their customers and markets. They had the resources to precisely gauge the demand for their product and what the competition was up to; therefore, they were less likely to make a serious business misstep. Small builders knew their communities, but they had little understanding of the broader economic and demographic forces shaping demand and supply for homes—a vital tool for success in such a sensitive business.

Shareholders and the global capital markets were also expected to impose discipline on the large construction firms, improving their performance. The smart money, it was believed, would ensure that egotistical builders didn't get carried away and put up more homes than the market could absorb. In the past, many smaller home builders had gotten into trouble erecting homes "on spec"—that is, with no bona fide buyer, only a local banker willing to put up the funds in anticipation of a sale. This sort of trouble wasn't going to happen again, or so it was thought.

The optimism was misplaced, however. On the contrary, publicly traded builders' access to freely flowing capital enabled them to put up homes long after housing demand had begun to wane. In the end, builders and their shareholders turned out to be about as good at gauging demand as Silicon Valley's tech gurus had been during the dotcom craze of the late 1990s. Like tech-company executives, builders had become intoxicated, as well as hugely wealthy, by their own lofty stock prices. Such prices could be justified and sustained only by building and selling more homes at higher prices.

The builders quickly forgot the pain experienced by their colleagues in the manufactured housing industry just a few years earlier. Mobile homes had gone upscale in the mid-1990s; the industry thought it had found a foolproof way to turn lower-income renters into homeowners while attracting older empty-nesters as well. At one point, manufactured housing accounted for an astounding 20% of all residential construction. But those soaring sales did not stem from genuine growth in demand or better product design—they were simply the result of very easy credit. Loans to buy mobile homes were being securitized and sold into global capital markets. Households were happy to borrow the nearly free money—they just weren't able to repay it. When global investors figured this out, the lending stopped. Without credit, unsold manufactured homes piled up on dealer lots, and the industry has never recovered. It was a sobering tale the home builders knew well; they just figured it didn't apply to them.

During the decade's housing boom, builders put up far too many single-family homes and apartments. At its worst, millions of empty units flooded the housing market. Builders were choking on unsold inventory, and investors who had purchased homes couldn't sell or rent them. There just weren't enough American households to fill all the vacant homes. And unlike past periods of regional overbuilding, such as Texas in the mid-1980s, these unsold homes weren't stick-like structures that could as easily be torn down as sold; they were large and well-appointed residences.

Builders had swallowed their own marketing hype. The industry's most vocal CEOs argued that demand for new homes would rise strongly ad infinitum, powered by a steady increase in foreign immigrants seeking a first home and aging baby boomers looking for a second one. Builders also had faith that Americans would rather own than rent, and that with low mortgage rates and ample credit, the national rate of homeownership could climb steadily higher. But their logic and arithmetic didn't add up. Home builders' enduring optimism, so instrumental in driving past housing cycles, had completely pervaded this one.

As the number of vacant homes mounted through 2006, 2007, and 2008, builders had no choice but to slash construction and house prices. It quickly became a matter of survival, and many builders didn't make it; bankruptcies and liquidations mounted. The

home-building cycle, which had powered the broader economy during the boom, cost it dearly in the bust. During the first half of the
2000s, rising home construction alone accounted for as much as a
third of the economy's growth; when construction collapsed in the
subsequent bust, it became the major cause of the 2008 recession.

Booms and Busts

Veteran home builders are much like wizened commercial fisher-
man—they have weathered many storms. Indeed, making it through
the housing market's ups and downs had been as tricky for builders as
navigating an Atlantic nor'easter could be for a sailor. Over the years,
rough economic weather had claimed as many builders as the ocean
storms had ships at sea.

A housing storm could be extraordinarily severe. In nine housing
busts since World War II, residential investment—the dollar value of
all new housing construction and remodeling by existing homeowners—had dropped nearly 25% on average.[1] Housing's booms have
been equally impressive, with average investment rising well over 50%
during periods of growth. Home building's swings dwarf those of the
broader economy, which rarely deviates from its long-term growth
trend by more than a few percentage points (see Figure 8.1).

% Change Year Ago

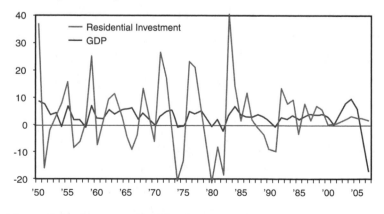

Figure 8.1   A very cyclical business

Housing busts through the early 1980s were particularly harsh, exacerbated by credit-crunch conditions—no loans available for anyone, no matter how good their finances. The problem: Only a banker could make a mortgage loan, and the banker could lend only as much as his depositors gave him. But depositors were fleeing traditional banks, which were barred by a Depression-era rule called Regulation Q from paying interest on checking accounts. As the Federal Reserve raised short-term interest rates to double-digit levels to quell the raging inflation of the 1970s, depositors moved their funds to money-market accounts and Treasury bills where rates were then far higher than in traditional bank accounts. As money flew out of the banks, mortgage credit for housing shut down.

Builders understood the dynamics of mortgage finance; they knew that when credit was ample they had to take advantage of it, putting homes up to market as quickly as possible. Economic rebounds produced plenty of pent-up housing demand, people who had put off home ownership during the lean times for lack of a loan.[2] Builders worked hard to make money during a boom so that they could survive the inevitable bust.

Housing booms didn't simply end after pent-up demand had been satisfied. Builders kept building as long as their bankers provided necessary up-front money to purchase cement and lumber and hire masons and electricians. Even if builders wanted to plan around the market, it was hard to gauge the strength of housing demand, or know how fast their competitors were adding to supply. Typically, builders misjudged and overdid it, constructing more homes than there were potential buyers. This set the stage for the next downturn.

The home building industry was largely a collection of small privately held firms, each one focused on just a few neighborhoods. It was difficult for a home builder to venture far, because his source of funding was a local banker, and banks were legally barred from crossing state lines to make a loan. If a builder wanted to expand to another state, he needed to find another banker. Local housing markets also tended to be idiosyncratic; building styles and desired amenities varied substantially from place to place. Knowing how to build center-hall colonials in New England suburbs wasn't of much use for constructing Spanish-style homes in the desert Southwest. Most builders stayed close to home.

Publics Ascend

Housing's storms have moderated over the decades—the recent downturn notwithstanding. Regulation Q was phased out during the 1980s, and mortgage securitizations came into its own, funneling capital from global financial markets to local U.S. mortgage and housing markets.[3] By the mid-1990s, mortgage loans were almost always available; it was a question of the interest rate, which was generally falling, and the loan terms, which were easing.

By the mid-1990s, the fragmented housing industry was ripe for consolidation. Many of the nation's smaller builders had failed or been severely hobbled by the late-1980s real estate bust and savings and loan crisis. Throughout Arizona, California, and the Northeast, it seemed as if the entire real-estate industry was in some stage of bankruptcy or liquidation. A nationwide homebuying market was also being created by the strong migration flows of households from the Northeast and Midwest to the South and West, and from California to the rest of the western U.S. demographically speaking, Florida had become more like New York and Seattle more like San Francisco. The stock market was beginning its 1990s' bull run, and investors were eager to finance the roll-up of small builders into large, publicly traded businesses. Those builders who were already publicly held had stock that was rising in value and could be offered to smaller builders to entice them to sell out.

Home building acquisitions multiplied. A handful of major deals were made during the first half of the 1990s, but more than 50 were done during the decade's second half. The merger wave spilled over into the first half of the 2000s, with such mega-mergers as Lennar's purchase of US Homes in 2000, Pulte's 2001 purchase of Del Webb, and Beazer's acquisition of Crossman in 2002. In 1990, public builders accounted for fewer than one in ten new home sales nationwide and generated no more than $10 billion in annual revenue. By 2000, their share of the market had surged to one new home sale in four, and at the peak of the boom in 2006, it had grown to nearly one in three, with sales of some one hundred billion dollars (see Figure 8.2).

Public Homebuilders Share of New Home Sales, %

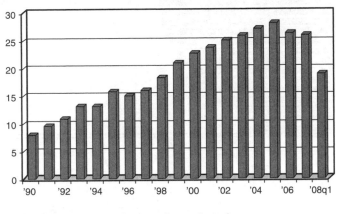

Figure 8.2   Public builders grab market share

As the publicly traded builders grew larger and their earnings seemed more predictable, their access to credit opened up, accelerating their expansion and tightening their grip on the industry. Construction and land-development loans—the money provided by bankers to finance home building—expanded three-fold during the first half of the 2000s to nearly half a trillion dollars. Major home builders could also tap the corporate bond market for cash; those borrowings soared from effectively nothing in the mid-1990s to well over $30 billion at the height of the housing boom.

The big builders concentrated on the nation's most lucrative and fastest-growing housing markets. Some two-thirds of their construction was in half a dozen states, including Arizona, California, Florida,

Nevada, North Carolina, and Texas. The big firms completely dominate building in these markets; they account for nearly all home building in places such as Orlando, FL, Fresno, CA, and Las Vegas, NV, and
over three quarters of house construction in San Diego, CA, Miami,
FL, and Phoenix, AZ (see Figure 8.3).

Public Homebuilders Share of New Home Sales, %

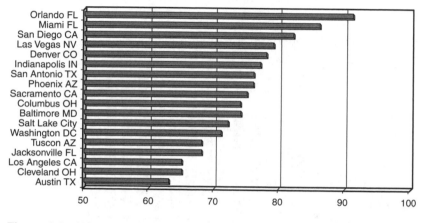

Figure 8.3   Where public builders build

Not coincidentally, these are the areas where the housing boom
turned into a bubble, and where the subsequent bust was especially
severe. Here the public builders were particularly aggressive about
seeking to control developable land; this significantly pushed up
prices for both land and houses, because in many areas, a home's price
is largely the cost of the land it occupies.[4] Builders either bought vacant lots outright or took out options to buy them in the future. Options were preferred because little cash was needed to effectively gain
control. In 2000, public builders owned or had options to buy 700,000
lots. By 2005, this had soared to 2.2 million lots, with nearly two-thirds
optioned. Builders meant to construct as many homes as they could
on this land, and that's exactly what they did.

Optimism Overflows

As the housing boom gained momentum, builders felt they could do no wrong. Sales volumes and house prices were hitting new records; builders' stocks tripled and then quadrupled in value, and there was plenty of cheap capital to finance more acquisitions and build out more communities. Builders were still like those fishermen, but now they were guiding large vessels equipped with satellite weather technology, and this made them certain they could avoid most storms and power through the rest. Some builders even seemed to believe that with their new financial tools and management acumen, they could make the housing storms go away permanently. It was certainly much easier to find a home buyer than a school of tuna.

Builders' optimism resembled that felt by technology entrepreneurs during the Internet bubble a few years earlier. Many newly minted dotcom firms had never generated a profit, but as long as Internet traffic and advertising were booming, shareholders were convinced payday would come eventually. Dotcom stock prices had soared; the value of Internet-related tech companies went from close to nothing in the early 1990s to nearly $1 trillion before the bubble burst.

Tech executives had woven compelling stories. "E-tailers" would sell everything from pet supplies to industrial equipment; virtual stores would overwhelm bricks-and-mortar retailers; advertisers would abandon newspapers and television for the Internet; and professionals of all types would work from home over the web, rather than in non-descript office parks. All these predictions rang true, and indeed, all have to some extent come to pass, but not necessarily as scripted in the 1990s.

Investors eventually grew tired of hearing the stories; they wanted the Internet to start producing profits. As the decade ended, demand was turning soft; new customers were harder to come by, and existing customers had already purchased as much technology as they could digest. The tech companies didn't give up without a fight, however. Some firms borrowed a trick from Detroit's automakers: They started providing their customers with financing to buy their products. This worked for a while, but even easy money couldn't keep increasingly stretched customers from cutting back forever. Some of those loans weren't being repaid, moreover. The Internet bubble burst.

On the face of it, home builders seem to be the antithesis of the tech companies. There is nothing virtual about a 3,000-square-foot home, and builders made plenty of money during the housing boom. Yet like the techs, the new publicly traded home builders became captivated by their own quickly rising stock prices. During the early 2000s, the stock-market value of all publicly traded home builders surged fourfold to $150 billion. While not in the same league as the tech boom, this was financially intoxicating for the builders. They realized the only way to hold on to their new-found wealth was by demonstrating that their firms could consistently generate strong annual growth—if not at the pace of the 1990s dotcoms, then something close to it.

The builders developed some appealing stories to tell investors. Strong foreign immigration was a favorite. More than a million immigrants come to the U.S. every year—legal and illegal—and builders pointed out that all these people would need places to live.[5] Given the period's low mortgage rates and ample mortgage credit, new immigrants would likely gravitate toward single-family homes. Then there were the aging and affluent baby boomers, all of whom, builders asserted, were looking either to trade up to new, larger homes or to purchase vacation homes. Florida and South Carolina golf courses, condo towers in downtown Boston or Washington D.C., and mountain resorts in Idaho and Colorado were especially popular.

The builders weren't wrong—these were indeed important sources of new housing demand—but they significantly overstated the case. The attacks of 9/11 crimped immigration more than they knew or let on, and many more boomers were worried about surviving in retirement than about finding the ninth tee.

As the home builders' stories bumped up against the reality of a peaking housing market, the builders did what the techs had done: They became their customers' bankers. Most builders had established mortgage lending units earlier, but now they ramped up these activities to ensure a steady flow of credit to their increasingly pressed buyers. The largest builders, such as Pulte Homes and Centex, financed nearly all the homes they sold during the height of the housing boom. It was one-stop shopping for homebuyers: a new home and the mortgage loan from the same place. The builders were glad to book profits from what was then a very lucrative lending business; but more importantly, they wanted to make sure sales weren't deterred for lack of mortgage credit.

Awash in Homes

Builders had been aggressively constructing homes early in the 2000s, but in the 2003 summer building season, they really let loose. The initial angst over the Iraq invasion had passed; fallout from 9/11 and the 2001 recession was fading, mortgage rates had fallen to new lows, and subprime lending was coming into its own. The number of new homes added to the market—including completed single-family houses, condominium and apartment units, and pre-fab manufactured homes—jumped to well over two million a year.

You can argue endlessly about what constitutes overbuilding, but two million units were clearly too many. At that pace, supply was growing substantially faster than demand. Fundamentally, housing demand equals the sum of all new households being formed, second or vacation homes, and homes being torn down for structural or economic reasons. This makes intuitive as well as mathematical sense: New households of whatever type—new college graduates, the newly married, or the newly divorced—must live somewhere. People who own second or vacation homes may not live there year-round, but have no immediate plans to sell. A torn-down home or one blown away in a hurricane adds to housing demand as well; whoever lived there now needs a new home. Throughout the early 2000s, total fundamental housing demand consistently ran near 1.8 million units a year (see Figure 8.4).[6] What had been a manageable gap between housing supply and demand early in the decade became an overwhelming gulf by the spring 2006 home building season when housing construction hit its all-time peak.[7]

Single and Multi Family Housing Starts, Thousands

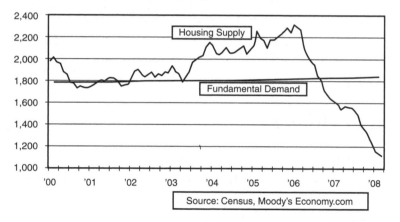

Figure 8.4   New housing supply and demand

Single-family home builders may have been initially fooled into thinking that the market could support a faster pace of building, because the effect of the early overbuilding had been felt mainly in rising vacancy rates for apartment rentals. The nationwide rental vacancy rate rose from 8% at the end of the 1990s to more than 10%, an all-time high, by the spring of 2004. The period's low mortgage rates and easy credit were prompting tens of thousands of apartment dwellers to become homeowners.

Overbuilding in the single-family market was also disguised by the arrival of housing flippers, people who buy homes as an investment only without intending to live in them. As the market heated up, these opportunistic buyers would purchase several homes in a new community, intending to sell them quickly at a profit. It seemed like easy money; builders were anxious to show prospective buyers that prices in their developments were rising so as to spur prospective buyers to act quickly. Flippers, however, took this as vindication of their own investment strategy. Builders quickly grasped the risks this posed for them; as more flippers started showing up, builders began demanding that buyers declare their intention to actually live in the home they were purchasing. Some builders also attempted to restrict quick resales in their contracts with buyers. But these efforts were no match for crafty investors who continued to gather up properties. Builders' sales agents were also conflicted; because their compensation was determined by sales volume, they had an incentive not to try too hard to weed out flippers. Better to make the deal, collect the commission, and move on.

The enormous magnitude of overbuilding in the United States thus did not become clear until the housing bust. Only after flippers stopped buying—and were only selling—and only after foreclosures began to mount, did the number of vacant homes for sale balloon. Even a well-functioning housing market has some unsold inventory, but a healthy level of inventory in today's housing market would amount to no more than 1.25 million homes, roughly the level seen during the first half of the 2000s. By early 2008, inventories had surged to more than 2.25 million homes and were still climbing (see Figure 9.5). Compared with the total number of homes nationwide, inventories have never reached anything close to this level.[8]

No one is more motivated to sell than a homeowner, banker, or builder trying to move an empty home. The property is generating no rental cash, and meanwhile there are property taxes and maintenance costs to pay, not to mention legal fees and a mortgage payment. Banks that take possession of homes dumped by flippers and hapless homeowners in foreclosure are exceptionally eager to sell. Homes sold in foreclosure generally go for about half of their previous sale price. The

Number of Vacant Homes for Sale, Thousands

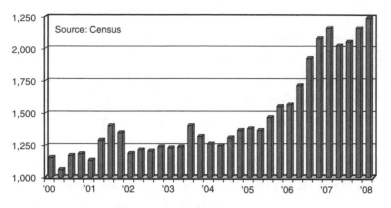

Figure 9.5   Awash in unsold homes

financial pressure on home builders awash in unsold homes isn't quite as intense, but they also tend to aggressively cut prices or offer large non-cash incentives, such as built-in appliances, to try to move their vacant units. One large publicly traded builder, Hovnanian, drew special attention in late 2007 for its "fire sale" offer of six-figure discounts for homes in some high-end communities. Other builders offered up new cars or even college tuition payments to make their homes more attractive.

This was a housing nor'easter as severe as any that ever had roiled the home building industry. The large public builders had not only failed to tame the economic weather, they helped create a storm so large it threatened to run nearly all of them aground.

9

As the Regulatory Cycle Turns

No part of the nation's economic life receives more legal and regulatory oversight than housing and mortgages. Federal and state government agencies have a say in nearly every stage of mortgage lending, from determining whether a loan is appropriate to how to foreclose on a defaulting homeowner. Yet regulatory supervision all but disappeared during the housing boom. Where were the regulators?

It wasn't as if regulators didn't understand subprime lending's risks. They had dealt with the issue in the mid- and late 1990s, when home equity lenders—that period's subprime pioneers—were aggressively making loans. Many of those home-equity loans defaulted and many of those lenders went belly-up by the end of the decade. Regulators responded in 1999 and again in early 2001 by "issuing guidance"—sending an official warning to lenders about the perils of such lending. The regulators told lenders to be sure they set aside adequate reserves to cover the potential losses on risky subprime loans and also warned lenders to avoid predatory lending.

Regulators carefully defined a "predatory" loan as one made without regard to the borrowers' ability to make timely payments.[1] Lenders had to do more than make sure the borrower's house was worth more than the amount of the mortgage; they also had to determine that borrowers had enough income to stay current on the loan. Loans that appeared designed mainly to generate fees for the lender were also declared predatory. A refinancing deal that did not lower the borrower's monthly payment or allow the borrower to take cash out of the house fell into the category of predatory practices, as did lying or withholding relevant information to make a loan to unsophisticated borrowers.

Yet as the subprime market heated up not long after the 2001 guidance was issued, predatory lending practices spread. Lenders appeared to be violating the rules' spirit, if not the letter. The nation's mortgage regulators largely went silent. They might slap the hand of a small lender for something particularly egregious; a few tweaks were made to the rules regarding property appraisals and mortgage fraud. But regulators had little of consequence to say during the housing bubble of the mid-2000s.

Not until late 2006, well after the bubble had begun to burst, did regulators issue their first formal guidance on what they called "nontraditional mortgage products."[2] Regulators had debated what to say in the guidance for more than a year, and what they finally agreed to still didn't directly address most subprime lending. Lenders limited their own definition of "nontraditional" mortgages to interest-only and negative-amortization loans, in which borrowers were allowed to pay less each month than the actual interest due, with the difference added to the principal amount of the loan. Most such deals were in fact prime—not subprime—loans.

The late 2006 guidance was much needed, but it was clearly too little and too late. It included some instructions that might have been considered common sense: lenders, for instance, should not qualify borrowers for a loan based on low introductory "teaser" rates, but rather ask whether a borrower had enough income to pay the higher rates that would kick in down the road. The guidance warned against making loans with no verification of income and savings, and it demanded lenders disclose whether a loan included a large prepayment penalty (as most loans did). The guidance was fashioned by federal regulators, but it quickly became national policy as mortgage-industry regulators at all levels of government adopted it. It was a laudable step; unfortunately, the mortgages whose defaults would precipitate the subprime financial shock had already been made.

Federal and state regulators finally addressed subprime lending formally in June 2007, just weeks before the financial shock hit.[3] In this guidance, regulators told subprime lenders to qualify borrowers assuming a loan's full monthly cost, not just at the low initial teaser interest rate. Borrowers hit with large hikes in their mortgage payments would also have to have at least 60 days to refinance into a more favorable loan before they could be charged a prepayment penalty. By the time this guidance went out, however, subprime lending was already evaporating; the new rules applied to a type of lending that was speeding toward extinction.

Too Many Cooks

One reason mortgage regulation is not more effective is simply the mishmash of regulators, all overseeing different aspects or regions of the market. Their sheer numbers muddied the response to the frenzy leading up to the subprime financial shock. Some regulators recognized that increasingly easy lending standards would soon be a problem; a few publicly warned of the risks. But with so many diverse groups involved, it was difficult to get a working quorum for decision-making.[4] At a time when oversight was most desperately needed on mortgages, half the nation's lenders were regulated at the federal level and half by the states (see Table 9.1).

The Federal Reserve Board is by far the nation's most important banking regulator. It is responsible for keeping an eye on the largest banks and financial holding companies (FHCs), which historically account for about a fourth of all mortgage lending. Another fourth comes from a hodgepodge of depository institutions, including commercial banks, savings and loans, and credit unions. The federal Office of Comptroller of the Currency (OCC), the Federal Deposit Insurance Corporation (FDIC), the Office of Thrift Supervision (OTS), and the National Credit Union Association (NCUA) oversee these lenders.

TABLE 9.1   Mortgage Lending Regulators

Regulator	Who It Regulates	Examples of Lending Institutions
Federal Reserve	Financial holding companies, bank holding companies, member state banks	Citigroup, JPMorgan Chase, KeyCorp, SunTrust Bank, Wachovia Corporation
Office of the Comptroller of the Currency (OCC)	Nationally chartered banks	Citibank, National Association; Mellon Bank, N.A.; PNC Bank National Association; Wells Fargo Bank, National Association
Federal Deposit Insurance Company (FDIC)*	State-chartered banks that are not members of the Federal Reserve System	BancorpSouth Bank, Bank of the West, Branch Banking and Trust Company, GMAC Bank
Office of Thrift Supervision (OTS)	Savings and loans associations (thrifts)	Countrywide Bank, FSB; Washington Mutual Bank; World Savings Bank, FSB
National Credit Union Administration	Federal credit unions	BECU (formerly Boeing Employees' Credit Union), Navy Federal Credit Union, Pentagon Federal Credit Union
State regulators*	State chartered banks, mortgage brokers, non-depository lenders	New Century Financial

*Banks regulated by the FDIC can also be regulated by the state they are located in.

Federally regulated lenders are not generally subject to state laws, but the states have more than their share of regulatory responsibility.[5] States are charged with monitoring the most aggressive mortgage brokers and non-bank lenders, including mortgage finance companies and real estate investment trusts, who accounted for the remaining half of mortgage lending during the boom.[6] Most states also require mortgage brokers to be licensed and registered; many, although not all, require the same for individual loan officers. Some loose coordination occurs among the states via umbrella organizations, such as the

Conference of State Bank Supervisors and the American Association of Residential Mortgage Regulators.

Other government agencies also have a voice in guiding the mortgage market. The Federal Trade Commission monitors mortgage lenders and brokers' compliance with anti-discrimination statutes and other federal laws. The Securities and Exchange Commission (SEC) oversees publicly traded companies, and the Office of Housing Enterprise Oversight (OFHEO) regulates Fannie Mae and Freddie Mac.

In some cases, more than one regulator is involved in overseeing a lender's activities. Wells Fargo & Company, one of the nation's largest mortgage lenders, is an example. The Federal Reserve watches over the bank's holding company, whereas its lending subsidiary is monitored by the OCC. In other cases, lenders receive very little scrutiny at all. New Century Financial, which made some of the most questionable subprime loans before it went bust, fell under California's state regulators and the SEC, neither of whom had the expertise nor interest in evaluating the company's mortgage lending policies.

Clear cracks exist in the regulatory patchwork that oversees mortgage lending, and the most aggressive mortgage lenders exploited them during the housing boom. Understaffed state regulators lacked resources to monitor a rapidly growing and increasingly sophisticated mortgage industry; they were the most vulnerable to the most aggressive and least scrupulous lenders, who were also among the biggest casualties when the boom went bust (see Table 9.2).

Why wasn't lending better regulated? Beneath the muddle of agencies and authorities was the nation's long-standing distrust of centralized government authority. The system might have worked well enough in an earlier time, when banking and mortgages were primarily local or at most regional businesses. Regulators knew the lenders in their jurisdiction intimately. As regional barriers to lending came down, the nation's Byzantine regulatory structure did not change, making its oversight of lenders increasingly unwieldy and ineffective.

TABLE 9.2   Regulators of Bankrupt Mortgage Lenders

Lender	Primary Regulator
Central Pacific Mortgage	California Department of Corporations
Eagle First Mortgage	Arizona Department of Financial Institutions
Mortgage Lenders Network USA	Connecticut Department of Banking
New Century Financial	California Department of Corporations
Ameriquest	California Department of Corporations
CoreStar Financial Group	State of Illinois Department of Financial and Professional Regulation
First Horizon	Tennessee Department of Financial Institutions
Homefield Financial	California Department of Corporations
Innovative Mortgage Capital	California Department of Corporations
Mortgage Tree Lending	California Department of Corporations
Columbia Home Loans	New York State Banking Department
No Red Tape Mortgage	California Department of Corporations
Heritage Plaza Mortgage	California Department of Corporations
Right Away Mortgage	California Department of Corporations
Oak Street Mortgage	Indiana Department of Financial Institutions
First Street Financial	California Department of Corporations
Alliance Mortgage Banking Corp	New York State Banking Department
Heartwell Mortgage	Michigan Office of Financial and Insurance Services
ACT Mortgage	Office of Financial Regulation, State of Florida
Altivus Financial	New Jersey Department of Banking and Insurance
Bridge Capital Corporation	California Department of Corporations
Steward Financial	California Department of Corporations
Freestand Financial	Arizona Department of Financial Institutions
Unlimited Loan Resources	Ohio Department of Financial Institutions
Starpointe Mortgage	Michigan Office of Financial and Insurance Services

TABLE 9.2   Regulators of Bankrupt Mortgage Lenders

Lender	Primary Regulator
Entrust Mortgage	Colorado Department of Regulatory Agencies, Division of Banking
American Home Mortgage	New York State Banking Department
Winstar Mortgage	Minnesota Department of Finance
Aegis	Texas Department of Banking
Mylor Financial	California Department of Corporations
Express Capital Lending	California Department of Corporations
Kirkwood Financial Corporation	Arizona Department of Financial Institutions
Lexington Lending	California Department of Corporations
Golden Empire Mortgage	California Department of Corporations
Spectrum Financial Group	Arizona Department of Financial Institutions
First Magnus	Arizona Department of Financial Institutions
Novastar	Missouri Division of Finance
First National Bank of Arizona	Arizona Department of Financial Institutions
Amstar Mortgage Corporation	Texas Department of Banking
Quality Home Loans	California Department of Corporations

Home Ownership Politics

Regulators' efforts to cool the lending frenzy were also fettered by America's fierce and long-running devotion to the ideal of home ownership for all. Since the Great Depression, politicians had viewed the percentage of American families who owned their dwellings as a key benchmark of economic success. Regulators were given an open-ended mandate to help drive that number higher. Any agency or administrator who did not actively pursue this vision was roundly criticized.

The pursuit of higher home ownership went into high gear beginning in the 1970s, as it also became a test of the nation's success in promoting civil rights. The 1977 Community Reinvestment Act had outlawed "redlining," historically the practice by bankers of defining neighborhoods—literally outlined on maps in red—where they would not make mortgage loans. Such neighborhoods were usually poor and most often home to minorities or out-of-favor ethnic groups. The Community Reinvestment Act (CRA) was meant not just to end, but to actively reverse the effects of such discrimination by offering banks both carrots and sticks to encourage lending in underserved areas. The CRA was given more teeth during the Clinton administration in the mid-1990s: regulators could now require banks to explicitly target disadvantaged neighborhoods for both business and home-mortgage lending.

About this time, the Federal Reserve also unveiled new statistical methods for detecting discrimination in mortgage lending.[7] Marrying data from mortgage loan applications and approvals (as required under the 1975 Home Mortgage Disclosure Act) with sophisticated econometric techniques, researchers at the Fed felt they could tell whether lenders were racially discriminating.[8] A bank tagged by the Fed's models could be denied permission to acquire or merge with another bank.[9] This was a period of active consolidation in the banking industry and any institution that could not be a shark quickly became a minnow. Only a handful of banks actually failed the Fed's test, but they were soon acquired, reinforcing the message from regulators to lenders to push home ownership aggressively.[10]

The Clinton administration was especially proud of the rise in home ownership during the 1990s, particularly among lower income and minority groups. While home ownership rose 7% among white households during the decade, it increased 13% among African American households and 18% among Hispanic households. This could not have happened without the regulators' blessing and encouragement.

President Bush readily took up the homeownership baton at the start of his administration in 2001. Owning a home became one pillar of his "ownership society," a vision in which everyone would possess a stake in the American economy. For millions, this meant owning their own home. In summer 2002, Bush challenged lenders to add 5.5 million new minority homeowners by the end of the decade; in 2003 he signed the American Dream Downpayment Act, a program offering money to lower income households to help with down payments and closing costs on a first home. Lenders gladly accepted Bush's challenge.

To reinforce this effort, the Bush administration put substantial pressure on Fannie Mae and Freddie Mac to increase their funding of mortgage loans to lower-income groups. Both Fannie and Freddie had been shown to have substantial problems during the corporate accounting scandals in the early 2000s, and both were willing to go along with any request from the administration. OFHEO set aggressive goals for the two giant institutions, which they met in part by purchasing subprime mortgage securities. By the time of the subprime financial shock, both had become sizable buyers of the Aaa tranches of these securities.

Democrats in Congress were worried about increasing evidence of predatory lending. Some noted that the 2001 rule prohibiting such lending only applied to federally regulated lenders. North Carolina had passed a law banning predatory practices in 1999, and the Democrats wanted a federal equivalent that would cover all lenders nationwide. The Bush administration and most Republicans in Congress were opposed, believing legislation would overly restrict lending and thus slow the march of home ownership; moreover, the Republicans argued, existing regulations were adequate to discourage the worst excesses. The last attempt to pass anti-predatory lending legislation occurred in 2005, but it was also stymied. It was thus up to regulators to strike the appropriate balance between promoting home ownership and ensuring prudent lending. All too obviously, they failed to strike that balance.

Greenspan's Regulatory Failure

The Federal Reserve not only sets monetary policy, it also plays a central role in guiding the nation's banking regulatory infrastructure. Without the Fed's leadership, other regulators could not take an effective stand against the frenzied mortgage lending of the early 2000s. But the Greenspan-led Fed was not anxious to use its considerable authority to significantly curtail mortgage lending.

The Fed's regulatory stature stems from its intimate relationship with the largest financial institutions, established as part of its monetary policy responsibilities. Given the importance of these institutions to the entire financial system, policies set by the Fed quickly radiate throughout the system. The Fed's leadership also stems from its enormous financial and intellectual resources; more economists work in the Fed system than in any other institution in the world. Most importantly, the Fed is largely independent: although not completely outside the political process, it is more able than any other regulator to adopt policies and positions without regard to what the president or Congress think.

Chairman Greenspan's reluctance to flex the Fed's regulatory muscles stemmed from his own oft-voiced skepticism about regulation. Greenspan believed a well-functioning market with the appropriate incentives could police itself more effectively than could government bureaucrats. Mortgage lending qualifies as such a market, Greenspan thought. Lenders ultimately had to answer to smart and self-interested global investors, who surely saw no lasting profit in making bad mortgage loans.

Greenspan wasn't the only policymaker who held such views; the 1980s and '90s had been marked by a steady march toward deregulation. The trend climaxed in 1999 with Congressional passage of the Gramm-Leach-Bliley bill, which overturned Depression-era banking laws barring banks from merging with securities dealers and insurance firms. The resulting financial holding companies were put under the regulatory domain of the Federal Reserve. The Basel II rules on banks' capital reserve requirements were being fashioned at about the same time. These rules rely heavily on market forces; how much capital banks need, and therefore how aggressive they can be in their lending, is determined mainly by the market value of their holdings. The fashion in banking circles was to let the market—not old-fashioned regulators—determine what was appropriate.

There was some notable dissent on this from within the Federal Reserve itself. Fed governor Edward Gramlich, a well-respected former economics professor from the University of Michigan, was notably vocal early in the lending boom. Gramlich, who was responsible for consumer affairs at the Fed, felt the central bank should take the lead in weeding out predatory lending by examining both the federally regulated banks under the Fed's auspices and their mortgage affiliates, which were not.[11] These proposals went nowhere. Chairman Greenspan argued that Gramlich's proposed examinations would not have stopped shady lending, and that they might inadvertently bestow on shady lenders the ability to claim the Fed's seal of approval.[12]

At various times, Congress also exhorted the Fed to address nagging concerns about excesses in the mortgage market. In 1994, the House and Senate passed the Home Ownership and Equity Protection Act (HOEPA), which authorized the Fed to prohibit unfair or deceptive mortgage lending.[13] Under the HOEPA, the Fed has the authority to prohibit predatory lending practices by any lender, no matter who regulates it. The Fed used these powers only sparingly, arguing against the need for blanket rules on unfairness or deception. Each case is different, Fed officials claimed.

Almost a decade later, Congressional Democrats pushed the Fed to use its authority under the Federal Trade Act to write rules on unfair and deceptive lending practices. Again, it was to no avail. Greenspan tossed the ball back to Congress, saying the legislature was better suited to define the practices it wanted to bar and make whatever laws were necessary. In other words, if there was improper lending going on, Congress would have to deal with it—not the Fed, and not, by extension, the nation's bank regulators.

Don't Worry, Be Happy

Although Greenspan ultimately acknowledged that he had erred in thinking that the market would discipline lenders, his doubts about banking regulation were not without merit. Among other problems, it is hard for regulators to avoid getting caught up in the same euphoria that envelops lenders during good times. Instead of restraining overly aggressive lenders in such periods, regulators may encourage them.

The housing boom period illustrates the point. Mortgage credit conditions couldn't have seemed better in those years. By 2005, with unemployment declining and house prices surging, delinquencies and defaults had dropped to record lows. Hardly a borrower in San Diego or Miami was even late with a payment. Regulators would have had great difficulty making the case to lenders that their lending standards were out of whack: the regulators had no tangible evidence to point to, even if they had wanted some.

Regulators also could not keep up with the explosion of new and increasingly complex mortgage loans. Although interest-only, nega-tive-amortization, and subprime loans had been around in some form for years, they had never been offered so widely to all kinds of borrow-ers in parts of the country where they had never before been available. Regulators didn't have time to evaluate all the new arrangements, let alone determine whether they were appropriate or what to do if they were not.

State regulators were particularly ill-equipped to confront lenders, especially in those states where housing was at its frothiest. Many state agencies were completely outmanned. At the peak of California's housing boom, for example, no more than 30 state exam-iners watched over nearly 5,000 consumer finance companies, includ-ing some of the nation's most aggressive mortgage lenders.[14] The massive workload effectively reduced examiners to bookkeepers who could only check to make sure that companies had adequate reserves and were not overcharging borrowers. Mortgage companies could expect an examination from state regulators about once every four years. When the bust came, some of the biggest casualties involved subprime lenders that had been examined just a few months before filing for bankruptcy.

Many state regulators also felt pressure from local politicians to keep mortgage credit flowing freely to their constituents. Examiners were asked to strike a difficult balance between regulating and encouraging home buying and lending. When house prices were high and mortgage delinquencies low, it was difficult enough to warn lenders that they might be overdoing it, let alone force them to rein in their lending.

Searching for a Voice

As mortgage loan quality weakened and foreclosures began to mount in 2006, regulators finally got their bearings. Federal agencies jointly issued the October 2006 guidance cracking down on nontraditional mortgage lending, and followed in June 2007 with a statement on subprime loans. The Federal Reserve, now under the leadership of Chairman Ben Bernanke, began a series of hearings about protecting mortgage borrowers. HOEPA had given the Fed the authority for this in the mid-1990s, but not until the housing bust was the central bank willing to take on the job in a comprehensive way.

Finally, in December 2007, the Fed proposed some common-sense lending rules. Firms that made "higher-priced" (mostly subprime) loans would have to consider the borrower's ability to repay, and verify the borrower's income and assets. Prepayment penalties were barred if a homeowner refinanced within 60 days after an adjustable loan reset, and borrowers would have to establish an escrow account for taxes and insurance.[15] Lenders could not compensate mortgage brokers for steering borrowers to higher-rate loans, nor coerce appraisers to overstate home values. Mortgage services would have to credit borrowers as of the date they receive payments. None of these rules were radical; indeed, it is hard to imagine that lending standards had eroded so badly that they were even necessary.

The Fed also began working to reestablish its leadership in mortgage and financial regulation. The central bank issued guidance in early 2007 along with other regulators, encouraging lenders to work with borrowers who were struggling to make their payments, particularly those facing steep adjustable-rate interest resets. Later in the same year, Chairman Bernanke threw his support behind expanding Fannie and Freddie's mortgage-lending authority, then still a politically controversial idea. The Bush administration and Congress eventually followed.

In early 2008, Bernanke also supported helping homeowners whose homes' value had fallen below the amount of their mortgages—a situation called "negative equity." Bernanke argued that such mortgages might have to be written down, reducing the principal until the homeowner no longer owed more than the home was worth. This was a particularly unpopular view in many parts of the mortgage industry, and in Washington, D.C. Some mortgage holders had agreed to help troubled borrowers by freezing interest rates or extending the term of their loans, but few were willing to shrink the amount of a borrower's debt. Much of the Bush administration, and some in Congress, also argued that such writedowns would amount to a bailout of bad borrowers and lenders. Bernanke countered that negative equity makes borrowers much more likely to default, and that writedowns might be necessary to keep foreclosures from spreading uncontrollably like dominoes, dragging down housing and the wider economy.

Some regulators were particularly forthright in their responses to the subprime shock. FDIC Chairwoman Sheila Bair was one of the first to advocate freezing interest rates for subprime adjustable-rate mortgage (ARM) borrowers facing payment resets; she also proposed writing-down borrowers' mortgage debts. John Reich, Director of the federal Office of Thrift Supervision, put forward a plan addressing some of the same concerns. Not only did such efforts illustrate the severity of the subprime shock and its implications for the nation's financial system, they also testified to the leadership void left over many years by dormant regulators at the Federal Reserve.

Regulators didn't create the subprime financial shock, but they did nothing to prevent it. This was a result of, first, policymakers' distrust of regulation in general, their enduring belief that markets and financial institutions could effectively police themselves; and second, of the nation's antiquated regulatory framework. The institutions guiding the nation's financial system were fashioned during the Great Depression, and as finance evolved rapidly, they remained largely unchanged. An overhaul was indisputably overdue.

10 —————————————

Boom, Bubble, Bust, and Crash

June 2, 1995: This is as good a date as any to begin the string of events that led to the subprime financial shock. On this day, the nation's housing market was enjoying a blessedly fortunate set of conditions—the best in at least 30 years, with fixed mortgage rates below 8%, adjustable rates below 6%, and a healthy job market. Combined with the relatively low house prices that prevailed into the mid-1990s, they made housing as good a bargain as it had ever been in the U.S. Sure enough, home sales, construction, ownership, and prices all climbed steadily through the remainder of the decade—and kept climbing, right through the 2001 recession and into the jobless recovery that followed.

Housing Boom

The period from the mid-90s through the early 2000s is best described as a housing boom. Consistently strong activity was driven by well-supported demand and disciplined new housing supply. Buyers of second homes or vacation homes had every intention of holding onto them; they weren't "flippers" looking for quick profit. House prices posted solid, steady gains—but those who wanted real action turned to the stock market. Anyone seeking a fast buck was focused on the price of Cisco stock or perhaps eBay—not a Miami Beach condo or San Diego ranch home. Speculation had taken over the stock market, but not yet the housing market.

A single-family home was a bargain in the late 1990s, and the job market was arguably stronger than at any previous time in the nation's history. In 1995, a median priced U.S. home could be purchased with a monthly mortgage payment of $675.[1] Because mortgage rates had fallen steadily, that monthly payment was no greater than it had been in 1980. Meanwhile, household incomes had more than doubled. Unemployment was falling, too; in 1995 it was near 5.5%, down from 7.5% early in the decade and half the level of the early 1980s. By the end of the 1990s, unemployment had reached a post-World War II low below 4%.

Minority groups were gaining meaningful access to mortgage credit for the first time. African-American and Hispanic households with incomes and savings, who may have been unable to obtain mortgage loans in the past, now finally could do so. This was a priority for the Clinton administration; it empowered and then pushed regulators to aggressively enforce requirements on mortgage lenders to extend more loans to previously excluded groups.

Foreign immigration also soared during the 1990s, pushing up the number of households and thus the demand for housing. Immigrants were attracted by the surging U.S. economy and all the available jobs, particularly in contrast to their own troubled economies in Latin America, Southeast Asia, and Eastern Europe. The terror attacks of 9/11 were still in the future, and security was a relatively modest concern. Legal and illegal immigrants were adding half a million households a year to the U.S. population; each household required a place to live. Almost one-fourth of the new homes constructed during the housing boom were for immigrants.

Despite the strong demand for new homes, builders were restrained from overbuilding. The large California and Northeast housing markets still felt the effects of the early 1990s savings and loan (S&L) crisis, when many builders failed along with their banks. The infrastructure for building homes—from obtaining construction permits to selling completed units—had been hobbled by the S&L bust.

Even as housing demand improved, it was difficult to put together all the moving parts needed to erect a home. California housing starts in 1995 were a third their level from a decade earlier. Not until the decade's end did the homebuilding industry begin humming again.

Housing Bubble

July 4, 2003: What had been a housing boom became a housing bubble (see Figure 10.1). There was no obvious warning: The war in Iraq still looked like an easy win; the domestic job market was finally regaining traction, fixed mortgage rates were closer to 5%, and adjustable rates had fallen firmly below 4%. Despite the solid rise of house prices in the preceding eight boom years, housing was still affordable. But this was also when homebuyers, lenders, and mortgage investors began looking skyward, assuming because house prices had been rising strongly in the recent past, they would continue to do so far into the future. Speculation began to grip the market.

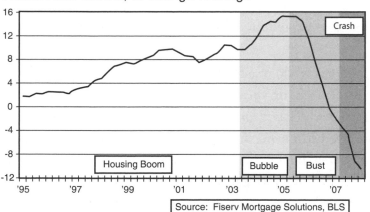

Figure 10.1   **Housing boom, bubble, bust, and crash**

The housing bubble was born out of the boom. The boom had been based on solid demand and supply fundamentals: things such as affordable homes, strong incomes, and ample household savings. The bubble developed when Americans started buying not simply because they needed someplace to live, but because they thought housing was a great investment. Prices had risen, therefore they would continue to rise. This is speculation. A bubble develops when an asset's price becomes disconnected from its fundamental value. Stocks derive their fundamental value from future corporate earnings. Housing derives its fundamental value from its future value as shelter or from the rent it generates.

Some regions are more susceptible to bubbles than others. Parts of the country where geography or zoning makes development land scarce—think California, Florida, or the Northeast corridor—are particularly fertile soil for speculation. When strong demand meets a restrictive building environment, houses can be bid up quickly, causing price appreciation to become divorced from the factors that caused the gains in the first place. Some of these areas had seen house-price bubbles in the mid-1970s, and again in the early 1990s. By contrast, in areas where new construction is relatively easy—Texas or Iowa— speculation is less likely. As soon as prices show any strength, builders rush in to add more houses and compete away the gains. Without dramatic price gains to point to, buyers' imaginations never drift toward the skies.

Conventional wisdom stated that although isolated regional housing bubbles might form, a nationwide bubble was all but impossible. The reasoning was based on transaction costs—the incidental expenses involved in buying and selling homes, from realtor fees to taxes. Speculative bubbles, it was believed, require frenzied buying and selling to fuel the price gains. Real estate transaction costs, however, were high enough to short-circuit such activity. Stocks, by contrast, were prone to speculation because the transaction costs involved in trading shares were much lower.

Yet the collapse of the Internet stock bubble at the turn of the century created the fodder for the subsequent national house-price bubble. With stocks reeling and the Federal Reserve slashing interest rates, many households wondered what to do with their savings. Because housing was still rising in price, the answer seemed straightforward: Buy a house, or maybe several houses. The idea grew even more appealing following 9/11, as travel began to seem less alluring than a barbecue in the safety of your own backyard.

Besides, almost anyone could get a mortgage loan. For those with unblemished credit histories, the rates resembled those our parents and grandparents talked about, much as they recounted hearing Elvis Presley or Jimmy Dorsey for the first time. Even better, those high transaction costs were falling fast. Competition among mortgage lenders and newfangled Internet technology had made shuffling all those documents much less expensive. There was no place like a brand new home, and sales soared to astonishing levels. At the apex in 2005, fully ten percent of all the homes in the country were bought and sold.

How Overvalued?

Economists often debate what constitutes a bubble and how to determine if one is forming. After all, the price for any asset, from a share of stock to a home, is based on forecasts of future returns by many buyers; and who can say that all those buyers are getting their forecasts wrong? There are some telltale signs, however, and the housing market circa 2005 exhibited all of them: A huge volume of home sales; available easy money for house purchases; and a lot of new theorists arguing that, yes, prices might have gotten too high in the past, but things were different now. To these theorists, the housing market made perfect sense. All you had to do was discard all those antiquated measurements and notions of what constituted an appropriate house price.

One such measure of housing valuation compares house prices with rents.[2] The logic is simple: Households can choose to own or rent their home, and are likely to choose whichever option is more cost-effective. The cost of ownership, of course, is closely tied to the sale price of the home. If house prices rise faster than rents over a long enough period, renting will become the cheaper option for many people—making house prices look overvalued. (The same relationship works in reverse: If house prices fall relative to rents over time, houses will likely be undervalued.) The relationship between house prices and rents depends on many factors, including interest rates and the availability of mortgage credit. Over sufficiently long periods of time, however, this relationship is quite stable.

Here's another way to think about it: The relationship between house prices and rents is much like a price-earnings ratio for stocks. PE ratios fluctuate as markets change, but since World War II, the PE on the S&P 500 stock index has averaged about 15—that is, stock prices have averaged about 15 times corporate earnings. At times a PE of more than 15 can be justified—such as when interest rates are low—but using the long-term average is a good rule of thumb for identifying whether the stock market is over- or undervalued. Just before the Internet-stock bust in 2000, for example, the PE on the S&P 500 peaked around 45. As subsequent events proved, it was clearly overvalued.

Nationally, the housing "price-to-rent" ratio hit an all-time peak of 25 at the end of 2005 (see Figure 10.2). On July 4, 2003, the day I've identified as the start of the housing bubble, the price-to-rent ratio was 18.5. This compares with an average over the past quarter century of 16.5, and a low of 12.5 during the mid-1980s. Although the overvalued national housing market in 2005 wasn't in the same league as the stock market in 2000, it was close in some metropolitan markets. The highest flyers included Miami, Washington DC, Phoenix, Orlando, most of Southern California and Sacramento, Las Vegas, and Long Island. Before the bubble ended, however, almost every major market in the country was deemed to be overvalued to some extent.[3]

Housing's Price-to-Rent Ratio

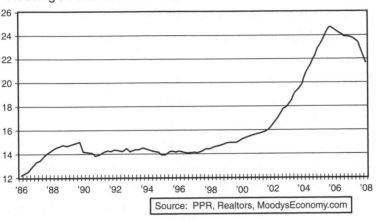

Source: PPR, Realtors, MoodysEconomy.com

Figure 10.2   An overvalued housing market

Housing Bust

April 10, 2006: On this chilly and wet day (at least in my neighborhood in suburban Philadelphia), housing was palpably overvalued from coast to coast. Housing affordability was sinking, dragged down both by soaring prices and by the Federal Reserve's recent series of interest rate hikes. The economy was looking robust, thanks largely to the soaring housing market, and low interest rates were no longer part of the central bank's prescription for balancing growth and inflation. Rising rates didn't prick the housing bubble immediately; mortgage lenders kept them at bay by offering even easier lending terms to borrowers. Eventually, lenders ran out of tricks for keeping monthly payments down. By the spring selling season of 2006, the housing bubble was starting to leak.

Nationally, house prices didn't fall much in 2006, but even the modest decline that occurred was unnerving. Not since the Great Depression had there been such an overall, coast-to-coast average price decline, and it got people's attention. Small- and medium-size real-estate speculators stopped buying and began selling—and when no one else showed up to buy, they began mailing their house keys back to their lenders. Mortgage loans made just a few months earlier began to show signs of trouble. Before long, a wave of mortgage defaults began the foreclosure process.[4] The pace of defaults rose from an annualized 775,000 at the end of 2005 to nearly 1 million by year-end 2006 (see Figure 11.3).[5] Many defaults involved recent buyers, who had made only one or two payments—or none—on their loans. Most were "flippers" who had taken out a mortgage expecting to pay it off quickly, after selling the house at a profit. When they couldn't sell or even rent their investment home, they defaulted.

First Mortgage Loan Defaults, Ths, SAAR

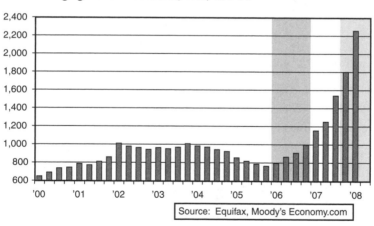

Source: Equifax, Moody's Economy.com

Figure 11.3   Three waves of foreclosures

A second wave of defaults and foreclosures began in the spring of 2007. Subprime mortgage borrowers who had obtained loans two years earlier choked as their mortgage payments jumped higher. Most had so-called 2/28 loans: For two years, the rate was low and fixed; after that, it adjusted generally every six months to levels reflecting prevailing short-term rates. Homeowners who hit their first rate reset in 2007 found themselves facing an average increase of $350 per month: Their average monthly payment shot from $1,200 to $1,550, often an unmanageable amount. The pace of defaults rose from 1 million per year at the end of 2006 to more than 1.5 million by summer 2007.

Nobody in the mortgage business had expected this. Many had understood it *could* happen—under the terms borrowers had agreed to, they could technically face a payment reset that would overwhelm their household finances—but almost no one thought it *would* happen. Surely such borrowers would be able to refinance; doing so was in everyone's interest. Mortgage lenders would collect more fees—often charging both to originate a new loan and a penalty for paying off the old one early. Mortgage investors would be happy to receive their money back; they had planned it that way and didn't want to worry about whether these shaky borrowers would default in the future. Borrowers would have a clean start.

Yet as credit conditions weakened, mortgage lenders and investors grew less willing to refinance hard-pressed borrowers facing resets. Suddenly, no one wanted to take on the risk, and subprime borrowers began defaulting en masse.

It was all too much for mortgage investors. They had been judiciously unloading their mortgage security holdings for more than a year, but by summer 2007 panic had set in, and the rout was on. The subprime financial shock was in full swing.

Housing Crash

July 30, 2007: As the opening bell sounded on Wall Street, news spread that investment bank Bear Stearns was shuttering two of its hedge funds, both of which had loaded up with subprime mortgage investments. The story pushed the housing market over the edge. Mortgage securities trading shut down; the pipeline from global capital markets to the housing market had been severed. Now mortgage lenders couldn't make a loan even if they wanted to. There were still

FHA loans and loans backed by Fannie Mae and Freddie Mac, but they could not fill the void left as private mortgage lending ceased. This was particularly true in places such as California and Florida, where government lending was virtually nonexistent.

Without mortgage credit, home sales plunged. At the start of 2007, new and existing home sales were running close to a 7.5 million unit pace a year, but by the end of the year the pace had fallen below 5.5 million. Psychology in the housing market had been turned upside down. Until this point, home builders and other sellers had believed that if they were flexible on pricing and patient, they would make a sale. It might take a few extra weeks or months, and perhaps an incentive such as a built-out basement or retiled roof, but eventually homes would sell for close to their initial asking price. Now, with mortgages and home sales evaporating, sellers realized they had no choice but to slash prices. Of course, those buyers who were still in the market sensed sellers' terror and turned coy; they didn't want to catch the proverbial falling knife.

House prices crashed. The national average price, which had fallen about 5% between the spring 2006 selling season and the summer of 2007, dropped another 10% by spring 2008. Prices were down more than 20% from their peaks around Washington, DC and on Long Island; more than 25% in Arizona and Nevada; and more than 30% in southwest Florida and the Central Valley of California.

Halfway through 2008, it was possible to foresee where house prices were headed using the price-to-rent analysis as a guide. If the ratio of prices to rents returned to its 25-year average, nationwide house prices were likely to fall an additional 10%. This would mean a total drop in house prices of about 25%—a tumble comparable to the one experienced in the Great Depression. Some large metro areas, moreover, were likely to experience total price declines of more than 35%, including Miami, Washington DC, Long Island, the Bay Area of California, Orlando, and Phoenix (see Figure 10.4).[6]

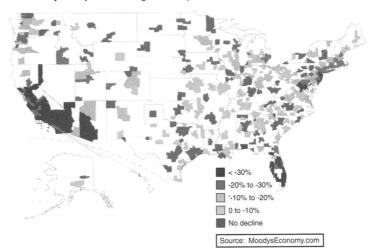

Figure 10.4   **Where house prices will decline most**

Where's the Bottom?

The free fall in house prices after the subprime financial shock brought on a third wave of mortgage loan defaults and foreclosures. This time, the catalyst for foreclosure was negative equity—the dilemma faced by a homeowner who owes more on a home loan than the home itself is worth.[7] With house prices falling back to 2004 levels, homeowners in most parts of the country who had purchased between 2005 and mid-2007 and put less than 10% down were lucky if they were still above water. By spring 2008, an estimated 8.5 million homeowners—one in seven of all those with a first mortgage—were indeed underwater. This was up from 3.5 million a year earlier and 2.5 million the year before that.

Some homeowners chose to just walk away. With their homes' value falling far below the amount of their mortgage, they lost hope of ever getting back their equity and simply handed both mortgage and house back to the bank. This was unusual, however. Most homeowners were willing to work hard to stay current and in their homes, even while in negative equity. Many didn't really know their homes' value;

others figured it was worth the wait until prices rose once again. It was a tenuous position to be in; one financial mishap, such as a temporary loss of income or an unexpected increase in expenses, could mean the loss of a home. The danger was compounded by lenders who couldn't or wouldn't renegotiate or modify the terms of a loan.

Many negative-equity households were also caught up in a rapidly weakening job market. Some were facing layoffs, others were losing overtime hours or settling for part-time work because full-time jobs weren't available. Predictably, regions with the worst housing troubles also saw the most severe job losses. The situation was precarious for those with negative equity; a fender bender, a busted water heater, or a child's broken arm could push families into delinquency and default.

From summer 2007 to spring 2008, first mortgage loan defaults soared from more than 1.5 million to 2.2 million. By spring 2008, an astounding 2% of the nation's households were in default on their mortgages. Default rates were measurably higher in California, Arizona, Nevada, Florida, the industrial Midwest, and in heavily populated regions of the Northeast corridor (see Figure 10.5).

Not all loan defaults forced families from their homes. In good times, fewer than half of defaults do. Homeowners and lenders are often able to work out a deal; lenders put homeowners on a repayment plan or modify the loan by lowering the borrower's interest rate or extending the term to make the loan more affordable. Many homeowners are able to recover and make good on their loans. But during times of economic weakness, things are different: well over half of defaults cause households to lose their homes. The end could be a short sale, in which the home is sold for less than the mortgage amount; lenders sometimes agree to accept this just to get rid of the problem. It could also be through a "deed in lieu," in which the homeowner simply hands their deed back to the lender and is freed from further obligation. More often than not, however, the lender eventually takes possession of the home, putting it into an "other real estate owned" (REO) account from which it is sold.

% of households defaulting on their first mortgage, '08q1

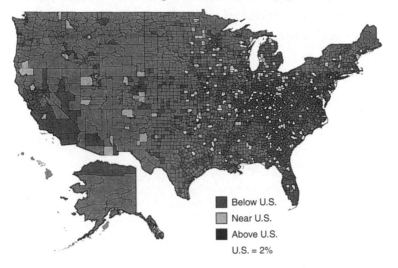

Figure 10.5   Defaults soar across the country

With so many homes going through this process, the number of vacant homes for sale surged. According the Census Bureau, by spring 2008 more than 2.25 million homes were vacant and for sale. During the housing boom, there were only 1.25 million such homes. In other words, the bust had turned more than 1 million homes into "excess inventory."

Such properties were often sold far below prevailing market prices. Lenders were absorbing big losses in maintenance, legal, and carrying costs, and wanted to sell their foreclosed REO property quickly, even if that meant writing off substantial sums. In early 2008, lenders were selling foreclosed property anywhere from 30% to 50% below prevailing market prices.

These distress sales were devastating for the broader housing market. A typical home sold in foreclosure reduces the value of surrounding properties by more than a full percentage point. Rising foreclosures were driving up inventories, which in turn were driving

down prices and homeowners' equity and thus creating more foreclosures. The housing market was trapped in a self-reinforcing negative
cycle. This had occurred, briefly, in California and New England in
the early 1990s, but never in so many parts of the country. There was
no obvious way out of the cycle, and no guarantee that house prices
would stop falling soon.

11

Credit Crunch

Watching a financial crisis feels much like watching a natural disaster—as long as you are watching from a safe distance. The raw, uncontrollable power of each is riveting. Although one is made by man and the other isn't, there is something deeply mysterious about each; it isn't quite clear how, or why, or why now. Of course, each can create enormous damage and can be heartbreaking for those directly involved. The repercussions last well beyond the immediate shock; nearly everyone is affected at least indirectly, and each leaves scars that never entirely disappear.

The subprime shock was as serious a financial earthquake as any the nation had seen since World War II.[1] There have been some big financial calamities through the years: the collapse of Penn Square Bank in 1982, the savings and loan crisis of the late 1980s, the collapse of hedge fund Long Term Capital Management in 1998, and the Internet stock bust at the turn of the millennium, to name a few. On the financial Richter scale, these other crises might rate a 5 or 6. The subprime shock was off the scale.

This was evident in the size of the losses suffered by global investors. Although the ultimate cost wouldn't be known for years, most reasonable estimates put the tab close to $1 trillion.[2] This includes both losses on thousands of defaulting mortgages and the decline in value of the securities backed by other shaky loans. The S&L crisis by comparison cost the country a mere $250 billion.[3] Even Japan's banking crisis of the 1990s, from which the economy has never fully recovered, doesn't measure up; its losses come in near $750 billion.

Nearly every sector of the financial system took a bath because of the subprime shock. Global banks have lost an estimated $475 billion; insurance companies and pension funds another $275 billion; and hedge funds and all other institutions $200 billion (see Figure 11.1). All kinds of institutions saw their residential mortgage and mortgage security holdings hammered—no surprise there—but the extent of their other losses was startling. There were write-downs on commercial mortgage holdings and on business loans and credit of all types; even consumer loans such as credit cards, auto loans, and student loans suffered big losses.

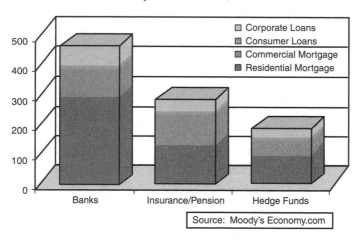

Figure 11.1   Financial sector losses mount

Every corner of the financial system was shaken. Trading in private residential mortgage securities came to a standstill along with the markets for collateralized debt obligations backed by asset-backed securities and for commercial mortgage securities. Low-rated "junk" corporate bonds and bonds backed by credit card loans were still issued, but investors now held out for a much higher interest rate before parting with their cash. Even the market for municipal bonds, where state and local governments raise money to build schools or sewers, was thrown into turmoil. It wasn't that municipal or state governments were suddenly likely to renege on their obligations, only that in panicked times, every deal seemed suspect.

The subprime shock was also noteworthy for its length. There were tremors beginning in early 2007, when the Chinese stock market swooned; but the shock struck hard in July 2007 and was still reverberating a year later. There were moments when the crisis seemed to ebb, but financial markets remained unsettled throughout. Historically, financial market crises begin and quickly abate in just a few days or weeks. Almost none last more than a few months.

The persistent angst that pervaded financial markets during the subprime shock was clearest in the London Interbank Offered Rate (LIBOR) market, where the globe's biggest banks lend each other money for short lengths of time. LIBOR is particularly important because so many other types of loans are pegged to it. Most subprime adjustable-rate mortgages, for example, carry interest rates tied to the 6-month LIBOR rate. Generally, LIBOR rates are not much higher than rates on U.S. Treasury securities of similar maturity. Treasuries are universally viewed as risk-free, and in normal times big banks don't see much risk in lending to each other, either. When LIBOR rates rise significantly above comparable Treasury rates, it's a signal that bankers are nervous about doing business with each other and want higher rates to compensate for the extra risk. When Long-Term Capital Management collapsed in the late 1990s, for example, the 3-month LIBOR jumped to more than a percentage point above the rate on 3-month Treasury bills (see Figure 11.2). There it remained for nearly a month. There was a similar increase in the LIBOR-Treasury rate spread in the early 1990s S&L crisis that lasted about three months. In the subprime financial shock, the rate spread reached nearly two percentage points at its apex and remained wider than a percentage point for a full nine months.

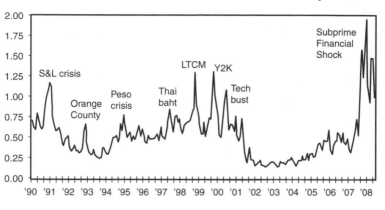

Figure 11.2   In a league of its own

But the most alarming feature of the subprime financial shock remains the fact that it was triggered by U.S. homeowners. There are 52 million American homeowners with first mortgages, and in a normal year, only about three-quarters of a million of them stop making their mortgage payments and default. In 2006, defaults reached an annual rate of almost 1 million. They rose to nearly 1.5 million in 2007 and were headed toward 2 million in 2008. This was a calamity for those losing their homes and also for the banks and mortgage security investors who owned their mortgages. Conservatively estimated, all those defaults would cost mortgage owners as much as $500 billion.[4]

Even at that size, it is still difficult to see how mortgages could have been the catalyst for such a wrenching financial crisis. In fact, $500 billion in mortgage losses equals not quite 5% of the $11 trillion in total U.S. mortgage loans outstanding, and that's not even a meaningful percentage of the $140 trillion in loans and debt securities held by banks, insurance companies, pension funds, hedge and mutual funds, sovereign wealth funds, and other institutions around the world.[5] How could the entire global financial system be undermined by subprime mortgage loans?

Re-Evaluating Risk

It wasn't the mortgage losses per se that ignited the shock, but what they meant more broadly: Global investors had taken on too much risk, not simply in their subprime mortgage security holdings, but arguably in all their investments. The mortgage losses crystallized what had long been troubling to many in the financial markets; namely that assets of all kinds were overvalued, from Chinese stocks to Las Vegas condominiums to the British government bonds known as "gilts" (short for gilt-edged securities). The subprime meltdown was simply a catalyst for a top-to-bottom re-evaluation of risk: Were investors being adequately compensated for the risks they were taking? Many quickly concluded the answer was no.

Global investors suddenly saw the entire U.S. housing and mortgage market in a new light. Although the number of homeowners struggling with mortgage payments was relatively small—only a few million—investors began to question the ability or willingness of all 52 million U.S. mortgage borrowers—subprime, alt-A, and even prime—to meet their obligations. The $11 trillion in U.S. residential mortgage debt outstanding had become a significant global financial influence, accounting for more than 8% of all the bank loans and securities in the world. In short, the world had made a huge bet on U.S. homeowners. In the mid-1990s, few overseas investors had ventured into the U.S. mortgage securities market. Those who did owned mostly debt backed by Fannie Mae and Freddie Mac, which was not much different than owning a U.S. Treasury bond. A decade later, foreign investors held some $3 trillion in mortgage securities, almost a third of all their U.S. financial holdings, including stocks. Some of this was backed by the U.S. government, but most was supported simply by the financial rectitude of the U.S. homeowner. This was seen as safe: Investing in an American household with a home and a mortgage wasn't supposed to cost investors any sleep—much less their shirts.

Investors also began looking critically at their other holdings, such as corporate bonds. It wasn't that businesses were defaulting on their obligations; the economy was still strong at the time. The problem was that investors were receiving returns that suggested no firm would ever default again. The rates were razor-thin compared to the potential risks. The difference between rates on risk-free Treasury bonds and on low-rated or junk corporate bonds narrowed to an all-time low in spring 2007 (see Figure 11.3). It is this interest rate difference—the spread—that measures how much compensation investors receive for the risks they take with their money. Not only wasn't there much of a spread in the prices of corporate bonds, but many bonds came with terms considered remarkably loose by historic standards. Traditionally, firms that issue bonds have to meet strict conditions, maintaining a certain level of cash flow or other financial benchmarks, to assure investors they can meet their interest payments. If the benchmarks aren't met, creditors have the right to demand their principal back. But in the 2000s, investors were so eager to throw their money around that many bought so-called "covenant-lite" bonds, which had fewer conditions and benchmarks for issuers. Terms became so easy that some businesses were allowed to make interest payments on their bonds by issuing additional bonds rather than paying in cash.[6]

Difference Between Junk Corporate Bond and T-Bond Yields

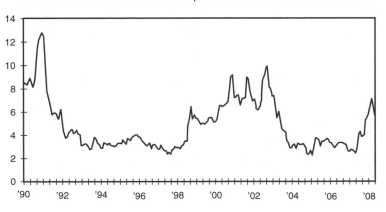

Figure 11.3   Junk spreads hit lows prior to shock

With corporate bond rates so low and terms so lax, it was incredibly cheap for private equity firms to finance their purchases of public companies. Firms such as the Carlyle Group, Blackstone, Cerberus, and Apollo Management were borrowing this cheap debt to buy out stockholders and take companies private. The plan was typically to reorganize a business, hopefully making it more profitable in the process, and later take it public again at a much higher price. Buyouts often worked purely because it cost so little to borrow in the bond market. To be more precise, private equity firms financed their purchases with bank loans that were then paid off after the bought-out business issued their junk bonds.[7] The bank loans were intended to be short-term bridge loans. These deals were all the rage in the lead-up to the subprime financial shock, and they helped drive global stock markets to record highs as private equity firms bid up stock prices.

The subprime meltdown brought it all to a swift end. Investors no longer wanted to buy corporate bonds with interest rates that effectively assumed there would never be another default. They had good reason: Such an assumption couldn't be right. Publicly traded automakers, retailers, and media companies were being taken private using a lot of debt. These were cyclical businesses—sales rise and fall, as do profits and the cash flow needed for interest payments. Some of these companies wouldn't make it and they would default. Investors lost interest in some deals entirely; for others, they wanted more compensation in the form of higher interest rates. The private-equity buyout mania fizzled; junk bond issuance fell off, and the spread between junk bonds and Treasury rates soared.

Investors were also nervous about their holdings of commercial mortgage-backed securities (CMBS). Like a residential mortgage security, a CMBS is backed by interest and principal payments on mortgages—but these are mortgages on office, retail, and industrial buildings, as well as hotels and apartments. Similar to the residential mortgage securities market, the CMBS market had expanded rapidly prior to the subprime shock as investors willingly purchased securities at increasingly narrow rate spreads. The CMBS market became a huge source of cheap cash for commercial property owners, who aggressively bought up office towers and strip malls. Property prices surged, encouraging even more borrowing in the CMBS-market, backed of course by the higher priced properties.

It sounded all too familiar to investors. If the residential securities market was unraveling, CMBS couldn't be too far behind. CMBS issuance came to a standstill and the yield spread between CMBS and Treasury bonds widened sharply. Even though commercial property markets weren't choking on empty space and rent growth was still sturdy in most areas, investors weren't willing to make fine distinctions between the commercial real estate market and the housing market. Commercial property prices were too high, vacancy rates would rise, rent growth would slow, and investors wanted compensation for the risk.

The new attitude toward risk rolled through other global financial markets, affecting everything from emerging debt–bonds issued by developing nations such as Argentina and Turkey to asset-backed securities, based on credit cards, auto loans, and student loans; to municipal bonds. Although the impact on these markets wasn't quite as harsh as in the junk bond or CMBS markets, fewer new bonds of any type were issued and interest rate spreads widened across the entire credit market.

When Insurers Need Insurance

Not all investors had been reckless. Some limited their purchases of mortgage securities to the top-rated Aaa tranches, and to be even more conservative, they had also purchased insurance. The insurance came from financial guarantors, also known as monoline insurers. These firms had traditionally insured municipal bonds against default; now they were also insuring the highly rated tranches of mortgage securities. The guarantors themselves were rated by the credit-rating agencies—guarantors had promised to make investors whole if anything went wrong with their bonds, so it was important that they be rock-solid Aaa firms. Yet after the subprime shock, the guarantors began to appear markedly less solid than their ratings had indicated. Monolines weren't failing to make payments on defaulting bonds, but with the pace of defaults soaring, it looked increasingly likely that some might not be able to meet their commitments in the future. As the mortgage securities they had insured were downgraded, odds were increasing that the guarantors would eventually have to make big payouts—bigger than their executives, investors, or clients had ever imagined would be necessary.

The rating agencies warned the guarantors to raise more capital or risk losing their Aaa-rating. It was a potent threat: Without that super-safe rating, the guarantors would be out of business and their insurance meaningless. No investor would trust them to be able to make payouts if needed. Most guarantors took the warning to heart and raised more capital. This wasn't easy or cheap because potential investors knew there was a reasonable chance the insurance firms might not survive. Nevertheless, the two biggest monolines, MBIA and Ambac, held on tenuously to their Aaa ratings.

The guarantors' problems exacerbated the nervousness in financial markets. A chain of events that had once seemed unimaginable suddenly began to loom as a possibility. It would work like this: Many large institutional investors, such as pension funds and insurance companies, are barred by law or their own rules from buying any securities rated less than Aaa. Without bond insurance, many securities would lose their Aaa ratings; thus pension funds and insurance companies would be forced to sell them. If a guarantor went out of business—or even lost its own Aaa rating—the securities it had insured could suddenly face such a downgrade. As the monolines' problems grew, so did the odds they would lose their Aaa ratings. The prospect of institutional investors suddenly flooding the markets with massive amounts of bonds began to haunt financial players.

Such worries reinforced the free-fall in mortgage securities and also pushed the formerly staid municipal bond market into turmoil. Perfectly solvent state and local governments and authorities found themselves having to pay interest rates reserved for high-risk borrowers. This was most clearly demonstrated by the disruption of the auction-rate securities market. In this out-of-the-way market, certain long-term municipal bonds were treated as if they were short-term investments, with interest rates set once a week in an auction run by large Wall Street investment banks. The rates were typically lower than for comparable fixed-rate bonds, making them attractive to municipalities issuing debt. The weekly auctions effectively turned long-term municipal bonds into more liquid short-term bonds, which appealed to investors such as money-market funds. Both features, however, depended on the success of the weekly auctions. So important were these auctions that, to ensure their smooth functioning, the investment banks would step in and buy the debt themselves if they failed to attract enough outside bidders.

In early 2008, spooked by the potential failure of the monolines and other worries, investors stopped participating in the auctions, causing scores of them to fail. Even the investment-bank sponsors, worried about their own financial exposure, refused to play their usual backstop role. As a result, the interest rates on auction-rate securities surged. Municipalities were suddenly forced to pay rates far higher than even junk corporate borrowers. Trust had broken down so thoroughly that municipalities couldn't even count on their own investment bankers. The subprime financial shock had engulfed even state and local governments.

Leverage and Liquidity

If the subprime shock involved no more than a massive reevaluation of risk, it still would have been a garden-variety financial event and not a global crisis. Investors took a hit, but this was seen early on as a healthy antidote to the housing bubble. Risk-taking had gotten out of control; financial decisions had made less and less economic sense. For instance, the private-equity firm Cerberus's leveraged buyout of the Chrysler Corporation, which involved piling a lot of debt onto the balance sheet of a very cyclical vehicle manufacturer struggling to sell big cars in the face of steadily rising gasoline prices, might be a case in point. Officials at the Federal Reserve and other central bankers weren't unhappy to see such excesses being wrung out of the financial system.

Views quickly changed as the shock's nasty side came into clearer relief. As the shock wore on and losses mounted, investors who borrowed money to pump up their returns in the good times came under increasing pressure to reduce their leverage. As this process of deleveraging gained momentum, the subprime financial shock turned from a therapeutic to a destructive process. To see the corrosive, self-reinforcing nature of financial leverage, consider the hypothetical example of an investment fund that bought mortgage securities by borrowing 85% of the purchase price, using its own equity for only 15% (see Table 11.1). The fund's leverage can be expressed as 85/15, meaning the power of its own investment has been magnified 5.7 times by leverage. Now suppose the securities owned by the fund fall in value by 5%. This isn't a very large decline, but it reduces the fund's equity to 10%, and its leverage jumps to 85/10 or 10.5 times. Because the fund agreed when it borrowed money from a broker-dealer to maintain at least 15% equity, it receives a notice known as a margin call, requiring it to either put up more cash or sell as much of the portfolio as necessary to get back to the agreed margin. Most funds are reluctant to put up more cash, particularly in a declining market, so they take the second option and sell. Brokers, meanwhile, can demand higher margins; if they believe the value of the underlying collateral is eroding, they might decide the original 15% percent is too low. If in this example the broker increases the margin to 25%, the funds have even more selling to do. Things get measurably worse if the fund's own investors start pulling out their money. These redemptions force more portfolio sales. In our example, the fund's value is ultimately slashed by more than 60% and its leverage plunges to 3 times. When leverage is involved, even a modest decline in asset values can provoke a rout.

TABLE 11.1   Corrosive Power of Leverage

	Asset Value	Equity	Borrowing	Leverage	Margin
Initial	100.0	15.0	85.0	5.7	15.0
5% Loss of Value	95.0	10.0	85.0	8.5	10.5
After Margin Call with a 15% Margin	66.7	10.0	56.7	5.7	15.0
Increase in Margin to 25%	40.0	10.0	30.0	3.0	25.0
10% Redemption Rate	36.0	9.0	27.0	3.0	25.0

Source: IMF

Now consider what happens when there are many such funds and all receive margin calls and redemptions at the same time. The wave of forced selling drives prices for assets such as mortgage securities sharply lower, further exacerbating investors' collective problems. This is exactly what happened as 2007 ended. Some funds, backed by larger financial institutions worried about their reputations, put up their own cash to meet margin calls. Others stopped accepting redemptions to try to stem the bleeding. None of it worked. They were overwhelmed by the tidal wave of deleveraging.

No financial institution avoided the fallout from the imploding securities markets. The list of casualties ranged from small boutique investment funds to the giant Swiss banks UBS and Credit Suisse to Wall Street titans Citigroup and Merrill Lynch. Each day seemed to bring another high-profile blow-up. Financial disaster seemed to lurk in practically every deal. Even making an overnight loan could be a mistake; a borrower could run aground between today and tomorrow.

An often-cited strength of the global financial markets had been their capability to diffuse risk widely; now this strength had become part of the problem. Risk was so widely scattered across the financial system that it was hard to tell who was bearing how much and what the danger of failure really was. Without clarity about which institutions had the bad investments and how much more financial damage was likely, there was going to be much less borrowing, lending, buying, and selling. As more institutions stumbled, the risk fog grew thicker until liquidity began to evaporate.

Liquidity—the ability to move money in and out of investments or among markets quickly and smoothly—is vital to all financial institutions. Some need it simply to survive. Banks, with their relatively stable deposit bases, weather liquidity storms best. Depositors tend not to move their money quickly (UK mortgage lender Northern Rock being a notable exception)[8] and even in times of crisis, they tend to stick with banks, particularly those covered by government deposit insurance. This gives such banks a reliable source of liquidity: money the bank can use to make loans or for other purposes whenever needed.

Other financial institutions also need ready sources of liquidity. Asset-backed conduits and special investment vehicles (SIVs)—institutions that warehoused and invested in mortgage and other securities—obtained theirs by issuing short-term commercial paper. When money-market funds and other investors became too worried to buy these IOUs, the conduits and SIVs lost their liquidity and were quickly forced out of business. Broker-dealers such as Bear Stearns and Lehman Brothers also relied on being able to raise money quickly. Because they were big, rich, seemingly healthy Wall Street firms, they typically had no trouble getting investors to buy their IOUs. It seemed unimaginable that this confidence would ever be shaken, yet in early 2008, Bear Stearns lost the faith of its creditors. By the middle of March, its funding sources had gone completely dry and the Federal Reserve stepped in to arrange an emergency sale of Bear Stearns to J.P. Morgan Chase.

Bad Marks

The entire banking system was now under pressure to reduce leverage. When conditions are good and borrowers are making their loan payments faithfully, banks are eager to increase leverage by building up their assets of both loans and securities relative to their capital. Higher leverage leads to big profits, at least in good times. When conditions grow difficult and borrowers fall behind on their debts, banks seek to cut back on leverage to limit losses and protect their capital. This ebb and flow in banking lending defines the credit cycle and gives rise to the old saw that a banker will give you an umbrella when there is plenty of sunshine, but wants it back as soon as it begins to rain.

Amplifying the credit cycle during the subprime financial shock was the use of an accounting standard called "mark to market."[9] It's based on a simple principle: When the market value of an asset changes, the bank or business that owns it must reflect that change on its books. Thus, if a bank makes a loan or buys a security and after a time that loan or security is only worth 50 cents on the dollar, the bank has to declare that on its balance sheet. Mark-to-market rules were adopted by financial regulators in response to the S&L crisis and were expanded and solidified after the corporate accounting scandals of the early 2000s when it came to light that Enron and other firms had been manipulating their books to disguise huge losses.

On the face of it, mark-to-market seems like a way to keep the financial system healthy as well as honest. If asset prices decline, those asset owners should have to acknowledge the losses and move on. Had more businesses done that in the 1980s, America might have avoided the S&L debacle, and Japan might not have lost a decade of growth during the 1990s when its banks were paralyzed by all the bad loans they refused to recognize and the economy starved for credit.

But as appealing as the theory behind mark-to-market is, it can present serious problems in practice. There are times, such as during the subprime financial shock, when marking to market is almost impossible because there are no market prices that make much objective sense. In the midst of the shock, prices for mortgage and other securities bounced around wildly or simply flat-lined as trading in these assets froze. Even the Aaa-rated tranches of mortgage-backed securities, which remained highly unlikely to suffer losses in the long run, were being traded at steep discounts or not traded at all. Yet under mark-to-market accounting rules, the banks that held these securities had to write their values down drastically. The distressed prices could have reflected investor fear or a temporary gap in trading and would thus eventually right themselves, but nonetheless the banks had to record the lower prices.

Some institutions tried a different tack: Rather than mark to market, they would "mark to model." In the absence of a functioning market for some highly complex securities, they turned to their own in-house mathematical models, used to calculate what the securities' values *should* be under normal conditions. Of course these models typically concluded prices should be higher; nonetheless, this tactic didn't play well with regulators, and the modelers eventually had to slash the value of their holdings as well. The losses were huge, at least on paper. Through spring 2008, the globe's biggest banks had collectively written down their assets by almost $275 billion (see Table 11.2). The losses were a direct hit to the banks' capital.

TABLE 11.2   Reported Write-Downs of Major Banks, March 2008

Billions $	
Total	261.7
Citigroup	40.9
UBS	19.2
Merrill Lynch	31.7
AIG (Insurance)	30
HSBC	12.4

TABLE 11.2   Reported Write-Downs of Major Banks, March 2008

Billions $	
Royal Bank of Scotland	15.3
Bank of America	14.8
Morgan Stanley	12.6
Deutsche Bank	7.6
Credit Suisse	6.3
JPMorgan Chase	9.8°
IKB Deutsche	8.9
Crédit Agricole	8.4
Washington Mutual	8.3
Other European banks	7.9
Wachovia	7
Société Générale	3.9
Mizuho financial	5.5
Other Asian banks	5.4
Barclays	4.5
Canadian Imperial	4.1
Bayerische Landesbank	3.6
Fortis	3.4

Source: Bloomberg and FT Research

Excluding the expected $9bn charge JPMorgan Chase will take to clean up Bear Stearns' balance sheet.

The banks' problems were aggravated further by the fact that even as losses eroded their capital, their assets were growing rapidly. This wasn't a conscious choice by the banks, and it made them appear even weaker and more risk-prone by increasing their leverage just when they needed to reduce it. Many had agreed earlier to prop up the as-set-backed conduits, structured investment vehicles, and broker-dealers in case they needed funds. Now these troubled institutions needed funds desperately, and some drew down long-standing credit lines with the banks. In other cases, bridge loans the banks had made to finance private equity deals just prior to the subprime shock were effectively converted into long-term loans; the troubled junk bond market had made it impossible to refinance or sell off the loans as originally planned. Banks were dragged into becoming the lenders-of-last-resort for much of the financial system. They didn't view it as an honor.

By mid-2008, the net result was that banks were hemorrhaging capital and were awash in assets they didn't want. Their leverage was rising at a time when they desperately wanted to reduce it. They had two choices: Either raise more capital, or shed any assets they could. They did both. With each quarterly round of earnings announcements, bank after bank reported billions in losses and followed this by announcing they had found an investor willing to take an equity stake in the bank. Many of these white-knight investors were sovereign wealth funds—large investment pools set up by foreign governments such as Abu Dhabi, Singapore, China, Korea, and Qatar, filled with the dollars these governments had earned from soaring energy prices and trade with the U.S. They were the only investors with the ready cash needed to fill at least some of banks' capital hole.

Even the sovereign wealth funds didn't provide enough capital to totally rescue the banks, and they remained under pressure to shrink their assets. Banks sold mortgage securities and much more; they tried to limit the credit they were extending to the bleeding conduits, SIVs, and broker-dealers, and became reticent even to lend to each other.[10] They also aggressively ratcheted up their standards for all new potential borrowers. New, rigid lending criteria applied not just to subprime or alt-A mortgage loans—those were simply unavailable under any circumstances— but to prime mortgage borrowers, credit card and student loan borrowers, and businesses of all sizes and stripes. Borrowers, who in more normal times would have no problem getting a loan, were now unable to get any bank's attention. According to a quarterly Federal Reserve survey of senior loan officers at the nation's major banks, lending standards were tighter than at any time since Jimmy Carter temporarily imposed credit controls on lending in 1980 (see Figure 11.4).[11] Marking to market, a much praised feature of the

modern banking system, had instead become part of the problem, reinforcing a vicious and self-reinforcing credit crunch.

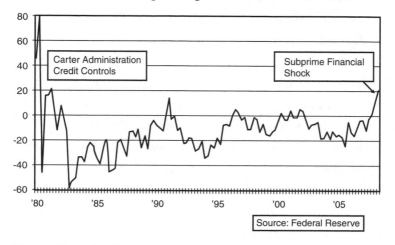

Figure 11.4   Credit crunch

12

Timid Policymakers Turn Bold

Policymakers' early response to the subprime financial shock was sometimes halting and, other times, confused. Policymakers misjudged the extent of the shock's economic and financial damage and were hamstrung by its complexity. They also feared bailing out undeserving homeowners, mortgage lenders, and investors; this would be unfair to people working hard to stay current on their mortgages and would embolden even more reckless risk taking in the future.

Instead of calming the financial turmoil, the tentative policy response fanned it. Investors didn't expect to be bailed out, but they were distressed by the government's reluctance to provide much help. The economic fallout spread, becoming an issue in the 2008 presidential campaign, and intensifying pressure on policymakers to do more. Eventually, they responded.

The Federal Reserve slashed interest rates and devised several novel mechanisms for providing cash to key financial institutions. Not only did commercial banks regulated by the Fed receive help, but so did unregulated investment banks. That aid came too late for some; the once powerful investment house Bear Stearns disappeared after the Fed backed an emergency fire-sale takeover by JPMorgan Chase. But the central bank's actions did forestall further major failures. Without such unprecedented moves by the Fed, the financial system could well have gone over the proverbial edge.

Congress and the Bush administration quickly came to terms on a fiscal stimulus package that included big one-time tax cuts for households and businesses. They agreed to aggressively expand the mortgage lending authority of the FHA, Fannie Mae, Freddie Mac, and the Federal Home Loan Bank, hoping to fill at least some of the void left by the collapse of private mortgage lending. The administration also pushed homeowners and mortgage owners to get together and negotiate changes to their mortgage loans that would prevent at least some of the foreclosures.

Financial markets responded favorably to these actions, but the markets remained anything but normal. Calls continued for more direct government intervention in the housing and mortgage markets; all the presidential candidates weighed in with their own plans. Legislation began to move through Congress that would alter contracts between mortgage holders—the investors who bought bundles of loans packaged into securities—and mortgage servicers—the firms that collected and processed homeowners' monthly payments. Proposals to have the government use taxpayers' dollars to buy mortgage loans and mortgage securities were hotly debated. And talks began on ways to fundamentally change the nation's Byzantine system of financial regulation to avoid similar crises in the future.

The subprime financial shock was the catalyst for a wide range of policy changes. Some of the more obvious changes were underway by mid-2008: licensing requirements for mortgage lenders, tougher regulations on the kinds of loans they can make, more and better information for borrowers. Other reforms followed. Clearly, financial regulators and policymakers would need to respond more aggressively to future credit crises before they undermined the wider economy. It wasn't just a matter of keeping interest rates low; borrowing costs rise and fall all the time. But if no credit is available even for solid, creditworthy borrowers, normal economic life can't go on. The Federal Reserve would need to monitor asset markets in the future, and if they were being infected by speculation and leverage, the central bank would need to respond. If bubbles develop, the Fed should use its regulatory authority to let some of the air out. An overhaul of the nation's regulators was also needed to fix a framework built during the Great Depression. Fundamentally, the financial system would work better with some modest regulatory fetters.

Fiddling While Markets Burned

The 2007 subprime financial shock seemed to surprise policymakers. The crisis had begun in earnest in mid-July, but the Federal Reserve didn't respond until more than a month later. Policymakers cut the federal funds rate target in September, and then again in October and December, but the total reduction by year end amounted to only 1 percentage point. More important for investors, the Fed hinted that each rate cut might be the last, saying inflation was too high to risk accelerating it by lowering rates aggressively. Even with the mid-December 2007 rate cut and financial markets clearly on edge, Fed officials were still hand-wringing about the inflation threat:[1]

> Readings on core inflation have improved modestly this year, but elevated energy and commodity prices, among other factors, may put upward pressure on inflation. In this context, the Committee judges that some inflation risks remain, and it will continue to monitor inflation developments carefully.

The crisis also surprised the Bush administration. The president maintained consistently that the economy was "fundamentally sound" for months after the shock hit. Treasury Secretary Paulson confidently forecast that the housing market had hit bottom just weeks before markets began to unravel. "I don't see [subprime mortgage market troubles] imposing a serious problem," Paulson argued. "I think it's going to be largely contained."[2]

The administration didn't respond concretely to the crisis until the end of August. Recognizing that foreclosures were mounting, the president proposed legislation to make it easier for troubled homeowners to sell out before they faced foreclosure. This was usually a preferable option, saving both homeowners and their lenders a costly trip through the legal system—but the tax code discouraged it by treating any mortgage debt forgiven by a lender as taxable income. A lender might be willing to let a distressed homeowner sell at a loss, writing off the difference instead of foreclosing, but the homeowner would need to pay taxes on that difference. Distressed homeowners with no cash to pay their tax bill had the Hobson's choice of going through foreclosure or stiffing the IRS. The Bush bill proposed to fix this by eliminating the tax liability on mortgage debt forgiven in a so-called short sale.

The president also unveiled a new program called Federal Housing Administration (FHA) Secure, designed to help homeowners who were delinquent on their mortgage loans as a result of a payment reset.[3] To qualify for the program, homeowners had to have been current on their payments prior to the reset, made at least a 3% down payment, and have sufficient income and a stable job. In announcing the plan, the president declared that "it's not the government's job to bail out speculators or those who made the decision to buy a home they knew they could never afford." Despite being well-intentioned, it quickly became clear that FHA Secure would be of little real help; the hardest-pressed homeowners didn't have the down payment or the necessary income to qualify. Even under the best of circumstances, the administration expected the program to help only a quarter-million households avoid foreclosure—a trivial number as foreclosure forecasts surged into the millions.

The administration followed up in October with a second program, called Hope Now. This was a consortium of mortgage lenders, services, and investors brought together to find an efficient way to modify mortgage loans. Millions of subprime borrowers were facing large mortgage payment increases at the time; the average reset was expected to be $350 per month, an overwhelming amount for most ordinary working families. The Hope Now agreement established rules to let lenders keep mortgage rates frozen temporarily, enabling these homeowners to keep paying under their original loan terms. The Treasury Department played a vital role, bringing together the diverse range of players who set loan terms, each with its own financial interests and understanding of the process. No one had ever contemplated the need to revise (or "modify") many millions of mortgage loans at once, and the system didn't seem up to the task on its own.

Hope Now helped open communications between stretched homeowners and mortgage servicers, but not as much as expected. Instead of substantially modifying many loans, mortgage services put most delinquent homeowners on repayment plans. This provided no relief; the plans simply let delinquent homeowners resume paying their mortgages with no change in terms; they also had to make up any missed payments and pay the associated penalties. Monthly payments actually rose in most of these repayment plans. Hope Now also failed as the nature of the problem changed. As the Fed aggressively lowered interest rates, the pending mortgage resets (which were tied to prevailing short-term interest rates) began to look less dire. Instead, homeowners now were struggling with plunging housing prices and negative mortgage equity. Hope Now's program did not involve lowering the principal on distressed mortgages; it only tinkered with their interest-rate terms. Now, with millions of homeowners underwater (their home's market value was less than the loan amounts), defaults rising, and policymakers searching for new ideas to keep people in their homes, financial markets began to writhe.

Policy Paralysis

Policymakers had significantly misjudged both the severity of the shock and its broader economic implications. At most, they assumed this would be a normal, even therapeutic, correction of financial markets that had simply become overvalued. They reasoned that although the housing market had been struggling for more than a year, housing prices had only begun to decline, and stock and bond prices had been rising almost continually since just after the tech-stock bust.

Markets were overextended, but policymakers had no idea how much. Prices had risen sharply in nearly all markets—not just housing, and not just in the United States. Prices for everything from Chinese stocks to European corporate bonds to U.S. commercial real estate were juiced up. Leverage had helped drive asset prices sky high; investors were borrowing aggressively to finance their trades. And this wasn't a matter of investors asking their friendly local banker for a loan; instead, investors were issuing short-term IOUs to faceless financial institutions across the globe. The web of financial relationships had grown so complex that it was hard to tell who was taking how much risk and what would happen if bets went bad. When they did go bad, a simple, healthy market correction rapidly turned into a rout, and policymakers were caught unaware.

Policymakers' confusion was exacerbated by their inability to gather timely and accurate information. Unlike past financial crises when most of the players involved were regulated and had to report regularly on their risks and financial health, rapidly evolving institutions that had little or no regulatory supervision were driving this crisis. Policymakers knew little to nothing about them. Global regulators did have discussions about whether and how these new institutions should report on their activities, but they had gotten nowhere. The U.S. Treasury was particularly uninterested in restricting the financial system; officials there believed the marketplace could discipline itself. The Bush administration's philosophy was to keep government out; financial markets should work out problems on their own. Yet without a regulatory structure in place, policymakers at the U.S. Treasury, the Federal Reserve, and elsewhere had no way to judge the severity of the shock, and they lacked the expertise to respond to it.

Adding to the policy paralysis were the Federal Reserve's worries about inflation. The Fed's legal mandate is to keep both inflation and unemployment low, but policymakers appropriately believe that focusing mainly on inflation is the most efficient way to ensure both objectives in the long run. Stable prices let the economy function efficiently, ultimately creating more jobs and holding down unemployment. Yet the broader forces shaping inflation have turned less positive in recent years: Productivity growth has slowed, the dollar is weaker, and commodity prices have moved higher. As the subprime shock loomed in 2007, interest rates were still low by historical standards, and with oil prices hovering over $100 per barrel, Fed officials reasoned that aggressively lowering rates in response to a financial crisis would only fan inflation more broadly. That was the last thing they wanted to do.

Policymakers also worried about something called moral hazard. This is a principle with roots in the insurance industry: It says that people are more likely to take risks if they are insured against the consequences. If your car is 100% covered against theft, you're less likely to lock your doors. Similar principles govern financial markets: If investors believe the Federal Reserve will cover or lessen their losses, for example, they will take greater investment risks. It is reasonable to argue that when the Fed cut rates aggressively in response to the 1987 stock market crash, the collapse of hedge fund Long-Term Capital Management in 1998, or even the tech stock bust in 2001, it planted the seeds of moral hazard, which led to the latest financial crisis. Therefore, Fed officials feared that lowering rates quickly in response to the subprime shock would only set the stage for bigger financial problems in the future, with complacent investors taking even bigger risks.

Other federal policymakers were less concerned about the moral hazard issue. The Democratic leadership in Congress wanted to do more to respond to the subprime shock—but acting quickly was all but impossible. Congress could pressure banking regulators to toughen their oversight of unscrupulous mortgage lenders, but passing legislation was a different matter. Some in Congress worried that they would overreach, citing Sarbanes-Oxley—the act that changed accounting and corporate governance rules in the wake of the Enron and Arthur Andersen scandals. Mortgage and financial service industry lobbyists also worked hard to slow any legislative action.

Policymakers were also receiving conflicting messages from their constituents. Homeowners who were facing foreclosure pleaded for government help, but others who were struggling but managing to stay current on their mortgages questioned the justice of such government assistance. Why provide relief to people who had gotten in over their heads with a big house purchase, while prudent families in smaller homes got nothing?

But while the government dithered, the financial turmoil worsened. The longer policymakers delayed acting, the more investor panic spread. The subprime shock had begun in the residential mortgage securities market, but now it was infecting the corporate bond market, the market for commercial mortgage securities, and even the normally low-risk municipal bond market. The stock market, which had held up well in the weeks following the shock—the Dow Jones Industrial Average hit a peak in early October 2007—now stumbled badly. By early 2008, stock prices had fallen almost 20%.

Even major global banks became reluctant to lend money to each other, demanding hefty interest rates for loans of any length. It was astonishing, but the world's largest financial institutions had suddenly become nervous that they wouldn't get their money back. Banks also worried that they might need the cash if their own investments went bad and their own long-standing lenders cut them off. The cash squeeze became particularly acute as the end of the year approached, normally a season when the demand for cash is greatest. London interbank rates—the interest rates banks charge each other for short-term funds—spiked (see Figure 12.1).[4]

Difference Between Rate on 1-Month LIBOR and 4-Week T-Bills

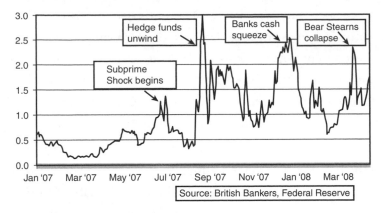

Source: British Bankers, Federal Reserve

Figure 12.1   Bankers panic.

Outside the Monetary Box

At the Federal Reserve, theoretical concerns over inflation and moral hazard were quickly being overwhelmed by practical concerns that a credit crunch was developing. Not only were people with clear credit problems no longer able to get loans, but even borrowers with solid credit histories faced usurious rates and onerous terms. This raised a new set of alarms among policymakers: Tighter credit for weak borrowers would slow the economy, but a crunch that affected creditworthy borrowers as well would likely bring on a recession.

The Fed began trying to ease pressures in money markets by en-couraging banks to use its discount window. This part of the Federal Reserve provides a way for some—but not all—financial institutions to borrow cheap money in times of need.[5] Although the subprime shock was clearly a time of need, institutions were reluctant to use the discount window. Historically, borrowing from the Fed that way had been a signal that a bank was in precarious financial health, and bankers feared it would scare away customers and other financial institutions, worsening their problems. The Fed tried lowering the rate on discount-window borrowing, permitted borrowing for a longer term, and even cajoled a few too-big-to-fail money center banks to use the discount window, just to show others it was okay. Nothing worked. Banks were hungry for cash, but they didn't approach the discount window, for fear of being seen as losers whom the market would let starve.

With the banking system increasingly cash-strapped and discount window borrowing at a standstill, the Fed became creative. In mid-December, the central bank unveiled an alternative to the discount window, which it called the Term Auction Facility (TAF). It enabled institutions to bid for short-term funds by putting up a wide range of securities, including mortgage-related instruments, as collateral (see Table 12.1).[6] In a TAF auction, the bids begin at a rate above the federal funds rate but well below the discount rate, thus providing institutions with at least the cover of a reason to borrow funds from the Fed other than potential financial stress. It worked; because no apparent stigma was attached to borrowing from the TAF, response was strong, beginning with the first auction. Although money markets were still not functioning normally by mid-2008, worries that the banking system might grind to a halt for lack of cash had faded.

In late January 2008, Fed officials took even more convincing action. In an unscheduled emergency meeting, the Federal Open Market Committee (FOMC) slashed the Fed funds rate target by three-quarters of a percentage point—the biggest such reduction in decades (see Figure 12.2). At their regularly scheduled January meeting a few days later, the committee cut rates again, by an additional half percentage point. For the FOMC, changing interest rates in between its normally scheduled meetings was a clear signal that the financial system was in crisis. And added together, the two rate cuts in January were unprecedented.[7]

TABLE 12.1   What's in the Federal Reserve's Monetary Toolbox?

	Who Can Borrow?	Accepted Collateral	Term of Loan	Interest Rate	Type of Loan from Fed	Reserve Impact
Primary Dealer Credit Facility (PDCF)	Depository institutions	Treasuries, investment grade municipal bonds, MBS, and ABS for which a market prices exists	Overnight	Discount rate	Money	Yes
Term Securities Lending Facility (TSLF)	Primary dealers	Treasuries, agencies, and AAA RMBS, CMBS, and CMOs	28-day funds auctioned weekly, up to $200 billion	Minimum fee bid set by the Fed	Treasuries	No
Term Auction Facility (TAF)	Primary dealers	Wide; ranging from Treasuries to CDOs	28-day funds auctioned bi-monthly, size determined by the Fed	Minimum bid rate set according to expected fed funds rate over the term of the loan	Money	Yes
Discount Window	Depository institutions	Wide, ranging from Treasuries to CDOs	Maximum maturity is 90 days	Discount rate	Money	Yes
Open Market Operations	Primary dealers	Treasuries, agencies, and agency MBS	Repos or reverse repos for a term up to 65 days	Fed funds rate	Money	Yes
System Open Market Account	Primary dealers	Treasury bills, notes, bonds, and TIPS	Overnight and auctioned daily	Minimum fee bid of 50-basis points	Treasuries	No

Sources: Federal Reserve Board, Moody's Economy.com

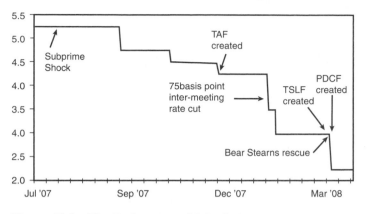

Federal Funds Rate Target

Figure 12.2   The Fed goes on high alert.

The Bernanke-led Fed was sharply departing from the Fed's pattern under former Chairman Greenspan, in which rate changes were typically incremental moves of one-quarter of a percentage point. Greenspan had cut rates by as much as half a point in times of stress, but never more. He had worried that if a larger cut didn't prove effective, his policy would be questioned, undermining confidence in the Fed. Chairman Bernanke jettisoned this concern; he signaled that he was willing to adjust monetary policy whenever the Fed's forecasts for inflation and growth changed.

Those forecasts were changing fast in early 2008. In just a few weeks, policymakers went from expecting the economy to slow modestly, to believing it would come close to stalling, to thinking a recession was likely.[8] Historically, when the economy has been in recession, the real funds rate have gone negative—the benchmark interest rate has fallen below the rate of underlying inflation.[9] The real funds rate went negative in spring 2008 as the Fed lowered the nominal rate to 2%, about the same rate as inflation (see Figure 12.3).

The Federal Reserve was now fully engaged in staunching the bleeding from the subprime shock, but its actions couldn't keep the crisis from spreading to other parts of the financial system over which the central bank had less influence. Most worrisome were the rumors swirling about potential liquidity problems among Wall Street's so-called broker dealers. These companies are investment firms that buy and sell securities, both for customers and for themselves (see Table 12.2). They often are highly leveraged, borrowing to make big bets on securities ranging from U.S. Treasury bonds to exotic and risky securities backed by mortgages. When they bet right, their profits can be huge—but when they bet wrong, they can end up as Bear Stearns did in mid-March 2008.

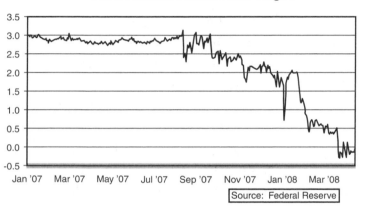

Real Federal Funds Rate Target

Source: Federal Reserve

Figure 12.3   The Federal Reserve girds for recession.

TABLE 12.2   Who Are the Broker Dealers?

BNP Paribas Securities Corp.

Banc of America Securities LLC

Barclays Capital Inc.

Cantor Fitzgerald & Co.

Citigroup Global Markets Inc.

Countrywide Securities Corporation

Credit Suisse Securities (USA) LLC

Daiwa Securities America Inc.

Deutsche Bank Securities Inc.

Dresdner Kleinwort Wasserstein Securities LLC.

TABLE 12.2   Who Are the Broker Dealers?

Goldman, Sachs & Co.

Greenwich Capital Markets, Inc.

HSBC Securities (USA) Inc.

J. P. Morgan Securities Inc.

Lehman Brothers Inc.

Merrill Lynch Government Securities Inc.

Mizuho Securities USA Inc.

Morgan Stanley & Co. Incorporated

UBS Securities LLC.

Bear Stearns bet big on the residential mortgage market. It not only issued mortgage securities, but it had also acquired mortgage-lending firms that originated the loans that went into those securities. Bear "made a market" in mortgage securities, meaning it would either buy or sell—whichever a customer wanted. It prospered during the housing bubble, but as the housing and mortgage markets collapsed, each of Bear's various business segments soured in turn, and confidence in the firm's viability weakened. Unlike commercial banks that collect funds from depositors, a broker dealer relies on other financial institutions to lend it the money it invests. If those other institutions lose faith and begin withdrawing their money, the broker dealer's only options are filing bankruptcy or—as in Bear Stearns' case—selling out.

During a tumultuous weekend in March 2008, the Federal Reserve engineered the sale of Bear Stearns to JPMorgan Chase. The Fed acted out of fear of what a bankruptcy could have meant for the financial system, given Bear's extensive relationships with banks, hedge funds, and other institutions around the world. Policymakers were legitimately worried that the system would freeze up. When it was finished, the Fed had agreed to absorb any losses on $29 billion in risky Bear Stearns securities that JPMorgan acquired in its takeover of the failed firm.

To quell fears that other broker dealers might follow Bear Stearns, policymakers established two new sources of credit for them—one called the Term Securities Lending Facility (TSLF) and the other dubbed the Primary Dealers Credit Facility (PDCF). The TSLF enabled broker dealers to borrow Treasury securities from the Fed in exchange for various other securities, including Aaa residential mortgage-backed securities, for up to a month. The PDCF provided overnight loans to broker dealers at the discount rate and accepted an even wider range of securities as collateral. The TSLF and PDCF lifted the pall over the broker dealers, provided much needed liquidity to the markets, and helped prevent a further unraveling of the financial system.

Although the Fed's early response to the subprime financial shock was tentative and contributed to the turmoil, its actions beginning in 2008 were without precedent. These efforts forestalled a more serious crisis, and although they would eventually benefit the housing and mortgage markets, and the broader economy as well, the benefits would not be seen quickly enough for those facing election that November.

Economic Stimulus

As the struggling economy soared to the top of voters' lists of concerns in early 2008, it quickly dominated the policy debate in Washington, D.C. The sense of political urgency was highlighted in early February, when in just a few days, the Bush administration and Congress came to terms on a sizable and reasonably well-designed fiscal stimulus package.[10] It was an astonishing show of bipartisanship; not only was there broad agreement that this was necessary, but very little debate occurred about what should be in the plan. Policymakers felt it critical to get something done quickly.

The package was worth $168 billion—equal to a little more than 1% of GDP. It included tax rebates for lower- and middle-income households, with checks to be mailed between May and July 2008, and tax incentives to spur business investment and put people to work. Economists debated just how large a boost the stimulus would provide—the administration said it would add about half a million jobs—but few believed the medicine would provide more than temporary relief if the housing market and financial system didn't begin to recover as well.[11]

The stimulus package did include some modest housing help; it significantly raised the caps on mortgage lending by the FHA, Fannie Mae, and Freddie Mac.[12] The previous caps made it all but impossible for these agencies to provide mortgage credit in areas of the country where high housing prices required large home loans.[13] These included places such as California, southern Florida, and around Washington, D.C., and New York City (see Figure 12.4). Because private lenders weren't making loans, perhaps these federal lenders could fill at least part of the void. This was a striking policy reversal for the Bush administration; only a few weeks earlier, the White House had emphatically said no to such a move. Until the crisis, administration officials had been intent on reining in these agencies, demanding that Congress pass reforms before expanding their lending powers. That the administration could forget its long-running feud with Fannie and Freddie—both institutions traditionally had much stronger Democratic support—and let them take on such a prominent role in solving the subprime financial shock was proof of how events had unnerved politicians of nearly all stripes.

% of Mortgage Originations Above Conforming Limit

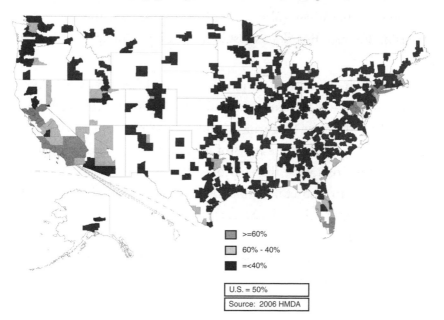

>=60%

60% - 40%

=<40%

U.S. = 50%

Source: 2006 HMDA

Figure 12.4   Government lending helps most here.

The administration even went along with relaxing Fannie and Freddie's capital requirements. This had been a contentious political issue earlier in the decade. A serious accounting scandal occurred at the two lending agencies; their books were so tangled that for years no one knew how much they were earning or losing. OFHEO, the agency that oversaw Fannie and Freddie, had issued penalties in the form of higher capital requirements—in effect, giving them less money to play with.[14] But now both institutions were suffering their own credit problems, and losses were making it harder for them to grow. The administration realized that unless it reversed OFHEO's rule and relaxed the capital requirements, Fannie and Freddie wouldn't be able to ramp up their lending and help ease the mortgage crisis.

The administration didn't stop there; it also granted Fannie and Freddie permission to increase their purchases of mortgage loans and securities. OFHEO had put limits on the growth in their holdings— also punishment for their past bad behavior—but with no one else buying, the mortgage securities market was choking. The Federal Home Loan Banks were also permitted by their regulator, the Federal Housing Finance Board, to substantially increase their security holdings.[15]

The Bush administration quickly retreated from its long-held positions in an effort to stem the financial crisis and developing recession. Markets weren't figuring it out by themselves—they needed government help. And the parts of government most valuable in addressing the crisis were the very ones the administration had previously wanted to restrict or dismantle. The administration viewed the FHA, Fannie Mae, Freddie Mac, and the Federal Home Loan Banks as, at best, anachronistic and, at worst, risks to the financial system; these institutions were now the centerpiece of the policy response to the subprime finance shock.

Government Intervention

By spring 2008, the Federal Reserve, the Bush administration, and the Democratic Congress were fully engaged in addressing the financial shock's fallout. This was certainly no garden-variety market correction, and worries about moral hazard, inflation, and fairness had been largely jettisoned.

Yet even the more aggressive policy steps seemed inadequate. For those facing an election in November, no assurance existed that the crisis and its fallout would fade by Election Day. Calls for more and faster government intervention in the housing and mortgage markets grew louder. Most of the proposals being considered involved lenders rewriting mortgage loans, reducing the amount of debt owed to less than the current house price, to enable homeowners to avoid foreclosure. Policymakers hoped this would stem the downdraft in housing prices and their ugly economic side effects.

One significant impediment to making this strategy work for many homeowners was the recalcitrance of junior lien holders. These were the lenders or investors who held title to someone's home equity loan or second mortgage (*second* meant their legal rights came after those of whoever held the first mortgage). The law gave second mortgage holders the right to veto loan modifications; yet in the kinds of loan write-downs being proposed, they stood to lose everything.[16] A fore-closure would be no better—junior liens would likely be wiped out in either case—but many second mortgage holders reasoned they had nothing to lose by vetoing a modification. And perhaps they could collect at least a few pennies on the dollar in exchange for getting out of the way. This financial game of chicken was a potential roadblock for hundreds of thousands of troubled loans, particularly subprime ARMs. During the housing boom, more than half of all such mortgages were issued with so-called simultaneous seconds—second mortgages issued to enable borrowers to avoid costly mortgage insurance.

Another problem impeding loan modifications was the fear of lawsuits. Specifically, mortgage servicers—people or firms hired to collect payments from homeowners and manage any associated problems—feared being sued by the mortgage holders who had hired them.

The problem was complex. Mortgage owners—investors who bought securities backed by mortgage loans—had a wide range of interests. Some had been seeking safe, high-quality investments. They had bought highly rated mortgage-backed securities with Aaa ratings. Others had been willing to take bigger risks for bigger returns; they had purchased low-rated or nonrated securities. Thanks to the Wall Street–devised system to package and slice up mortgages to suit different risk appetites, both high- and low-risk investors now shared an interest in the same pools of loans. This made it very hard to reach agreement about a change in the rules.

Low-risk Aaa investors were typically willing to let loans go into foreclosure because the losses that would result from that process would hit the high-risk investors first. In a loan modification, on the other hand, those who held the riskier securities would continue to be paid, and the probability of a future default—in which even the Aaa investors might lose—would remain high. Complicating matters further, many Aaa investors didn't trust their mortgage servicers, some of whom were also investors in the high-risk portions of their loans. By mid-2008, the first lawsuits were already being filed.

Congress tried to smooth these impediments and jump-start more loan modifications. To resolve conflicts between mortgage servicers and investors, it introduced legislation to indemnify mortgage servicers from investor lawsuits, provided they could show that a modification would be less costly than a foreclosure. Congress also debated changing the bankruptcy rules, to allow judges to rewrite the terms of some mortgages originated during the bubble period. Historically, first mortgages were exempt from any such changes, a provision designed to prevent homeowners from using bankruptcy to avoid foreclosure. Now proponents argued that changing the rules would put pressure on mortgage owners to renegotiate; otherwise, the borrower could go to bankruptcy court and find a judge who would rewrite the mortgage without the mortgage owner's input.

Industry groups and the Bush administration strongly opposed both pieces of legislation; in mid-2008, they seemed unlikely to pass unless the crisis intensified. Such legislation seemed a second-best solution. It is no small matter for the government to alter contracts between private parties—between servicers and investors, or between homeowners and mortgage owners—even in times of crisis. Doing so would likely increase borrowing costs in the future because lenders and investors would require compensation for the extra risk that the government might intervene again. As distant as that notion might have seemed in the middle of the mortgage crisis, it was real; given the principles involved, it seemed far better for the government to intervene by providing incentives for homeowners, servicers, and mortgage owners to voluntarily modify loans.[17]

A plethora of voluntary mortgage write-down plans was put forth. Among the notable ones was a proposal by Massachusetts Congressman Barney Frank and Connecticut Sen. Christopher Dodd giving mortgage owners the option of having the FHA refinance their distressed loans. The mortgage owners would have to reduce the loan's principal to 85% of a home's current appraised value,[18] but this might still be less costly than putting the home through foreclosure, particularly in a sinking market for home sales. Homeowners would end up with smaller, fixed-rate FHA mortgages, and if they stayed put for five years, they would be able to keep any future price appreciation if home values rose.

The Frank/Dodd plan was a good effort, but it had several limitations. First, it saddled the federal government with a substantial amount of credit risk. Although homeowners with smaller FHA loans were more likely to remain current on their loans, the potential for default was still significant. Second, it was unclear whether many mortgage owners would accept the government's offer. It seemed difficult for mortgage owners to tell which homeowners would default without a significant write-down. Instead of accepting a substantial write-down with the Frank/Dodd plan, many mortgage owners might take their chances with standard, and less costly, loss-mitigation techniques. Third, it was unclear how many homeowners would meet the plan's criteria for residency and income. Fourth, the plan did not address the possible objections of second mortgage holders or investors. Finally, the FHA—historically a cumbersome government agency— might not be able to refinance a large number of loans quickly enough.

The official response to the subprime financial shock had gone from timid to bold. In summer 2007, the Federal Reserve had been uncomfortable lowering interest rates; by spring 2008, policymakers were gearing up for the largest government intervention in the financial system since the savings and loan crisis of the early 1990s. The failure to act decisively early in the crisis had contributed to the need for even more aggressive action later. The fast-approaching presidential election surely had something to do with this transformation; voters demanded that policymakers act. However, just as important was the realization that the subprime financial crisis was bigger than the market's ability to manage it.

13 ———————————————————

Economic Fallout

The subprime financial shock hit in summer 2007 and by early 2008 the U.S. economy had come unhinged. Economists and policymakers debated whether the nation was in recession, but for the majority of Americans, there was no debate. They were worth measurably less and their incomes didn't stretch nearly as far.[1] For them this was a recession.

As summer 2008 approached, Americans' anxiety regarding the economy and their own financial affairs was as high as it had been in more than a quarter century. Surveys of consumer sentiment concurred that the collective psyche had not been so fragile since the early 1980s, when inflation and unemployment were both in double digits.[2] Though both were still relatively low, it was telling that people felt as bad as they had in that earlier dark period.

Little was going right: There were fewer jobs available, and part-time work was replacing full-time. The stock market was down and, for the first time in a while having trouble getting back up. Gasoline prices were rocketing past $4 per gallon. The cost of bread, milk, and other staples was rising quickly as well. Millions were losing their homes to foreclosure; and house prices were in free fall. American consumers, whose collective spending might had powered the global economy since World War II, had no choice but to tighten their belts.

For the economy to be pushed into recession by scared consumers was unprecedented. Historically, recessions had been caused by businesses that had overextended in the good times and had to pull back when things didn't go as planned. An event such as 9/11 or the Gulf War could trigger a recession, as they had in 2001 and 1990. Disruptions in oil supplies did the trick in 1973 and 1980. Those downturns began when firms had been forced to lay off workers and cut investment. But that wasn't the cause in 2007 and 2008. First, homeowners stopped paying their mortgage bills and other debts; then they stopped spending altogether. Economists had long counted on the American consumer to power the economy's growth; to never, as they put it, underestimate the hedonism of the American consumer. That old adage no longer appeared to hold true.

Yet the subprime financial shock's significance goes beyond the recession it started. The shock was, in fact, an inflection point in the nation's economic history. Before it hit, most households saved little, and many borrowed aggressively and spent beyond their incomes. Between 1980 and 2005, the personal saving rate—the percent of after-tax income that is not spent—fell steadily from 10% to essentially nothing (see Figure 13.1). The decline was due in part to wealthier households saving less. Affluent Americans had built up their nest eggs during years of strong stock and real-estate gains. The 1987 stock market crash, the tech-stock bust, and the housing crash had been only temporary setbacks.[3] Millions of families didn't have to worry about paying for the children's college education or their retirement, they were set. Why save?

Saving also declined as the borrowing power of poorer households increased. Steadily falling interest rates since the early 1980s and financial innovation had made credit available to households that had not previously had access to credit cards, car loans, or mortgages. By going from a 3-year to a 5-year car loan or taking on a 2/28 subprime mortgage, these households could add debt without seeing their monthly payments rise, at least for awhile. Borrowing allowed them to maintain a level of spending despite having tenuous jobs and volatile incomes.

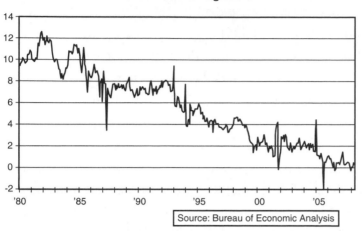

Figure 13.1   **Personal saving fades away**

The subprime shock signaled an end to all this. No longer would wealthier families be able to count on outsized gains in the stock or real-estate markets to do their saving for them. No longer could poorer households easily get another loan when the cash from the previous one ran out. The subprime shock marked the denouement of a half century of global economic history driven by the American consumer.

Housing's Tentacles

The bursting of the housing bubble and the waves of mortgage defaults that followed brought on the subprime shock; conversely, the shock and subsequent credit crunch accelerated the housing crash. With mortgage lending at a standstill, home sales collapsed and foreclosures soared, forcing builders to cease construction and home sellers to slash prices. Because housing is such an essential part of the economy—no other industry is arguably as important to the business cycle—the housing crash choked the economic expansion. Recession followed.

The severity of the housing crash was without parallel, save perhaps for the Great Depression. By spring of 2008, housing starts had fallen nearly 60% from their peak in late 2005; home sales were off 35% (and closer to 50% if foreclosure and other distress sales were excluded), and house prices had dropped by 15% on average nationwide. For historical context, in the early 1980s' housing downturn, the industry's previous low-water mark, home sales fell about 50% peak to trough, and housing starts fell 60%, but the average sales price of American homes prices never declined.[4]

The most obvious link between housing and the economy is construction. During the housing boom, residential investment, which includes the value of homebuilding, renovation, and remodeling, steadily rose. When homebuilding peaked in late 2005, its value as a percentage of GDP was at an all-time high; residential construction had never been more important to the economy.[5] Three years later, building as a share of GDP was plumbing a record low.

The wild swing in homebuilding had a dramatic impact on the nation's overall growth. Residential construction had added nearly half a percentage point to real GDP steadily during the boom; it *subtracted* a full percentage point from yearly growth during the crash. In 2007, real GDP growth came in at 2.2%, but it would have been 3.2% if homebuilding had simply remained unchanged that year. But this is just a partial measure; it doesn't count all the ripple effects that occur when homebuilding falls off: Demand, and thus production, fall for steel, cement, gypsum, lumber, tools, plumbing fixtures, and electrical apparatus; there is less work for surveyors, truckers, and retailers; fewer roads, bridges, and schools are built, and on and on.

A less obvious link between housing and the economy runs through state and local government finances. Property taxes account for more than two-thirds of local governments' tax receipts, while states depend on various transfer fees and capital gains taxes on home sales for their revenue. Government coffers overflowed during the housing boom as rapidly rising house prices fueled gains in revenue. Those coffers didn't dry up right away, thanks to the time lag between house prices, property assessments, and tax payments. But it was clear the housing crash would be a drag on government finances for a long time. Budgets for the fiscal year 2009 already showed the first effects as more than half the nation's states reported sizable shortfalls. States had been relatively prudent during the boom and fattened up rainy day funds, but it wouldn't be long before those would be drained, forcing states to cut back spending to balance their budgets. All government services, from schools and universities to hospitals and roads, would be pinched. In addition to the institutional pain that would cause, the economy as a whole would feel the drop in such spending. Government isn't a huge contributor to the economy but it is a consistent one, and when other sources of growth fall off, it can be important.

Perhaps the least understood link between housing and the economy is via house prices and their impact on homeowners' net worth. As we saw in Chapter 4, "Chairman Greenspan Counts on Housing," the wealth effect of rising house prices lifted consumer spending during the housing boom. During the crash, this same wealth effect went into reverse. Because a home is most households' most important asset, a drop in real estate prices affects consumers' sense of their own net worth and strongly influences decisions on spending. When house prices were high, for example, the equity in a home might have been enough to pay for a year or two of a child's college; but with prices down, there was enough for room and board at best. With the echo-boom generation reaching late teens and the credit crunch suddenly making student loans more difficult to get, there was no other option but to spend less and save more—and quickly.

Amplifying the financial angst was the extra debt many homeowners had taken on during the boom via home equity lines and cash-out refinancing deals. When prices were soaring, this had seemed essentially like free money. Even if some thought their rising real-estate wealth was a bit too good to be true, they were confident that at worst, house prices would only plateau rather than fall. It was inconceivable that home values would drop and keep dropping, past 10%, 20%, or even 30%. The average homeowner's equity in their dwelling was roughly $75,000 when house prices peaked in spring 2006.[6] By early 2008, this figure had fallen to almost $50,000. And house prices were still declining. If nationwide average home prices bottomed out 25% below their peak—the widespread consensus among economists at the time—then an average homeowner would have only $45,000 left in equity.[7] But these numbers mask a wide distribution in homeowners' economic fortunes. Millions of wealthier and generally older homeowners had built up hundreds of thousands of dollars in equity through the years; millions more owned no equity at all—they owed more than their homes were worth. As of early 2008, an estimated 8.5 million households had more than $200,000 in homeowners' equity. Another 8.5 million were completely underwater on their homes.

To fully appreciate the implications of the negative wealth effect on consumer spending and the economy, consider the behavior of three types of households: renters; wealthier homeowners who did not dip into their home equity for cash during the boom; and lower- and middle-income households who did. The saving rate for those who rent has long been close to zero (see Figure 13.2).[8] Rising and falling house prices mean little to them directly, so their spending and saving is not affected by ups and downs in the housing market. Wealthier homeowners who did not cash out also have a zero saving rate; but while this has fallen over the years, it was also about zero when the stock market was at its peak at the turn of the millennium. This group's spending and saving is more dependent on the vagaries of stock prices than on house prices. This is not so for lower and middle-income homeowners who cashed out. For them, movements of house prices are crucial; nothing affects their financial decisions more. As prices took off in the late 1990s and early 2000s, they borrowed so aggressively that their saving rate reached an astounding negative 10%—in other words they were collectively spending 10% more than their income. Rising home equity was fueling this binge; as the fuel ran out in the housing crash, they were forced to become more prudent spenders, at the very least matching their spending with their income. This was a tough adjustment for an economy whose growth had become dependent on consumers' earlier habits.[9]

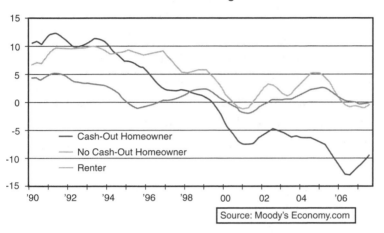

Personal Saving Rate

Source: Moody's Economy.com

Figure 13.2   Cashing out homeowners dis-save

Falling $, Record Oil

Amplifying the economic fallout from the subprime shock was a dramatic fall in the value of the U.S. dollar. The two were related: The housing bust had occurred in the U.S. at a time when financial and economic conditions elsewhere around the world were measurably better. Global investors who had been eager to put their cash into U.S. markets prior to the shock were now just as eager to get out. As a result, the dollar tumbled in value against other major world currencies. The euro moved up from $1.35 to almost $1.60; the Canadian loonie rose from 85 U.S. cents to $1-for-$1 parity (the first time since the early 1970s); and instead of needing 125 Japanese yen to make $1, traders needed only 100. Together, the dollar's value (measured against the currencies of America's major trading partners) fell more than 10% in just a few months in late 2007 and early 2008. This was on top of a 15% decline during the Iraq invasion and deflation scare earlier in the decade. The dollar was worth about one-fourth less than at its peak.

This wasn't an entirely bad thing. There were clear economic benefits to the weaker dollar. When combined with stronger growth overseas, the U.S. trade deficit narrowed. The imbalance between U.S. imports and exports had, in fact, peaked with the housing market in late 2005; by early 2008 it had been cut by a fourth.[10] The nation's agriculture, aerospace, machine tools, and technology industries gained new market power overseas and shipped record amounts of goods to Asia, South America, and Europe. After years of weighing down the economy, trade had become a key source of growth.

The dollar's sharp drop in the midst of the financial turmoil did more damage than good, however. It helped ignite another surge in oil, food, and other commodity prices. Since most commodities trade globally in dollars, a fall in the dollar's exchange value means the dollar price of these commodities must rise to maintain a balance between global demand and supply. Given the increasing values of the euro, yuan, and rubble vis-à-vis the dollar, without a higher dollar price for oil, wheat, and copper, the Europeans, Chinese, and Russians will consume more, throwing demand and supply off kilter. As a result, a barrel of oil that sold for $65 in the weeks leading up to subprime shock had doubled in price by spring 2008.[11] The dollar price of other commodities ranging from gold and wheat to copper and coca beans didn't rise quite as much, but most were still hitting record highs.

Commodities weren't being powered by a weaker dollar alone. The financial bedlam created by the subprime shock also contributed. Global investors were truly confused about where to put their money. Real estate was certainly out, bonds seemed like land mines, and stocks appeared shaky at best. Each new explosion in the financial markets drove investors to seek safer investments—mainly U.S. Treasury securities and commodities. Some investors reasoned commodity prices tended to move in the opposite direction of other asset prices and would thus help diversify their portfolios. Other short-term investors, so-called momentum players, simply bet that because commodities had been consistently rising in price, they would rise even further. The commodity markets were like any other asset market in an age of easy trading and excess liquidity; here too, prices could be subject to speculation and bubbles.

For the economy, surging oil and other commodity prices were too much to bear. The price of a gallon of regular unleaded gasoline, which had averaged $2.75 nationwide on Labor Day 2007, reached $4 by Memorial Day 2008 and kept rising. Each penny increase increased Americans' driving costs by more than $1 billion. Washington's $100 billion tax rebate—part of the fiscal stimulus passed a few months earlier to try to stave off recession—began arriving in Americans' mailboxes just as gasoline crossed $4, and was effectively gobbled up by the higher cost of fuel. Observers noted a bitter irony: The U.S. Treasury had sold bonds to raise the cash to pay the tax rebates which were spent to buy oil from the same nations that had purchased the bonds. It's not much of an exaggeration to say that countries such as Saudi Arabia had essentially financed the purchase of their own oil.

Energy wasn't the only thing that was rising quickly in price. Food prices were also up sharply. This was driven partly by the higher cost of moving farm products to store shelves as diesel prices soared; but it also reflected the weak dollar and strong global demand for all U.S. agricultural products. Imported goods of all kinds cost more. Even prices for goods coming from China, which had fallen for years, were now on the rise. It was the reverse of the late 1990s, when the Asian financial crisis had sent investors scurrying to the safety of the U.S. This lifted the dollar and slashed the price of imports to U.S. consumers. The subprime financial shock induced global investors to flee American markets, undermining the dollar and raising prices for anything not made in the U.S. Consumers were rightly panicked, realizing there was no way out and that recession was unavoidable.

Cracked Nest Egg

A temporary period of slack in U.S. growth was hardly the net impact of the subprime shock, however. Henceforth, American consumers would have to find ways to live within their means; their unlimited freedom to spend, as well as their dominant role in the global economy, had reached an end.

The era of U.S. consumer dominance can be tracked through the rise of household spending as a share of the total economy. In 1980, consumer spending stood at 62% of GDP—about where it had been since the end of World War II (see Figure 13.3). By 1990, that share had risen to 66% and by the turn of the millennium, it was 70%.[12] This is the flip side of the falling personal saving rate. Consumer spending rose as a share of GDP throughout this period because households were willing and able to spend above their incomes.

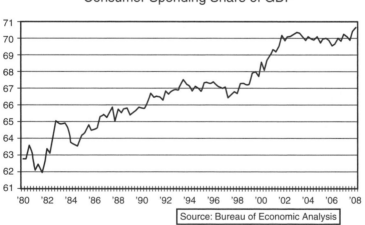

Consumer Spending Share of GDP

Source: Bureau of Economic Analysis

Figure 13.3   Consumers power the economy

Underpinning this quarter-century of aggressive consumer spending was the steady deceleration in inflation and the resulting decline in interest rates. The early 1980s was a period of stagflation, characterized by double-digit inflation, unemployment, and interest rates. The oil price shocks of that time—the Iranian revolution had occurred in 1979—had ignited a spiral in which rising prices begat increased wages which begat yet higher prices. Consumer price growth and the 10-year Treasury bond yield both peaked about this time at close to 15%. Almost 25 years later, inflation had been wrung out of the economy by years of stringent monetary policy, stable and low oil prices, and China's rapid ascent. Inflation and interest rates fell into the low single-digits.

These conditions helped ignite an increase in asset prices: stocks, bonds, and real estate all increased smartly in value. Interest rates play a crucial role in determining any asset's value because they affect the present value (what its' worth today) of the asset's future income. For a share of stock, for instance, that income is the future profits of the company that issued it. For real estate, it's rents for landlords and the benefits of living in the home for homeowners. When interest rates fall, the present value of this future income rises and thus so does its price. Lower rates mean asset prices will rise relative to the future income they are expected to generate—the price-to-earnings ratio (PE) increases. As the 10-year Treasury yield fell from 15% in 1980 to less than 5% in 2005, asset prices rose strongly, and the economy's collective PE ratio—measured by ratio of the value of all household assets to GDP—went from 3.5 to more than 5 (see Figure 13.4).[13]

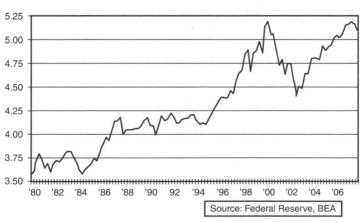

Ratio of The Value of Household Assets to GDP

Source: Federal Reserve, BEA

Figure 13.4   The economy's PE has peaked

The increase in asset prices and PE ratios is evident in the stock market. The S&P 500 PE rose from less than 10 in 1980 to closer to 20 by 2008. Stock prices rose about 10% annually during this period, despite some major setbacks such as the 1987 crash and the bursting of the Internet stock bubble. House prices also enjoyed a solid run, rising more than 5% annually. As with stocks, the housing PE rose from a low of 10 to near 20—even after including the post-2005 housing market crash.

The financial benefits of these outsized asset price gains have gone almost entirely to higher income households. The data is a bit sketchy, but those households who are among the highest 40% of income earners saw their share of overall wealth rise from 79% to 83% in the 15 years between 1989 and 2004.[14] The median net worth of these households was above $600,000 in 2004, up from less than $400,000 15 years earlier. The share of wealth going to the lowest 60% of income earners fell commensurately, from 21% to only 17% (see Table 13.1). Their median net worth of $35,000 in 2004 was not much different from what it had been 15 years earlier, and it was lower still after accounting for inflation.

TABLE 13.1   The Wealthy Get Wealthier, The Poor More Indebted

	Share of Net Worth		*Share of Debt*	
	1989	2004	1989	2004
Percentile of Income				
0-20	0.27	0.49	1.90	3.33
20-40	3.73	2.30	5.74	7.46
40-60	6.33	4.76	13.21	14.82
60-80	10.14	10.61	25.81	23.67
80-100	79.50	81.8	53.33	50.72

Source: Federal Reserve Board

About the time the housing market peaked in 2005, many wealthy Americans thought they were financially set. If their nest eggs were not quite large enough to sustain a comfortable retirement and meet other obligations, they would be assuming that asset prices continued their recent pace. This seemed a reasonable assumption: Assets had risen on average in the high-single-digits for as long as this generation could remember.

The subprime financial shock put an end to this kind of thinking. The super-wealthy had no concerns. They were indeed set, but the simply well-to-do realized now that their nest eggs were insufficient. The subprime shock dashed beliefs and hopes that asset prices would consistently appreciate faster than the income those assets were likely to generate. This was clear in the post-shock collapse in house prices. The tech-stock bust had similarly made it clear in the stock market. With interest rates unlikely to go lower for long, the most reasonable assumption was that asset prices would grow about as fast as the income those same assets generated. That is, PEs would not continue to rise. Across all asset classes—stocks, bonds, and real estate—the best forecast was that asset prices would increase at a mid-single-digit pace, about the same as the expected growth in GDP. Even higher income households had some saving to do.

Debt Millstone

Lower income households faced a far more difficult adjustment. For a quarter century, these households benefited from steadily increasing access to credit. By borrowing more, they could supplement their constrained incomes to maintain their spending at a relatively high level. The subprime financial shock signified the end of such free-flowing credit. Lower income households had little choice but to match their spending with their incomes; their living standards would inevitably suffer.

It was tough to get a loan in the early 1980s. For most households, that period's double-digit interest rates made borrowing prohibitively expensive. Credit cards were still new (they were not mass-marketed until the late 1960s) and still were used by a minority of households. Vehicle loans lasted at most three years and were exclusively intended for car buyers with pristine credit. Mortgages were almost entirely plain-vanilla 30-year, fixed-rate loans.

Over the subsequent 25 years, the availability of credit ballooned, powered by steadily declining interest rates, rapid financial innovation, and government policy. The lower rates were vital to increased borrowing as households could take on more debt and not have to make larger payments. Lenders also extended the length of loans to keep payments down; minimum payments on credit cards fell, most car loans evolved into 5-year loans, and 40-year mortgages became increasingly common. Credit scoring, direct marketing, and securitization came into their own, and lenders grew emboldened to provide credit to new groups of consumers. Risk management techniques improved dramatically, enticing lenders to provide more credit to less creditworthy borrowers. There was also mounting regulatory pressure to provide more credit to minority and disadvantaged borrowers. Ongoing changes to the bankruptcy laws making them steadily more lender-friendly may have also empowered lenders to extend more credit.[15]

While all income groups took on more debt, lower income groups were particularly burdened. In the fifteen years between 1989 and 2004, households in the bottom 20% of income earners increased their indebtedness by 3.4 times.[16] Those in the next lowest 20% bracket boosted their debt levels 2.2 times. Households in the top 20% of income earners also borrowed more, but their debt increased only 1.3 times.

Some of this reflects a judicious use of credit by households getting their first taste of it. Higher income households have long had the luxury of financing purchases of big-ticket items—a car, a dishwasher or even a big-screen TV—that they will consume over a long period. They use debt to more efficiently pay as they consume—laying out cash (via debt repayment) as they go. Of course there are interest charges included in this plan, but for many it is well worth it. There is no reason why lower-income household shouldn't enjoy the same privileges, and that's how many have used their access to credit.

Over time, lower-income households have increasingly used debt to supplement their constrained and volatile incomes. It's not hard to understand why: After inflation, incomes for those on the bottom rungs of the income and wealth ladders barely grew after the early 1980s, and didn't grow at all through the late 1990s to the mid-2000s. While globalization—including immigration and trade—had been a boon to the overall economy, it was hard on those with lesser skills and education. In the competition with cheaper labor from all corners of the world, lower-skilled U.S. workers were losing. Borrowing more took the financial sting out, and while debt burdens were getting weightier, these households could manage it as long as lenders continued to extend them credit.

By the time the subprime financial shock hit, debt loads were at record highs. The average American household was paying almost a fifth of its after-tax income on financial obligations—everything from the mortgage payment to the auto lease—to avoid going delinquent on those obligations. For subprime homeowners, who were forking over more than 35% of their after-tax income to meet their obligations, this was an overwhelming burden (see Figure 13.5). It all came undone in the housing crash and the subprime financial shock. Many poorer households were now completely cut off from credit; and while lending to this group would eventually be reborn, these households would no longer be able use credit as a ticket to a better lifestyle.

Financial Obligation Ratio, % of Disposable Income

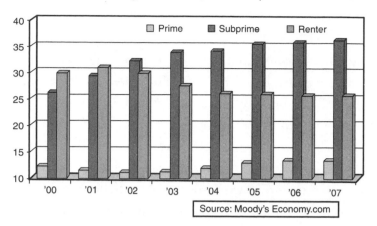

Source: Moody's Economy.com

Figure 13.5   Weighty household debt loads

14

Back to the Future

As this is being written, about a year after the subprime financial shock hit, the worst of the crisis appears to be over. The financial turmoil reached an apex in mid-March, when the Federal Reserve stepped in to engineer the sale of Bear Stearns—then on the brink of collapse— to JPMorgan Chase. While conditions have improved since then, the shock continues to reverberate: House prices are still declining, foreclosures continue to mount, the economy hasn't found its footing, and the financial system remains unsettled.

Falling house prices are particularly unnerving. With no clear bottom in site for the residential real-estate market, financial institutions remain unsure of their losses on mortgage loans and securities. Many have already written down their portfolios by large amounts, subtracting from their balance sheets both the estimated losses from defaults and declines in the market value of their remaining loans and securities. Some institutions believe the market has grown overly pessimistic and that those securities will eventually rise again in value; thus the write-downs might simply reflect a temporary hysteria from the subprime shock. Whether this ultimately proves correct depends on how far house prices eventually fall. The same applies to the fate of the monoline insurers, who are still trying to raise enough capital to maintain their Aaa-ratings and thus survive. Another wave of financial turmoil looms if they cannot.

It is also disconcerting to find many banks without enough capital to withstand the credit losses that were still to come. The nation's community and regional banks appear especially vulnerable, as credit problems spread from residential mortgages to other types of lending. There have never been so many auto repossessions, and credit card and student loan delinquencies are rising quickly. Banks also have loans out to troubled home builders and have sizable commercial loan portfolios that could soon face problems from weakening rents and falling commercial property prices.

The big banks continue to suffer from indigestion, even as the rest of the cash-strapped financial system relies on them for credit. The shadow banking system—made up of asset-backed conduits, structured investment vehicles, finance companies, broker-dealers, and so on—continues to have difficulty funding itself and has turned to banks for help. This means that assets that had been deliberately kept off banks' balance sheets are moving back on them. Combined with the banks' own massive write-downs, this will sorely strain banks' available capital. Even with sovereign wealth funds offering billions in new equity capital, banks still don't have the resources necessary to both backstop the entire financial system and also provide enough credit to their own household and business customers.

It is also possible that previously unaffected parts of the financial system will soon feel the widening ripples of the subprime shock. One likely candidate is the mammoth market for credit default swaps. While CDS on mortgage-related securities are relatively well understood, a much larger portion of the market involves default swaps on corporate bonds. These have been unaffected thus far because corporate bonds have experienced relatively few credit problems. However, if corporate bond defaults rise (which seems likely) the default-swaps market will surely be tested. That could set off a new and more powerful shock to the financial system.

There are other potential new shocks as well, but it remains unclear which pose the greatest threats and to which institutions. Financial markets remain disturbingly opaque, making it hard for financial players to identify or prepare for additional threats. If financial institutions are worried and uncertain, they will remain cautious and restrict credit and raise its cost for nearly everyone, good borrowers and bad. Until credit flows more freely and cheaply, the economy will not get its groove back.

Subprime Policy

Much still depends on policymakers. Their response to the subprime shock has grown bolder and more effective, but it has not yet proved able to stop the fallout from the subprime crisis. A prudent approach dictates that policymakers plan as if their efforts will be insufficient to the task ahead—because there were reasons to believe they won't be.

The Federal Reserve's dramatic interest-rate deductions in early 2008 were less than effective because the principal near-term link between monetary policy and the broader economy is the housing and mortgage markets, and those are not functioning normally. Housing is the part of the economy most sensitive to rate changes, but lower rates will not jump start home sales if mortgage credit remains largely unavailable. Further rate cuts seem unlikely because of mounting inflation concerns amid sharply rising energy and food prices.

The Fed's new credit facilities and its willingness to help resolve the Bear Stearns collapse has improved the financial system's functioning, but these measures have also stretched the central bank's mandate. The Bear Stearns affair sparked particular criticism from analysts who warn that investors will expect the same treatment in future crises. That danger still seems small compared with the disaster that might have followed an actual collapse of Bear Stearns; still, such concerns have reduced the Fed's latitude in responding to the subprime shock.

The tax rebates mailed in the summer of 2008 as part of the fiscal stimulus package will also prove less potent than expected because of record gasoline prices. Every penny increase in the price of a gallon

costs American households just over $1 billion in extra annual spend-
ing. With average national gas prices rising from $3 a gallon at the be-
ginning of 2008 to over $4 by mid-year, the nation's annual gas bill rose
by more than $100 billion: just about the amount of the tax rebates.
Although the rebate money comes all at once and the extra gasoline
costs will stretch over a year, it is clear the rebates won't provide quite
the economic pop for which Congress had hoped. Moreover, what
happens in 2009 after the rebates are spent if credit markets and the
banking system fail to stabilize and the economy is still sputtering?

Any hope that financial markets will repair themselves with the
help of the Fed and the Treasury Department may prove overly opti-
mistic. Parts of the financial system are in serious disrepair: The
private mortgage securities market, for example, is in shambles. The
originate-to-distribute model (described in Chapter 7, "Financial Engineers and Their Creations") propelled the housing and mortgage
frenzy is bankrupt. Even if home prices and foreclosures stabilize,
investors will not purchase a private mortgage security without clear
guarantees that the mortgage loans behind it are properly underwrit-
ten and that the underwriter has some financial stake in the loan's performance. This seems a long way off.

Policies to promote work-outs between mortgage lenders and
troubled borrowers, such as Hope Now and Project Lifeline, are also
being overwhelmed by the magnitude of the problem and the shifting
forces behind it. When these programs were established in late 2007,
the main driver of foreclosures seemed to be the prospect of huge interest-rate resets on subprime ARM loans. Yet this possibility faded as
the Fed's aggressive rate cuts drove down current interest rates, so
that by the time their reset clocks ran out in early 2008, many subprime homeowners ended up facing no big jump in payments at all.
Foreclosures have continued to increase, but now the biggest problems are negative homeowners' equity and rising unemployment.
Hope Now was not designed to tackle these issues, and as of mid-2008
there has been no other policy response from Washington.

Policymakers have also yet to address the future. This is understandable given the pressing demands of the subprime shock, but it is important that we focus before long on how to avoid the next crisis. The following "top ten" list summarizes what I believe needs to be done, starting with the most pressing items and ending with the most complex:

Policy Step #1: Adopt a voluntary mortgage write-down plan

Many troubled mortgages could be salvaged if lenders would agree to modify them, typically by reducing the principal owed. The borrower would get to stay in the house, the lender would avoid a costly foreclosure, and the economy might avoid falling into a destructive self-reinforcing cycle in which house price declines beget foreclosures which beget still more price declines. Thus it seems both reasonable and urgent to encourage this wherever possible. While there is no silver policy bullet that will address this problem, a number of proposals have circulated that could help. Most involve a small commitment of taxpayer dollars.[1]

Passage of an effective mortgage write-down plan faces several hurdles, including reasonable concerns that it would end up helping those who least deserve it. Lenders who faithfully observed sound underwriting methods would not benefit; nor would those homeowners who are working hard to keep their mortgages current despite financial strains. The counter-argument is that the housing problem is so serious that it threatens the honest and diligent as well as those who made big mistakes. The cost to the overall economy in lost jobs, wealth, and tax revenue if troubled borrowers do not receive financial help will almost certainly be greater than the cost of bailing them out. Although there is no guarantee that such a plan will be adequate to the problem, it is worth the effort.

Policy Step #2: Establish clear mortgage lending rules

A number of steps have been proposed that could prevent a repeat of the housing meltdown once the current crisis is past. Most notable would be the Federal Reserve's adoption of clear guidelines for appropriate mortgage lending: Under the Fed's proposed rules, lenders must consider the borrower's ability to repay and also verify the borrower's income and assets. Prepayment penalties are barred if a homeowner refinances within 60 days after an adjustable loan reset, and borrowers must establish escrow accounts for taxes and insurance. These commonsense lending rules would apply to all mortgage lenders given the Fed's broad authority.[2]

Policy Step #3: License mortgage brokers

There is widespread agreement that all mortgage brokers must be licensed. Unregistered brokers were among the most unscrupulous lenders during the housing boom. State banking regulators are working to set tougher standards for brokers by requiring applicants to pass proficiency tests and to be fingerprinted by the FBI.[3] State regulators have also launched a nationwide lender information system: an Internet database with pending enforcement actions and background data for all licensed mortgage brokers and lenders.

Policy Step #4: Expand data collection

A lack of timely and accurate information hobbled policymakers' ability to respond to the subprime financial shock. Data on mortgage delinquencies and defaults comes from a variety of mostly private sources, making it nearly impossible for regulators or others to see the crisis as it grew. No government agency tracks the number of mortgage foreclosures, for example, and the various private sources of such information are limited in various ways.

A ready mechanism for expanding the government's data collection already exists under the data collection efforts required by the Home Mortgage Disclosure Act. HMDA requires most mortgage originators to report some information on all loan applications and approvals. This includes data on the lender, location, income, and ethnicity of the borrower, whether the loan is a first or second lien, whether it is a purchase loan or refinancing, as well as the loan's amount and its interest rate.

Reporting requirements should be expanded to include mortgage servicers, who in most cases are also the lenders already reporting under HMDA. Servicers can provide information on delinquencies and defaults as well as on whether various types of loans and borrowers are having credit problems. Reporting under HMDA should be more frequent—it currently occurs annually—and data releases should be accelerated. The HMDA data for 2006 wasn't fully released until the Fall of 2007. More frequent updates and more rapid reporting would help policymakers and lenders spot credit quality problems earlier and allow them to respond better to developing problems.

Policy Step #5: Reform the fractured foreclosure process

The current mortgage foreclosure system is a complex mélange of laws and rules that varies substantially from state to state. The foreclosure process generally entails three steps: First, a loan default, no more than 6 months after the first missed loan payment, then a foreclosure auction, and finally a sale of the property by the bank. The average time between the first and last steps ranges from about 7 months in Virginia to 20 months in New York City.

The federal government streamlined the bankruptcy code in 2005 to make it more uniform across states, and it should do the same for foreclosures. A federal foreclosure system would substantially reduce the cost of the foreclosure process, be more equitable to borrowers and lenders, and allow for the more accurate collection of data and information.

A federal foreclosure process should standardize the time between a mortgage loan default and an auction. One year would be reasonable because that is approximately the median current length of time among states. A year would be sufficient to give borrowers who have hit hard times—perhaps due to unemployment or illness—a meaningful opportunity to work with their lenders and turn things around. It also allows lenders to foreclose within a reasonable time if borrowers are unable or unwilling to meet their obligations.

A federal process should also favor the judicial form of foreclosure, even though the costs are greater. Requiring a lender to file a lawsuit gives consumers greater protection against abuse. Lenders could recoup some of their extra expenses by obtaining deficiency judgments, which hold borrowers liable for the difference between the price a home fetches in a foreclosure sale and the amount of outstanding debt.[4]

Federal foreclosure should eliminate the right of redemption, which gives the original homeowner a chance to repurchase a foreclosed home for up to a year after it is auctioned. This right can add delay and uncertainty to the process and reduce the value of the foreclosed home. A one-year period between default and foreclosure offers homeowners sufficient time to negotiate with lenders or to find the cash to keep their homes if they are able.

Policy Step #6: Invest in financial literacy

Americans aren't as smart about money as we should be. Financial illiteracy was a fundamental cause of the subprime financial shock. Yes, many people knowingly stretched to buy an expensive home with a subprime ARM loan, figuring they could either sell quickly at a profit or refinance before the payment reset hit. But many more barely understood what they were getting into. According to Federal Reserve surveys done prior to the subprime shock, almost half of lower-income homebuyers (mostly subprime) couldn't describe basic features of their mortgage, such as how their interest rate was determined or whether it was capped. Many trusted their brokers to get them a mortgage they could afford, believing it was the broker's responsibility to look after their financial interests.

The nation's general financial illiteracy contributes to a wide range of poor decisions on borrowing, saving, and investment. This may have been less dangerous 10 or 25 years ago when there were fewer financial products to choose from, thus it was harder to make a financially catastrophic mistake. But ignorance of the basics is certainly perilous today. Some of the mortgage options presented to homebuyers during the housing boom were mind-numbingly complex and confusing; even an economist adept at manipulating spreadsheets would have trouble calculating future payments on an interest-only or "option" ARM loan.

It is both bizarre and tragic that American high schools today are more likely to offer students cooking classes than personal finance courses. Such courses should be required—period. A meaningful investment in the financial acumen of young people would pay enormous dividends by reducing the likelihood that future households will take out bad mortgages or not save adequately for retirement.

Policy Step #7: Modify mark-to-market accounting

Past financial crises have often resulted from lax accounting rules. Ironically, the subprime shock is partly the result of rules that were too rigid. Mark-to-market accounting standards, implemented widely in recent years, need to be adjusted. The rules put pressure on financial institutions to quickly adjust the book value of their assets to reflect market prices. The practice stems from the reasonable argument that it is better to deal with problems quickly and move on, even if the adjustment is painful. But what happens when institutions own assets whose prices can't be found, or for which the market price reflects temporary panic? In the midst of the subprime shock, trading in the mortgage securities market literally froze. With no buyers, even Aaa rated prices for these securities went into free fall.

Of course such a plunge could—and did—reflect weakening housing and mortgage markets, but depressed prices may also simply reflect fear and distressed selling. If so, these prices would eventually rebound, but not until after institutions marked down their assets. In the subprime shock, markdowns were so large and cut so deeply into some institutions' capital that it threatened their survival.

To keep this from happening in the future, mark-to-market accounting rules could be tweaked so that changing asset prices are phased in over time, say over one year. Instead of marking an asset to the price that prevailed last quarter, institutions could use the average market price of the asset over the past four quarters. Banks would still have to lower the value of their holdings as prices fell but not as rapidly. This would also limit accounting gains if prices were to shoot up quickly for whatever reason, helping restrain institutions from overextending credit when markets are hot.

Policy Step #8: Raise financial transparency and accountability

Both transparency and accountability are vital to a well-functioning financial system. Both were thought to be present until the subprime financial shock occurred.

Transparency means timely, meaningful, reliable, and complete information is available regarding financial products, institutions, and markets. In transparent markets, financial players borrow, lend, and buy and sell aggressively. In opaque markets, players are uncertain, and they tend to panic in times of trouble, just as they did during the subprime shock.

Financial products were anything but transparent. Complex mortgage loans were offered to homebuyers and nearly incomprehensible mortgage securities were sold to investors. Too many financial institutions hid in the shadows and outside the regulatory light. Large global banks took on risks that they kept off their books until forced to take responsibility. No one really knows what most hedge funds are up to. At times it was all but impossible to reasonably price most mortgage securities. Even the integrity of the LIBOR interest rate, a daily financial benchmark used to calculate financial costs all over the world, has been called into question.

Accountability means someone is ultimately responsible if mistakes are made. No one bore responsibility for the performance of mortgage loans made during the housing boom, and as a result, many bad loans were made. The mortgage securities market remains in disrepair partially because it is unclear how to apportion responsibility for the performance of the underlying loans. Someone must have enough financial skin in the game to want to be sure that good loans are originated and securitized.

Ensuring transparency and accountability requires confident regulatory oversight, which, in turn, must be empowered by Congress and the executive branch. Now that the Federal Reserve has explicitly backstopped the broker-dealer industry via its new credit facilities and its resolution of the Bear Stearns collapse, the quid pro quo should be a more watchful and questioning eye on that industry's capital and activities. This will also provide a better window into the hedge fund industry. The SEC must also become more aggressive about policing financial statements, audit opinions, credit ratings, and analyst reports.

There is a balance to be struck between the benefits of transparency and accountability and the costs of greater disclosure by financial players. The subprime shock showed how unbalanced things had become. It is up to regulators to set it right.

Policy Step #9: Overhaul financial regulation

The regulatory framework overseeing the nation's financial system needs a good overhaul. The current byzantine regulatory structure contributed to the subprime financial shock, allowing the most aggressive lenders to avoid regulatory scrutiny. Regulators were also hamstrung in efforts to impose greater discipline on the industry given the difficulties coordinating among themselves.

Regulatory oversight tends to be pro-cyclical. That is, when credit quality is good and lenders are aggressive, regulators have difficulty imposing discipline; when quality is poor and lenders are tightening, the disciplinary screws are tightened. This tends to exacerbate shifts in lending standards and credit availability. In part it stems from regulators' inability to respond quickly, but it also reflects the influence of politics on regulation. Lenders find it much easier to keep regulators at bay when credit conditions appear robust, though this is generally when increased regulatory oversight would be most beneficial.

The U.S. Treasury Department's "Blueprint for Financial Regulatory Reform," is a reasonable roadmap.[5] In the wake of the mortgage debacle, the plan would establish a commission to create minimum licensing requirements for lenders and assess the caliber of state regulators. It would also give one regulator, probably the Federal Reserve, authority over mortgage lending laws, superseding all other federal and state regulators.

In the long term, the Treasury's plan proposes consolidation of the current regulatory structure into three principal agencies. The basic concept of regulation would shift; instead of agencies monitoring specific types of financial institutions, regulators would specialize in various types of risks and activities. The Federal Reserve would look out for the stability of the entire financial system; its mandate would include any risk that threatened the system, whether it involved banks or hedge funds. The Fed is uniquely suited for this task given its central position in the global financial system, its significant financial and intellectual resources, and its history of political independence. A second regulatory agency would oversee any financial institution receiving an explicit government guarantee. Lenders couldn't choose their regulator as they do now and would have consistent standards to work with. The third regulatory agency would aim to protect consumers by monitoring how all financial institutions market their products.

Financial institutions and their products no longer fit in narrowly defined boxes. The risks they take cut across markets and extend around the globe. The regulatory structure needs to adapt or it will be as irrelevant in the next financial crisis as it was in the subprime financial shock.

Policy Step #10: Pay attention to asset bubbles

It has long been conventional wisdom that the Federal Reserve should not worry about asset bubbles: setting monetary policy without regard to the price of investments such as stocks or real estate. Those who hold this view doubt it's possible to identify investment bubbles anyway. Thus they believe the Fed should stick to worrying about inflation and the real economy; if a bubble does burst, the central bank's role is to clean up afterward and limit the economic damage.

Recently this prescription has not worked particularly well, however. In the wake of both the late-1990s tech-stock bubble and this decade's housing bubble, the Fed was forced to slash interest rates with doubtful consequences for both financial markets and the real economy. The Fed's ultra-low rates after the stock bubble burst helped inflate the subsequent housing bubble, and the low rates in the wake of the housing collapse may contribute to a developing bubble in energy and other commodity markets. Ignoring bubbles may abet their creation.

Cleaning up the economic mess from bursting bubbles has also proved difficult for the Fed. The financial system is the key conduit between monetary policy and the economy, and it is invariably a casualty of plunging markets. Lower rates can't help a struggling economy if they don't quickly translate into more and cheaper credit for businesses and households.

It may, in fact, be possible to accurately identify bubbles. Not only are these characterized by rapidly rising prices, they also involve increased leverage, surging trading volumes, and the arrival of less sophisticated buyers to a market where they have little experience. It is true that bubbles are always born out of something fundamental— be it the Internet's debut for stocks, low interest rates for housing, or

Chinese demand for oil—making it difficult to conclude in real time they are indeed bubbles. Yet policymakers are often asked to make judgments of equal, if not greater, difficulty. Will record oil prices undermine inflation expectations and result in higher underlying core inflation? Is a 2% funds rate target an appropriate response to the subprime shock? Was putting the Fed's balance sheet on the line to resolve the Bear Stearns collapse beyond the Fed's mandate? Asking whether there is a bubble in the housing market is not a more difficult question than these.

Yet policymakers might argue credibly that higher interest rates are too blunt an instrument to wield against bubbles. And so we are back to a regulatory response. Bubbles need lots of credit, and regulators have many ways to affect the flow of credit. A Federal Reserve that determines the nation's monetary policy and is also its chief financial regulator could reduce the odds of future financial crises through deft use of its regulatory powers. This, however, requires that the central bank also demonstrates the courage of its convictions.

Personal Challenge

Policymakers won't enact all the reforms on my top-ten list soon; nevertheless some substantive policy changes are coming. The financial and economic damage emanating from the subprime financial shock is a powerful catalyst for change. The mortgage lending industry will face new rules, and Wall Street will live with new standards and oversight. Work will also begin on making the regulatory framework more effective in a globalized financial system.

Financial institutions and markets have also begun the task of repairing themselves. Wall Street is reengineering the subprime loan (soon to have a new name) and is refashioning the process of securitization. Banks are feverishly writing off bad loans and raising new capital. Funds are raising billions from institutions and wealthy individuals to prepare to buy up distressed properties and securities.

Policymakers' efforts along with investors' renewed enthusiasm will eventually prevail; financial markets will settle and the recession will end. Although the next financial crisis is not in sight, there is no question that another one will arrive eventually. If there is one lesson the subprime financial shock teaches, it is that that no matter how sophisticated financial institutions, markets, and products become, those animal spirits—aka hubris—cannot be kept down long. Future generations will come again to believe that this time things are different but will ultimately overstep.

The most daunting challenge is thus a personal challenge. We must each prepare for the next financial crisis by carefully considering the condition of our own balance sheets. No longer can we count on rapid gains in stock and house prices. Lenders will be less forthcoming with credit, particularly to those who already have taken on their share. Social Security and Medicare benefits will almost certainly be cut for most of us. We will all have to save more and be more careful how we invest. Instead of piling into the next new thing, we should be diversifying away from whatever is appreciating quickly. These are simple principles that have long been the basis for sound personal finance as well as of high finance; principles that many of us seemed to forget in the frenzy that produced the subprime financial shock.

ENDNOTES

Chapter 2

1. This is based on data from the Federal Reserve Board's Flow of Funds.
2. The FHA is part of the Department of Housing and Urban Development.
3. This is based on data collected from the 2006 Home Mortgage Disclosure Act.
4. This is based on credit scores calculated by credit bureau Equifax and is analogous to the more ubiquitous FICO score.
5. This is based on data from the Mortgage Bankers' Association.
6. Loans held in bank portfolios are likely to be less than prime given the very thin spread between rates on prime loans and their cost of funds. They are also likely to be of higher quality than securitized loans, however, given the risk of holding them on their balance sheet.

Chapter 3

1. Between the late 1800's and 1940, the homeownership rate remained essentially unchanged at just under one half of households.
2. Like the FHA, Fannie Mae and Freddie Mac, the VA does not originate mortgage loans but provides insurance on loans to vets originated by private mortgage lenders.
3. The Bureau of Labor Statistics' Consumer Expenditure Survey is the basis of this statement.
4. The Federal Reserve Board's Flow of Funds is the source of this data.
5. While sizable, this is down from $105,000 when house prices were at their peak.
6. The Treasury loses approximately $85 billion a year from the mortgage interest deduction, $20 billion from the deduction for property taxes, and $30 billion for the favorable treatment of capital gains.
7. This is based on a 6.5% fixed mortgage rate.

8. The FHLB was established in 1932, the FHA in 1934 and Fannie Mae in 1938. Freddie Mac was established in 1968 when Fannie Mae was converted into a private corporation to provide competition to Fannie and further facilitate the availability of cheap mortgage credit.

9. This is well documented in "Do Homeowners Know Their House Value and Mortgage Terms?" Brian Bucks and Karen Pence, Federal Reserve Board of Governors, January 2006. http://www.federalreserve.gov/pubs/feds/2006/200603/200603pap.pdf

10. This is based on data from the Bureau of Census. http://www.census.gov/const/C25Ann/sftotalmedavgsqft.pdf

11. The sources and uses of cash from mortgage equity withdrawal is presented in this Federal Reserve study http://www.federalreserve.gov/pubs/feds/2007/200720/index.html

12. This is based on data collected as part of the Home Mortgage Disclosure Act.

Chapter 4

1. This assumes a 20% down payment and property tax payments equal to 1.5% of the home's value.

2. Savings and Loan were given explicit authority to originate adjustable rate mortgages in 1982 by the Federal Home Loan Bank.

3. As of 1980, the S&L industry held approximately one-half of all residential mortgage debt.

4. See "Understanding Household Debt Obligations," speech by Alan Greenspan to the Credit Union National Association 2004 Governmental Affairs Conference, February 23, 2004. http://www.federalreserve.gov/boarddocs/speeches/2004/20040223/default.htm As it turns out, the basis for Greenspan's argument that ARMs are a bargain for homeowners, at least the one he provided in the speech, turned out to be incorrect. He estimated that fixed rate loans had an option adjusted spread that was as much as 1.2 percentage points greater than that of an ARM loan. In other words, even after accounting for the benefit to borrowers from being able to refinance a fixed rate loan it still cost borrowers substantially more than an ARM. In fact, however, there was no meaningful difference between the OAS spread on a fixed rate and ARM loan. Greenspan's analysis was improperly based on the OAS between 30-year fixed-rate mortgage-backed securities and Treasuries. This was significantly biased, however, by the dramatic decline in Treasury yields during the period when the federal government was running a surplus and the supply of Treasury bonds was dwindling.

5. Cost of funds or COFI ARMs were prevalent in the western U.S. and based on an average of the cost of various types of deposits at Savings & Loan institutions.

6. In this case, the so-called user cost housing is negative. That is the buyer believes that he will make a profit given that the return on owning the home is greater than his cost of financing it. Moreover, the greater his conviction in future house prices gains, the greater his incentive to take on as large as mortgage as possible.

7. The real funds rate, which equals the difference between the funds rate and expected inflation and is a better gauge of just how aggressive the Fed is conducting monetary policy, declined from 4% in late 2000 to -1.5% by early 2003. There are only a handful of times since World War II that the real funds rate has been as high as 4% and as low as -1.5%.

8. Stock investors borrow from their brokers to finance the purchase of more stocks. Investors currently can borrow up to half the value of their stock holdings in margin debt.

9. See "Monetary policy and the economic outlook," testimony before the Joint Economic Committee, U.S. Congress, June 17, 1999. http://www.federalreserve.gov/boarddocs/testimony/1999/19990617.htm

10. See "Home Mortgage Market," speech before the annual convention of the Independent Community Bankers of America, March 4, 2003. http://www.federalreserve.gov/boarddocs/speeches/2003/20030304/default.htm

11. See "Issues for Monetary Policy," speech before the Economic Club of New York, December 19, 2002. http://www.federalreserve.gov/boarddocs/speeches/2002/20021219/default.htm

12. This is effectively as low as the federal funds rate can go without creating substantial problems for various parts of the financial system.

13. It is also worthwhile to point out that the deceleration in inflation experienced during the period was also likely due in some large measure to the monetary easing itself. See "Examining Contributions to Core Consumer Inflation Measures," Bauer, Haltom, and Peterman, Atlanta Federal Reserve Board working paper, April 2004. http://www.frbatlanta.org/invoke.cfm?objectid=27CDD5D8-E72D-7303-E60DDF476993E68E&method=display

14. According to the Federal Reserve's Flow of Funds the value of housing owned by households rose from $10.4 trillion at Y2K to $18.7 trillion by year-end 2005.

15. The most recent paper is "Sources and Uses of Equity Extracted From Homes," Greenspan and Kennedy, Finance and Economic Discussion Series, Federal Reserve Board of Governors, March 2007. http://www.federalreserve.gov/pubs/feds/2007/200720/index.html

16. The transaction costs include everything from points on the mortgage to the cost of title insurance.

17. The home equity line of credit has generally been more popular. It has an adjustable rate that moves with the prime rate and is thus more attractive when short-term rates are lower. The prime interest rate was historically the rate charged bank's best business customers. In more recent years it has became a commonly used rate for consumer loans such as the home equity line of credit and has been set by banks to 3 percentage points over the federal funds rate.

18. The increase in home equity debt outstanding also reflects the increasingly popular use of piggy-back seconds during the housing boom as a way to avoid paying mortgage insurance.

Chapter 5

1. That long-term rates remained so low throughout this period despite much stronger economic conditions was dubbed a "conundrum" by Chairman Greenspan. In early 2005 testimony before Congress he speculated that this was due at least in part to the global forces considered in this chapter. See http://www.federalreserve.gov/boarddocs/hh/2005/february/testimony.htm

2. The Chinese authorities determine the value of the yuan and have intentionally kept it cheap relative to other currencies such as the U.S. dollar to promote exports and foreign investment in their country. Since the summer of 2005, the Chinese have been allowing the yuan to appreciate slowly in value, but it still remains undervalued by an estimated 20-25% against the dollar.

3. Imports from China into the U.S. of some products, such as women's lingerie, doubled within a few months. U.S. textile producers objected loudly, setting off a trade dispute some called the "bra war." It ended quietly, with some import restrictions being re-imposed on Chinese textiles.

4. More precisely, Chinese imports accounted for 11% of consumer spending on non-energy and food durables and non-durables.

5. Treasury bonds are also owned by various government entities that are not publicly-trade – the most significant being the Social Security trust fund.

6. It could be argued that Chinese purchases of U.S. Treasury bonds have effectively financed the U.S. war efforts in Afghanistan and Iraq. The cost of those wars now total about $500 billion, which equal the increase in Chinese Treasury holdings.

7. The U.S. economy accounts for approximately one-fourth of global output and the remaining fourth is in other developed economies including Europe, Canada, and Japan.

8. Most emerging economies have also managed their new riches well, paying off their previously existing debt and investing the rest.

9. The average central bank target rate is calculated as a weighted average of target rates across central banks where the weights are equal to the nation's GDP on a purchasing power parity basis.

10. The Bank of Japan felt it had to strongly commit to its zero interest rate policy and the strong money growth it implied to rid the economy of deflation.

11. Global financial liberalization has been important in breaking down the so-called home bias in investing in which populations have a bias in investing in their own countries. While this bias is still strong it had been fading until the current subprime financial shock.

12. The stock PE ratio in the U.S. had risen, but well below the record high set in the technology-stock bubble of the late 1990s. This is a key reason why U.S. stock prices have not fallen more sharply in the wake of the financial shock.

Chapter 6

1. Depository institutions are financial institutions that take deposits that are insured by the FDIC. Most depositories are commercial banks, thrift institutions and credit unions.

2. Most have a license for those who wish to be a "Broker Associate", a "Brokerage Business", and a "Direct Lender".

3. Since 2005, a third of the top 30 have either been acquired (Countrywide is now part of Bank of America) filed for bankruptcy or been liquidated. Since 2005, a third of the top 30 have either been acquired (Countrywide is now part of Bank of America) filed for bankruptcy or been liquidated.

4. This is from the Federal Housing Finance Board and it may overstate the decline as the period was characterized by a refinancing boom and fees and points on refis are lower than on loans made for the purchase of a home.

5. Interstate banking became a reality with passage of the Riegle-Neal Interstate Banking and Branching Efficiency Act of 1994. More specifically the legislation allowed adequately capitalized and managed bank holding companies to acquire and merge with banks in any state.

6. The largest refinancing boom in history occurred in 2002-2003. Some $5 trillion in mortgage debt representing some 30 million homeowners refinanced their mortgage during those two years.

7. A REIT is a corporation that invests in real estate that allows its owners to avoid corporate income taxes. For this benefit, REITs are required to distribute 90% of their income to the owners of the firm. REITs were designed to provide a similar structure for investment in real estate as mutual funds provide for investment in stocks.

8. Gresham's law is named after Sir Thomas Gresham, an English financier in Tudor times. Gresham's law says that any circulating currency consisting of both "good" and "bad" money (both forms required to be accepted at equal value under legal tender law) quickly becomes dominated by the "bad" money. This is because people spending money will hand over the "bad" coins rather than the "good" ones, keeping the "good" ones for themselves.

9. Fannie Mae's AU model is known as Desktop Underwriter and Freddie Mac's model is called Loan Prospector.

10. Perhaps as importantly–at least from their perspective ? if they were misjudging, then their competitors with less capable models were certainly doing worse.

11. The most common credit score is known as the FICO score, named after Fair Issac, the company that commercialized credit scores. Each of the credit bureaus also constructs scores which they sell, as do most large lenders who customize the scores for their own specific purposes.

12. Credit bureaus and scoring companies have gotten wise to this practice and are working to shut-in down.

Chapter 7

1. "Banks" is used here to refer to all depository institutions, including commercial banks, savings and loans, and credit unions. This is the traditional banking system in which institutions use households' deposits to at least partly finance their lending and other investment activities.

2. The consumer price index and prime interest rate were consistently in the double-digits between the early 1970s and early 1980s.

3. The banks were largely recycling "petro-dollars" from the Middle East and other oil-producing nations earned in the period's high and rising oil prices to Latin American nations. There is some similarity to the recent experience as flush oil producers were putting their cash to work financing U.S. subprime mortgage loans.

4. The Resolution Trust Corporation was established in 1989 and closed its doors in 1995. It ultimately resolved close to 750 thrifts with assets of nearly $700 billion in today's dollars. The total cost to taxpayers of the S&L crisis was ultimately $250 billion.

5. This occurred in the large 1986 tax reform law.

6. This is a form of what is known as credit enhancement, which also includes overcollateralization in which the face value of the securities is less than the value of the underlying loans.

7. In the investment management vernacular, diversification benefits accrue if returns on the bonds are not correlated.

8. It's ironic that the first CDO was issued in 1987 by the infamous investment bank of junk bond fame, Drexel Burnham Lambert.

9. Synthetic CDOs were constructed so that the CDS included in the CDO mimicked the cash-flow patterns of the residential mortgage securities being insured.

10. The first Basel Accord on minimum capital standards for banks was reached in 1988 and implemented globally during the 1990s. Basel II provides much more comprehensive guidelines and was implemented during the early 2000s.

11. The Treasury deal involved establishing a "super-SIV" that would be funded and owned collectively by the big global banks and would buy assets from the failing SIVs at some undetermined discounted price.

12. The ABX is an asset-backed securities derivatives index constructed by Markit.

13. The hedge funds were euphemistically called the Bear Stearns High-Grade Structured Credit Fund and the Bear Stearns High-Grade Structured Credit Enhanced Leveraged Fund.

14. These securities are said to be negatively correlated.

Chapter 8

1. This calculation does not include the current housing bust.

2. Pent-up demand represents the demand for a product that develops during recessions as nervous and financially pressed households put off spending they would do given their income, wealth, and demographic circumstances.

3. Regulation Q was phased out with the passage of the Monetary Control Act of 1980.

4. Nationwide, land prices accounted for an estimated 60% of housing values as of 2005. This varied from 30% in Pittsburgh, PA to more than 90% in San Francisco. This calculation is based on a methodology presented in "The Price of Residential Land in U.S. Cities," David and Palumbo, May 2006. Finance and Economic Discussions Series, Federal Reserve Board. http://www.federalreserve.gov/pubs/feds/2006/200625/200625pap.pdf

5. The Bureau of Census estimates that legal immigration averages approximately 1 million annually and illegal immigration averages about 250,000.

6. The 1.8 million homes in annual fundamental demand is composed of 1.25 million in household formations, 200,000 in second homes, and 350,000 in obsolete homes.

7. Home building peaked in early 2006 in part due to rebuilding in the wake of Hurricane Katrina, which had destroyed well over a quarter million homes in New Orleans, LA and Gulfport-Biloxi, MS.

8. The homeowner vacancy rate hit a record 2.9% in the first quarter of 2008 according the Census Bureau. The long-run average of the vacancy rate was 1.7%.

Chapter 9

1. The definition of predatory mortgage lending is clearly defined in this January 2001 regulatory guidance http://www.federalreserve.gov/boarddocs/press/boardacts/2001/20010131/default.htm.

2. The "Interagency Guidance on Nontraditional Mortgage Product Risks" was issued by regulators in October 2006 http://www.federalreserve.gov/newsevents/press/other/20061018a.htm.

3. The "Statement on Subprime Mortgage Lending" was issued by regulators in June 2007 http://www.federalreserve.gov/newsevents/press/bcreg/20070629a.htm.

4. Former Fed Governor Susan Bies did warn early on of pending mortgage credit problems. See "A Supervisor's Perspective on Mortgage Markets and Mortgage Lending Practices," June 14, 2006. http://www.federalreserve.gov/newsevents/speech/bies20060614a.htm. FDIC Chairwoman Sheila Bair was also outspoken on the topic before most others. See http://www.fdic.gov/news/news/speeches/archives/2006/chairman/spsep2706.html, September 27, 2006.

5. This is through the doctrine of preemption, which was extended in an early 2007 Supreme Court ruling clarifying that federal regulation applies to operating subsidiaries of national banks, and not just the national banks themselves.

6. These entities may be regulated both in the state where they are headquartered and in other states where they operate.

7. See the Boston Federal Reserve study "Mortgage Lending in Boston: Interpreting the HMDA data," working paper, October 1992.

8. HMDA has been amended since the 1970s to increase the mortgage lenders required to report on their lending activity and also to expand the information reported.

9. See Boston Fed Study. For a critique of this study, see "Is the Boston Fed Study on Mortgage Discrimination Flawed," American Banker, March 1993, Mark Zandi.

10. The largest bank to fail the Fed's discrimination test was Hartford CT based Shawmut bank. Soon after that, it was not granted permission to acquire another smaller bank and it was acquired by the Bank of Boston.

11. Gramlich's views on subprime lending are expressed in a December 2000 speech "Subprime Lending, Predatory Lending,"http://www.federalreserve.gov/boarddocs/speeches/2000/20001206.htm.

12. The Greenspan-Gramlich disagreement came to light in Wall Street Journal interviews with both. See http://online.wsj.com/article/SB118134111823129555.html?mod=todays_us_money_and_investing, June 9, 2007. While Gramlich later stated that he generally thought subprime lending was positive as it supported increased home ownership, and he probably even thought the criticism Chairman Greenspan received on the subject unfair, his view that the Fed should take on a leadership role in addressing predatory lending practices was rebuked.

13. HOEPA was passed in 1994 as an amendment to the Truth in Lending Act in response to Congressional testimony about predatory home equity lending practices in poor and other underserved markets.

14. In California, the Department of Real Estate oversees mortgage brokers and the Department of Corporations is responsible for finance companies in addition to regulating more than 300,000 corporate entities in a wide range of financial businesses.

15. A higher-priced mortgage was defined as a loan with an annual interest rate of three percentage points or more above a comparable Treasury note. These rules apply to first mortgage loans secured by the borrower's principal dwelling.

Chapter 10

1. This assumes a 20% down payment and a fixed rate mortgage at prevailing rates for a prime borrower.

2. Another common approach is to compare house prices with household incomes. Because people generally want as much housing as they can afford given their incomes and saving, it makes sense that incomes and house prices should increase at about the same rate. There are more sophisticated econometric approaches, but all of them reach roughly the same conclusions.

3. This is of the nation's sixty largest metropolitan areas based on population.

4. The mortgage foreclosure process is long, complicated, and varies substantially across states. The average length to move through the entire foreclosure process from default to a home sale is about one year.

5. These are first mortgage loan defaults based on consumer credit file data supplied by credit bureau Equifax. They are measured at an annualized rate; the number of loans that would default over a year given the default rate at that time.

6. It is worth noting that given the house price declines that have already occurred, there are now a few markets that appear undervalued by this analysis. They include Detroit, Cincinnati, Cleveland and Indianapolis.

7. See "Mortgage Put Options and Real Estate Markets," Pavlov and Wachter, April 2008, forthcoming in the *Journal of Real Estate and Finance*.

Chapter 11

1. The 1929 stock market crash leading to the Great Depression was measurably more serious as it was part of a global financial and economic meltdown. The subprime financial shock has affected the entire globe, but not nearly to the same degree.

2. The IMF has also come up with a similar loss estimate. See "Global Financial Stability Report," April 2008. http://www.imf.org/External/Pubs/FT/GFSR/2008/01/index.htm.

3. These loss estimates are in 2007 U.S. dollars. It is important to note that the $1 trillion loss estimate include both cash-flow and mark-to-market losses. For example, for mortgages it includes the losses on defaulted mortgages and the losses on the value of mortgage securities.

4. This is based on the assumption that national house prices would fall 25% from their peak. It includes about $100 billion in losses on mortgage loans and $400 billion in losses on mortgage securities.

5. According to the IMF, in 2006 total global bank loans were more than $70 trillion and the value of debt securities was just under $70 trillion.

6. These are known as payment-in-kind or PIK bonds.

7. The banks' loans were also securitized into collateralized loan obligation or CLOs and then sold to investors.

8. Northern Rock was one of the United Kingdom's largest mortgage lenders prior to suffering a run on the bank by depositors who had lost faith in its capability to pay them back. The British government was ultimately forced to take over the bank to quell the run in September 2007.

9. This is also known as fair value accounting and is defined by the Financial Accounting Standards Board in FAS 157, http://www.fasb.org/st/summary/stsum157.shtml.

10. The previously discussed wide LIBOR-Treasury spread thus reflected worries banks had about not getting repaid, but it also reflected their desire to reduce their leverage.

11. The credit controls were imposed in a failed effort to stem the period's high and accelerating inflation. The logic behind the plan was that a consumer borrowing binge was fueling spending and price pressures. The plan was quickly jettisoned as the economy quickly began to sputter and recession ensued a few months later.

Chapter 12

1. See http://www.federalreserve.gov/newsevents/press/monetary/20061212a.htm for the FOMC statement from the December 12, 2006 meeting.

2. This statement was made after a speech to The Committee of 100, a business group promoting better Chinese relations. See http://uk.reuters.com/article/marketsNewsUS/idUKWBT00686520070420

3. The press release announcing the plan is available at http://portal.hud.gov/portal/page?_pageid=33,717219&_dad=portal&_schema=PORTAL FHA also announced the adoption of risk-based premiums for FHA insurance beginning at the start of 2008. This in theory allows FHA to help provide mortgage credit to more financially stretched households.

4. More precisely, LIBOR rates spiked relative to risk-free Treasury rates. The bigger the difference in LIBOR and Treasury rates the greater the angst among banks.

5. Commercial banks, thrift institutions, and domestic branches of foreign banks are permitted to borrow from the discount window.

6. The same financial institutions able to use the discount window are also permitted to use the TAF.

7. Similarly big moves in the funds rate did occur in the early 1980s, but during that period of hyper-inflation the Fed was managing policy by targeting the growth in the money supply and not the funds rate.

8. Bernanke's first public reference to "recession" occurred in the Q&A period during testimony before the Joint Economic Committee of Congress on April 2, 2008. See http://www.federalreserve.gov/newsevents/testimony/bernanke20080402a.htm

9. More precisely, the real federal funds rate is equal to the difference between the funds rate and inflation expectations. Inflation expectations as measured in the market for Treasury Inflation Protected Securities have remained low and stable at close to 2%.

10. The package satisfied the criteria for a well-designed economic stimulus plan; namely that it was timely, it was a one-time cost to the government, and the benefits were targeted to those households most likely to spend them quickly.

11. This estimate of the job impact is similar to that determined by Zandi in "Fiscal Stimulus Plan 2008," Mark Zandi, Dismal Scientist, January 22, 2008.

12. The stimulus plan also authorized more tax-exempt bond issuance by states to fund efforts to refinance hard-pressed homeowners into new more manageable loans.

13. The new mortgage loan caps vary by metropolitan areas and equal 125% of the median priced home in the highest priced county within the metro area but can not bigger than $729,000.

14. OFHEO is the Office of Federal Housing Enterprise Oversight.

15. The 12 member banks of the Federal Home Loan Bank system are normally permitted to hold no more than 300% of their capital in mortgage securities; this was increased to 600%.

16. If there are other lien holders on the property, they too have to subordinate their claim on the property before a modification can occur.

17. See testimony by Mark Zandi before the House Judiciary Committee in support of the bankruptcy reform legislation on November 19, 2007.

18. The plan states that mortgage owners must writedown to 90% of the new appraised value, but there is also a 5% insurance fee paid to the FHA that can not included in the calculation of the 90% LTV. Similar plans, at least in spirit, have been put forth by other groups including the Office of Thrift Supervision, the National Community Reinvestment Coalition, and various investment banks and academic economists.

Chapter 13

1. A recession is defined as a broad-based and persistent decline in economic activity and is determined by a committee of economists at the National Bureau of Economic Research based on examining a wide range of economic data. The rule of thumb is that a recession is defined by two consecutive quarters of declining real GDP. This is a rule of thumb and not a rule.

2. Consumer price inflation peaked at over 14% in early 1980 and the unemployment rate peaked at close to 11% in late 1982.

3. Despite the 1987 stock market crash and the tech-stock bust at the turn of the millennium, stock prices had risen by over 10% annually during the period. Despite the housing crash, house prices had risen 5% per annum.

4. This was a period of double-digit inflation. Real house prices fell modestly, but nominal prices did not.

5. Residential investment's share of GDP was briefly higher immediately following World War II when homes were built for returning U.S. soldiers.

6. This is the median homeowners' equity; half of homeowners have more equity in their homes and half less.

7. A 25% peak-to-trough decline in house prices would wipe out $5 trillion in homeowners' equity.

8. The saving rate calculations are based on data from the Federal Reserve's Flow of Funds and Survey of Consumer Finance using a methodology described in "Disentangling the Wealth Effect: A Cohort Analysis of Household Saving in the 1990s," Maki and Palumbo, April 2001, Federal Reserve Finance and Economics Discussion Series. http://www.federalreserve.gov/pubs/feds/2001/200121/200121abs.html

9. While each group of households account for about one-third of the population, renters account for only about one-tenth of total consumer spending, homeowners who have never tapped their equity account for just over half of spending, and homeowners who have done so account for the remainder.

10. This is the real trade deficit. The nominal trade deficit had also fallen but not nearly as much given the rising prices for oil and most other imported goods.

11. This is the price for a barrel of West Texas Intermediate

12. Adding in residential investment—which is not counted as consumer spending even though it is a household decision—the share of GDP rises from 66% in early 1980s to 76 percent at it peak at the apex of the housing boom in 2005.

13. GDP equals the value of all the goods and services produced by the economy and thus is a good proxy for the income generated by all of the economy's assets.

14. Wealth is measured by net worth, which is equal to the difference between all assets and liabilities. This data is based on the Federal Reserve's triennial Survey of Consumer Finance. The 2007 survey results will not be made available until early 2009. The survey was conducted before 1989 but significant changes in the survey make the results difficult to compare to the survey results beginning in 1989.

15. This culminated in the late 2005 bankruptcy reform legislation, which among other things implemented an income means test to determine who was eligible for a Chapter 7 liquidation or a lender-preferred Chapter 13 workout.

16. The Federal Reserve's Survey of Consumer Finance is also the source for these statistics.

INDEX

FINANCIAL TIMES

In an increasingly competitive world, it is quality
of thinking that gives an edge—an idea that opens new
doors, a technique that solves a problem, or an insight
that simply helps make sense of it all.

We work with leading authors in the various arenas
of business and finance to bring cutting-edge thinking
and best-learning practices to a global market.

It is our goal to create world-class print publications
and electronic products that give readers
knowledge and understanding that can then be
applied, whether studying or at work.

To find out more about our business
products, you can visit us at www.ftpress.com.